D1272141

ROYAL HISTORICAL SOCIETY
STUDIES IN HISTORY
SERIES
No. 29

THE JUDICIAL BENCH IN ENGLAND
1727-1875

The Reshaping of a Professional
Elite

Recent volumes published in this series include

23   John Russell, First Earl of Bedford: *Diane Willen*
        One of the King's Men

24   The Political Career of Sir Robert Naunton   *Roy E. Schreiber*
        1589-1635

25   The House of Gibbs and the Peruvian   *W. M. Mathew*
        Guano Monopoly

26   Julian S. Corbett, 1854-1922 : Historian of British   *D. M. Schurman*
        Maritime Policy from Drake to Jellicoe

27   The Pilgrimage of Grace in the Lake Counties,   *S. M. Harrison*
        1536-1537

28   Money, Prices and Politics in Fifteenth-   *Angus MacKay*
        Century Castile

For a complete list of the series please see pp. 209-10

THE JUDICIAL BENCH IN ENGLAND 1727-1875

The Reshaping of a Professional Elite

Daniel Duman

LONDON
ROYAL HISTORICAL SOCIETY
1982

The Society records its gratitude to the following, whose generosity made possible the initiation of this series: The British Academy; The Pilgrim Trust; The Twenty-Seven Foundation; The United States Embassy bicentennial funds; The Wolfson Trust; several private donors.

The publication of this volume has been assisted by a further grant from the Twenty-Seven Foundation.

Printed by
Swift Printers (Sales) Ltd
London E.C.1

To Marion

CONTENTS

		Page
	Preface	viii
	List of Tables	x
	Introduction	1
1	The Organisation of the Legal Profession 1727-1785	7
2	The Preparation for a Profession	28
3	Beginning a Career	50
4	Progress, Promotion, and Politics	72
5	Incomes and Investments	105
6	At Home and in Society	145
7	Professionalization and the Law	173
	Appendix: The Judges of England 1727-1875	183
	Bibliography	190
	Index	200

PREFACE

Despite their central place in the history of England in the eighteenth
and nineteenth centuries, the judges of England have escaped the
scrutiny of researchers until recently. Here I have attempted to trace
the development of this leading professional elite during a period of
profound social change. This is not a legal history but a collective
social history of members of the English judiciary appointed to the
bench between 1727 and 1875. I hope that the product does justice to
that history.

During the past seven years, the judges of England have been an
integral part of my life. They have accompanied me on my travels from
Baltimore to London to Jerusalem, finally coming to rest in the desert
city of Beersheva. I have incurred many debts during these years
which I would now like to acknowledge. First I would like to thank my
former supervisor at Johns Hopkins University, Professor David
Spring, who introduced me to English social history and guided me
during the research and writing of my doctoral dissertation which
forms the basis of this book. I would also like to thank Professor
Robert Forster for his time and patience in reading the early drafts of
this work and for his invaluable suggestions. Similar appreciation is
due to Professors Robert Kargon and J.W. Howard of the Johns
Hopkins University, and to Professor W.R. Cornish of the London
School of Economics. Naturally any remaining errors are my
responsibility alone.

There are numerous individuals and institutions without whose
help this project would never have been completed. I am most grateful
to those institutions which made the records in their care available to
me, including the Public Record Office, the Library of University
College London, the Kent County Council, the Merioneth Record
Office, the Norfolk Record Office, the Berkshire County Library, the
Northumberland Record Office, the British Library, the Cambridge
University Library, the Bodleian Library of Oxford University, and
the Buckinghamshire Record Office. In addition to the aforementioned,
I would like to thank the current representatives of the families whose
papers I consulted in these repositories, including the Marquess of
Camden, the Earl Bathurst, Viscount Ridley, Lord Coleridge, Lord
Monk Bretton, Lord Walsingham, Sir George F. Pollock, and
Commander Richards of Caerynwch. A special appreciation is due to
Lord and Lady Kenyon of Gredington, Shropshire and Mr. and Mrs.
M.A. McLaggan of Merthyr Mawr, Glamorganshire, for making
their family papers available to me and for their hospitality.

I would also like to extend my thanks to the staffs of the Milton Eisenhower Library of The Johns Hopkins University, the Jewish National and University Library at the Hebrew University of Jerusalem, the Zalman Aranne Library of the Ben Gurion University of the Negev, and the Institute of Historical Research at the University of London.

I am also indebted to The Johns Hopkins University for the fellowship which allowed me to pursue my research in England, and to the Faculty of Humanities and Social Sciences of the Ben Gurion University for the research grant which allowed me to prepare the final draft of this monograph.

Two members of my family deserve special acknowledgements for their efforts: my mother, who devoted so much time and energy to typing the early drafts of this study; and finally, my wife Marion, who has been my editor, proof-reader, typist, and companion through all the stages of this project. For all this and more, this volume is dedicated to her.

LIST OF TABLES

1. Schools attended by future judges   *p.* 38
2. Universities attended by future judges   43
3. Inns of Court affiliation   45
4. Socio-occupational origins of the judges 1727-1875   51
5. Judges' legal activities other than the Bar   61
6. Judges' counties of origin, 1727-1875   66
7. Law officers and Welsh judges among the judges of the High Court   76
8. Income at the Bar 1735-1871   106
9. Salaries and emoluments of the judges 1750-1832   112
10. Annual value of judicial estates 1727-1875   128
11. Size and distribution of the judges' personal estates 1760-1875   140
12. Real and personal wealth of the judges 1790-1875   142
13. The fortunes of English judges in the nineteenth century   143
14. Judges' London residences 1760-1875   146
15. Personal and professional expenses of Sir John Nicholl in the years 1813 and 1820   155
16. Lord Mansfield's expenses 1786   157
17. Social origins of judges' wives   163
18. Occupations of judges' sons   166
19. Professional ideology and structure in eighteenth- and nineteenth-century England   178

Figure 1. Judicial bequests and settlements.   169

INTRODUCTION

Eighteenth-and nineteenth-century Britain witnessed the concurrence of political stability with dynamic economic and social transformation. Despite enormous stresses within the nation, continuity was unbroken, although on several occasions the government felt threatened by revolution and resorted to political and legal repression of dissident groups. The royal and ecclesiastical courts of England and the judges who presided over them constituted one of the leading political institutions in the transition from the old society to the new. The courts held the central position because they combined for much of the period the judicial and legislative functions of the government. They attempted to keep the peace by administering the civil and criminal law. They were quick to check political, social, or economic revolts, such as the Swing or Luddite uprisings, the Gordon riots, and English radical support for revolutionary France, by meting out harsh sentences to participants. Finally, the courts were responsible for developing new legal codes required by the new society during a period in which Parliament was unable or unwilling to perform this function, most especially during the eighteenth century when 'nearly all the important developments in Private Law and many of the developments in Public Law were due, not to the Legislature but to the lawyers. The chancellors, the judges, and the civilians of Doctors' Commons settled the principles of equity, of common law, and of ecclesiastical and admiralty law. . . . They accomplished this work mainly through the decisions of the courts'.[1]

Despite the prominence of the members of the legal profession and especially of the judiciary in the eighteenth and nineteenth centuries, there has been a singular lack of historical research on the social and occupational history of the bar and bench during this period.[2] The only full-length social history of the legal profession in the eighteenth century is a study of the attorneys.[3] The upper branch has been treated in Sir William Holdworth's monumental *A History of English Law* and in Edward Foss's *The Judges of England.* It is hoped that this study will serve to illuminate one small chapter in the social history of England in the age of industrialization.

---

[1] Sir William Holdsworth, *A History of English Law,* XII (London, 1938), p. 3.

[2] J.H. Baker, 'Counsellors and Barristers - An Historical Study', *Cambridge Law Journal* 28 (1969), 205; C. Neal Tate, 'Paths to the Bench in Britain', *Western Political Quarterly* 28 (1975), 101-29; Jennifer Morgan, 'The Judiciary of the Superior Courts 1820-1968', (unpublished University of London M. Phil. thesis, 1968).

[3] Robert Robson, *The Attorney in Eighteenth Century England* (Cambridge, 1959).

A complete history of the bar and bench in the modern period will be written one day. My more limited goal is to write a social and occupational analysis of the judges appointed to the equity, common law, and civil law courts in England between 1727 and 1875.[4] However, despite the emphasis on the bench, the bar as a whole must figure prominently in any such study. This follows naturally from the fact that the English judiciary, unlike some of its continental counterparts, did not comprise a separate occupational group, but was an integral part of the upper branch of the legal profession.[5]

No attempt has been made to write a legal history of the judiciary, and I leave to specialists the important task of analysing the legal decisions of the judges. My goal is to elucidate the structure of the élite of an old and important English profession. To this end I investigate the social composition, education, career patterns, wealth and income structure, methods of judicial selection, patronage, life style, political involvements, non-legal activities, family structure, and self-conceptions and attitudes of the English judiciary. The choice of a small and relatively well-known élite (the total number of judges appointed between 1727 and 1875 is 208) was made in order to rectify a flaw which has tended to call into question the findings of other quantified professional studies. The relative anonymity of the members of these professions means that in a large proportion of the cases, little or no personal information is available, especially in the most easily accessible sources, and therefore one often finds that fifty or sixty per cent of the data in a given category is listed as unknown. With such a high proportion of unknown data, conclusions are at best very tenuous and are frequently little better than meaningless. The members of the group I am studying, on the other hand, are well-known so that in most cases an enormous amount of personal data is available; in addition, the group is small enough to allow for investigation of a range of sources which would be made prohibitive if the sample under examination were very large. Thus, I have been able

---

[4]This study deals with all those judges whose offices were included in the Supreme Court of Judicature established by the Judicature Acts of 1873 and 1875. In the Court of Chancery they are the Lord Chancellor, Master of the Rolls, Lords Justices of Appeal and Vice-Chancellors; in the three common law courts, Queen's Bench, Common Pleas, and Exchequer, the Chief Justices and the puisne judges and barons, and in the ecclesiastical courts the Judge of the Prerogative Court of Canterbury and Dean of the Arches and the Judge of the Court of Admiralty.

[5]In a number of continental countries, the judges are members of the civil service rather than of the legal profession, and very early on in his career the young barrister must decide which profession he wants to join. This division did exist in England during the thirteenth century, but by the end of that century had begun to dissolve, and thus a single legal profession developed in England of which both the lawyers and the judges are members. For a complete discussion of this issue see Theodore F.T. Plucknett, *A Concise History of the Common Law* (London, 1956), pp. 236-7.

to reduce the missing data to a minimum: in most cases it does not exceed between fifteen and twenty per cent, and is frequently as low as between five and ten per cent.

The type of data which was used in this study is of two distinct varieties, requiring very different methods of analysis. The first is biographical data which is available for all or most of the 208 judges, such as length of career, social origins and educational background. This data has been collected from genealogical handbooks, school registers, university registers, Inns of Court registers, newspaper obituaries, biographical dictionaries, professional registers, city directories, and works of contemporary biography.[6] The resulting data has been divided into twenty-five variables which have been cross-tabulated by means of a pre-packaged computer programme. The derived tables will facilitate the statistical elucidation of phenomena such as the social and occupational structure of the judiciary, the investigation of career patterns, influence of politics and patronage on judicial appointments, and patterns of social mobility, among others.[7] The second type of data was drawn primarily from printed and manuscript memoirs and from personal letters, account books, professional and legal documents, and estate papers. This data is available for only some of the judges and therefore cannot be treated statistically. It can, however, be used as exemplary evidence of life style, patterns of investment and the level of judicial involvement in non-legal activities, which are just as necessary as the quantifiable data in creating a complete portrait of the judges of England as a social group. I hope in this way to correct what I see as a basic fault in a number of previous professional studies; that is an unequal emphasis on either the quantitative aspect or the exemplary aspect of the social group under investigation.

[6] The major sources used in compiling the quantitative material used in this study are: *Dictionary of National Biography; Burke's Peerage; Burke's Landed Gentry; Walford's County Families of the United Kingdom;* F. Boase, *Modern English Biography;* G.E. Cokayne, *Complete Peerage;* J. Venn, *Alumni Cantabrigenses;* J. Foster, *Alumni Oxonienses, Men-at-the-Bar,* and *Register of Admissions to Gray's Inn, 1521-1889; Register of Admissions to the Middle Temple; The Records of the Honourable Society of Lincoln's Inn;* E. Foss, *The Judges of England; The Times; Eton College Register* and other school registers; *Kelly's Hand-Book of the Titled, Landed, and Official Classes;* J. Whishaw, *A Synopsis of the English Bar; Haydn's Book of Dignities; Dictionary of Welsh Biography;* and various London and Provincial directories.

[7] Care must be taken in the utilization of the statistical data in this study, especially when evaluating the changes from period to period. In fact the universe of 208 judges is quite small, and these men are further divided into five chronological groups as follows: 1727-1760 - 44 judges; 1760-1790 - 32 judges; 1790-1820 - 29 judges; 1820-1850 - 44 judges; and 1850-1875 - 59 judges. As a result of the size of these groups, small changes in the percentages, all of which have been rounded off to the nearest per cent, are probably not very significant.

The social history of the English judiciary that I have sketched will be studied over a 148 year period, that is from 1727 to 1875. The starting date, 1727, corresponds to George II's accession to the throne, while 1875 was chosen as the final date because it was in that year that the Supreme Court of Judicature was established in approximately its present form. The intervening years have been divided into five periods and each judge has been assigned to one of them according to the year of his appointment to the bench. The first period corresponds to the last years of pre-industrial Britain and ends in 1760 with the accession of George III, the second, 1760-1790, corresponds to the early years of the industrial revolution, the third, 1790-1820, to the French Wars, the fourth, 1820-50, to the age of social upheaval and social reform, and the final period, 1850-75, to the period of Britain's economic supremacy. By using this quinque-partite time division it will be possible to evaluate the effects of changing social, economic and political environments on the English judiciary.

Throughout this study, the concept of professionalization will serve as a central theme in the description and analysis of the social and administrative history of the judiciary between 1727 and 1875. Unfortunately, despite the frequency with which the term professionalization has been used by historians and sociologists of the professions, there appears to be no completely satisfactory existing definition which will adequately serve our needs. As a result, a working definition is suggested, which may serve as a guide to the various uses of the word and the contexts in which it can be found in the history of the nineteenth-century professions.

The term professionalization can be used to describe three separate but related processes which transformed the English professions in the eighteenth and nineteenth centuries. The first process can best be described as internal professionalization, which includes the creation of a new system of intra-professional standards. The most important developments in this regard were the addition of classroom training, entrance examinations, and qualifying examinations to the pre-existing systems of general education in élitist schools or in the universities, and professional apprenticeship.

The initial series of these internal reforms was begun in the first third of the nineteenth century by the most prominent of the lower professions — the solicitors, the apothecaries and the surgeons. These professions, unlike their more gentlemanly contemporaries — the barristers, physicians, military officers, clergymen, and government officials (later to become civil servants) — had to make special efforts to substantiate their claims to professional status. Consequently, they were in the vanguard of the movement to standardize entrance, training, and socialization of new recruits as a means of assuring the public of a practitioner's miniminal competence.

By the middle of the nineteenth century, the new standards which had been voluntarily adopted by the lower professions began to be imposed on the upper professions and on the universities through the agency of parliamentary commissions, legislation, or the threat of legislative action. In documents such as the 1846 Report of the Select Committee on Legal Education or the 1855 Northcote-Trevelyan Report, the importance of substituting systematic lectures and examinations, which were theoretically based on merit and skill, for the old criteria of social background, patronage, and purchase was publicly recognized.

The second aspect of professionalization was the establishment or restructuring of institutional and administrative bodies and offices closely connected to the professions. Beginning in the 1820s and 1830s, Parliament began to apply the measure of utility in an ongoing process of reform. Salaries of government office holders were standardized, useless sinecures were abolished, and the leading professions felt the impact of parliamentary examination and legislative reform. The church, the courts, the army, and the civil service were all subjected to thorough-going reforms whose goal was the rationalization of professional institutions. As a result, by 1887, the year of Queen Victoria's Jubilee, little remained of the professional world which had existed in 1760 at the accession of her grandfather, the vast majority of the professionalizing reforms having been instituted since her own coronation fifty years previously.

The third and final aspect of professionalization was neither the result of voluntary reform nor of legislation imposed on the professions by Parliament. It encompassed a series of changes in the social composition and attitude of professional men which resulted in the emergence of the professions as a unique and independent social group. This does not mean that all professions or professional men were recruited from the same social milieu or that they all adopted a single point of view with regard to their occupations and social positions. However, there seems to be little doubt that by the middle of the nineteenth century, if not earlier, the members of the professions had begun to distinguish themselves from both the business and the landed classes. They had established the ideal of service as a central part of their occupational creed. In addition, they emphasized the unique qualities of the professions by stressing the technical skill, the specialized training and the ethical standards which, they maintained, separated them from other occupational groups.

6

Between 1727 and 1875 the judiciary, as shall be demonstrated, underwent three processes of professionalization. All three types — internal reform, administrative reorganization and changes in social composition and attitudes — can be recognized in the transformation of the judiciary in the eighteenth and nineteenth centuries. The first two processes have been examined in detail elsewhere and they will be employed here as a means of providing a notion of the scope of the professionalization of the law and its institutions.[8] Attention in this monograph is centred on the third of the three processes and its implications for the creation of a modern judiciary.

[8]See Holdsworth, *History of English Law,* XIII, XV, XVI, *passim;* Brian Abel-Smith and Robert Stevens, *Lawyers and the Courts* (London, 1970), *passim.* Robert Stevens, 'The Final Appeal: Reform of the House of Lords and Privy Council 1867-1876', *Law Quarterly Review* 80 (1964), 343-69; and Alan Harding, *A Social History of English Law,* (Harmondsworth, 1966), chapters 12, 13, and 14.

1

THE ORGANIZATION OF THE LEGAL PROFESSION 1727-1875

Geography, Dimensions and Status

London was, in the eighteenth and nineteenth centuries, the heart of legal England. Temple Bar, the spot where the City and Westminster meet and where Fleet Street becomes the Strand, was the centre of the legal district of London which extended from Whitehall, St. Martin's Lane and Monmouth Street on the west, to Queen Street on the east, and from the Thames on the south to Theobalds Road, Newgate and Cheapside on the north. A barrister in 1800 who halted momentarily at Temple Bar could see from his carriage a number of London's most important legal buildings. Immediately to the south he could see the gateway to the Temple which housed two of the four Inns of Court; to the north was the Serjeants' Inn on the corner of Chancery Lane, and a bit further up the Lane, the residence of the Master of the Rolls as well as Lincoln's Inn. If he were so inclined, our barrister could visit all the other major sights of legal London which were conveniently situated only a few minutes away by carriage, including Westminster Hall — the home of the common law courts and the House of Lords — Doctors' Commons, and Gray's Inn. Almost every barrister in the eighteenth and nineteenth centuries spent the major part of his professional life in this circumscribed area of two square miles. The court system in England was extremely centralized, and until the formation of the county courts in 1846 there was no permanent system of intermediate courts between the quarter-sessions presided over by justices of the peace, who were laymen for the most part, and the high court presided over by the judges of England. The most important exceptions were the *ad hoc* courts of requests which had been established by private Acts of Parliament throughout the eighteenth and early nineteenth centuries in large towns for civil causes.[1]

The ecclesiastical and equity courts always sat in London, while the common law courts, which were also headquartered there, dispensed justice to the provinces by means of a system of six regional circuits which the twelve common law judges travelled twice a year. As a result of the geographic concentration of the courts in London, it is not surprising that the barrister who practised solely in the

---

[1]W.D.H. Winder, 'Courts of Requests', *Law Quarterly Review* 52 (1936), *passim;* Holdsworth, *History of English Law,* I, p. 680-4.

provinces was rare,[2] and could not hope to be a recipient of the highest honours and rewards of the legal profession.

The legal profession was divided into two main parts: On the one hand, common law and equity, centred around the Inns of Court; on the other, ecclesiastical and admiralty, centred around Doctors' Commons. The training, organization, and basic law followed by these two divisions of the profession were completely different, yet their jurisdictions often overlapped. The common law barristers were theoretically trained at the Inns of Court, while the civil lawyers were trained at the universities. The common law and equity courts were based on English common law, while the ecclesiastical courts were based on Roman civil law. The two parts of the legal profession were finally united in 1857 when the common law courts absorbed the jurisdictions previously enjoyed by the ecclesiastical courts.

The first profession to issue an annual register of practitioners was the legal profession. Begun in the late 1770s, these lists included the names of barristers, advocates, special pleaders, conveyancers, and London and provincial attorneys. These registers, known as the *Law List*, enable us to estimate, at least in general terms, the dimensions of the bar. According to the *Law List*, there were 257 barristers in 1780, 880 in 1810, and 3,268 in 1850, while there were 9 advocates of Doctors' Commons in 1785, 28 in 1815, and 25 in 1835.[3]

Unfortunately the figures for the number of barristers cannot be accepted without serious reservations. Many men who went to the Inns of Court and who were called to the bar never earned a penny from legal practice, but as barristers they were entitled to have their names included on the *Law List*. Some of these men, who were heirs to landed estates, enrolled as students at the Inns prior to inheriting their fortune. They took this step probably with the hope of acquiring some knowledge of the law which would be of use in the management of their estates and beneficial to their participation in local and national society, for example as justices of the peace or members of Parliament.[4] Others may have hoped to make a living at the bar but

[2]In 1850, out of 3268 men listed on the Law List, no more than 60 were provincial barristers and many of this small group were not full-time barristers.

[3]Rudolf Gneist, *Das heutige Englische Verfassungsund Verwaltungsrecht*, I, (Berlin, 1857), 503, as partially quoted in Elie Halevy, *England in 1815*, (London, 1961), p. 23, Holdsworth, *History of English Law*, XII, 3, Peter Brown, *The Chathamites* (New York, 1967), p. 238, and the *Law List*.

[4]For an example of a barrister who inherits an estate and becomes a J.P., see Smollett's rather uncomplimentary portrait of Mr. Pimpernel, which also includes a mid-eighteenth-century view of the attorney. *The Expedition of Humphry Clinker* (Harmondsworth edn., 1971), p. 205. See also Sir William Blackstone's discussion of the benefits landed gentlemen could derive from the study of the law in *A Discourse on the Study of the Law. Being an Introductory Lecture Read in the Public Schools, October 25, 1758* (Oxford, 1758), pp. 4-7.

were unsuccessful, for competition was stiff. Still others left the law for other professions soon after being called to the bar.

If we are primarily concerned with the bar as a practising profession, and not merely with paper qualifications, then it is necessary to separate the non-practising barristers from those men making a living from the law. Whether the figure of 257 barristers for 1780 represents just the practising bar or not is uncertain, but the figures for the nineteenth century are undoubtedly inflated by the inclusion of non-practising barristers. Fortunately we do have some estimates by contemporaries which provide very rough approximations of the number of barristers earning a living in the profession during the 1850s. One authority on the professions, writing in 1857, states that of the 4,035 barristers and advocates appearing on the *Law List* in 1855: 'I believe that not more than 250 are profitably employed in the practice of that branch of law [Common Law]. If to this we added 250 as successful equity lawyers, conveyancers, and advocates in Doctors' Commons, it may be fairly said that the country, in its present condition, supports only 500 advocates.'[5] Additionally, in evidence given before a parliamentary committee in 1850, Sir John Jervis, the Attorney-General, estimated that the number of barristers earning a living at the bar was between 100 and 1,000, which adds credence to the 1857 estimate.[6] However, even if we accept the higher estimate of 1,000 practising barristers as accurate, it is still only a third of the number of barristers appearing on the 1850 *Law List.*

Even in absolute terms, disregarding for the moment the problem of non-practising barristers, the bar was a small profession. The *Law List* in 1850 includes the names of slightly more than 3,200 barristers as compared with 13,256 attorneys and solicitors, 2,238 physicians, 15,163 apothecaries and surgeons, 11,087 army and naval officers, 29,785 local government officers, 3,708 men in the Indian civil service, 37,698 in the home civil service, and more than 28,000 clergymen of whom 18,587 were of the established church, 8,521 dissenters, and 1,093 Roman Catholics.[7]

In fact the influence of the bar in eighteenth- and nineteenth-century England was out of all proportion to its size. This was due to the

---

[5]H. Byerley Thomson, *The Choice of a Profession, A Concise and Comparative Review of the English Professions* (London, 1857), pp. 96-97.

[6]*Report of the Select Committee on Official Salaries,* PP, XV, (London, 1850), p. 180.

[7]Thomson, *Choice of a Profession,* p. 6.

essential services provided by the judges and barristers, their leadership role in government and society, and the high status of the profession. The bar, like clergy of the Church of England, officers in the army and navy, and perhaps members of the civil service, was classed as a 'higher profession' in the mid-nineteenth century and probably before then as well. On the next level stood the 'lower professions' which included doctors, solicitors, artists and engineers.[8]

Despite the status differences between the professions, as a group they were considered superior to business. In comparing the higher professions in particular with business, H. Byerley Thomson wrote in 1857 that 'the member of the higher profession . . . at once takes a place in society by virtue of his calling; the poor man of business is nowhere in social position, yet the poor curate is admitted readily to the coveted country society that the millionaire has even to manoeuvre for. . . '.[9] By the standards of the eighteenth and nineteenth centuries, the bar, along with the other higher professions, was clearly a gentlemanly occupation. This distinction meant that these professions were suitable for sons of the landed as well as the middle classes.

Structure of the Bar

Of the two branches of the legal profession, the common law and equity side was by far the larger and more important. Within that branch there was a further sub-division between the barristers on the one hand and the solicitors and attorneys on the other. These two groups, each with its own clearly defined functions, were separated by a barrier which was infrequently surmounted: membership in the Inns of Court. Every barrister had to be a member of one of the four Inns which had a monopoly on calls to the bar. Only a barrister could act as an advocate in proceedings in the royal courts. However, by a convention, which was firmly established by the middle of the nineteenth century, litigants were rarely in direct contact with the barristers, but could employ their services only through the medium of an attorney or solicitor.[10] The attorneys (who practised in the common law courts) and the solicitors (who practised in the equity courts) who were not members of the Inns and who could not plead in court, were in charge of all the pre-trial details of a case. They would

[8]W.J. Reader, *Professional Men* (London, 1966), pp. 150-1.

[9]Thomson, *Choice of a Profession,* p. 16.

[10]Abel-Smith and Stevens, *Lawyers and the Courts,* p. 222.

retain a barrister on behalf of their client, draw up the brief, and pay counsel his fee. Thus we have a clearly defined division of legal labour, in which the attorney is very much a general practitioner and has charge of the case, while the barrister is a specialist whose sole function is to plead the case in the courts.

The bar itself exhibited a corporate unity which was almost unaltered by the passage of time. Dr. Ives's description of the profession in the late Middle Ages could as easily be used for the eighteenth or nineteenth centuries: 'Not only was the unity of the profession encouraged by the education and life of the Inns, by the fellowship of the legal quarter of London and by the conditions under which lawyers worked, but the action of the courts was bound to produce the same effect.'[11] The entire professional milieu of the barrister and judge created a unique occupational outlook. The socialization process was so thorough that Henry Sumner Maine could write of the English judge that 'his tastes, feelings, prejudices, and degree of enlightenment were inevitably those of his order'.[12] In a similar vein, Tocqueville sees lawyers as members of a distinct social class, since 'they naturally constitute *a body;* not by any previous understanding or by agreement that directs them to a common end; but the analogy of their studies and the uniformity of their methods connect their minds as common interest might unite their endeavours.'[13]

Corporate unity, however, did not prevent the emergence of a highly structured professional hierarchy containing numerous ranks and offices which continued to change during our period. Every prospective barrister was aware that from the day he was called to the bar he was a participant in the most competitive professional lottery in England. Throughout his career he would be required, if he met with success, to make many crucial decisions on the course he should follow, any of which could be his making or breaking.

Some men chose to postpone their debut at the bar. By obtaining a certificate which entitled them to practise as a special pleader or conveyancer, they were enabled to earn a living in their profession, and at the same time make connections which could be most useful in the future, without having to contend with the severe competition at the bar. The function of both the special pleader and the conveyancer was

[11] Eric William Ives, 'Some Aspects of the Legal Profession in the Fifteenth and Sixteenth Centuries', (unpublished Ph.D. thesis, University of London, 1955), p. 169.

[12] Henry Sumner Maine, *Ancient Law* (London, 1930), p. 70.

[13] Alexis de Tocqueville, *Democracy in America,* I (New York edn., 1954), 283-4.

to assist attorneys and barristers; the special pleader drafted complex pleadings, while the conveyancer drafted documents connected with the transfer of real property. Some men chose to remain 'under the bar', acting in one of these two capacities for their entire careers, while for others it was merely a temporary expedient before they were called to the bar.

Upon being called, the fledgling barrister had to begin to chart his professional course in earnest. In the eighteenth century the system was less specialized, and even the separation between the equity and common law barrister was indistinct. Most barristers joined one of the six English or two Welsh circuits, although some later confined themselves to the equity courts. By the nineteenth century, barristers began to specialize immediately, and only those intended for the common law bar joined a circuit. The equity barrister often served as an equity draftsman and conveyancer during his early career, trying his luck in the various equity courts. Once he gained a reputation, he often decided to limit his practice to a particular court.

If a man was a success as a junior barrister, he then had the opportunity to advance to a more senior position in the profession. By the middle of the nineteenth century the most natural course was to apply to the Lord Chancellor for an appointment as a King's (or Queen's) Counsel. In fact this rank was a modern one by the standards of the English bar. Dating from the seventeenth century it had but a few members until the reign of William IV. The men who held the rank of King's Counsel prior to that reign have been described as 'sound lawyers in full employment, but the immediate cause of their elevation was almost always some political consideration'.[14] The King's Counsel as a senior member of the profession was granted the right of precedence at the bar, allowed to wear a silk gown instead of the stuff one, required (from the nineteenth century) to have a junior as an assistant when he appeared in court, and was prohibited from holding briefs against the crown without a special patent. As we shall see, receipt of this office, which frequently served as one of the keys to the highest honours and incomes of the profession, could also spell the end of a successful career at the bar.

Alternatively, the successful junior might have been made a serjeant-at-law. This order, which dates from the early history of the

---

[14]John C. Jeafferson, *A Book About Lawyers,* II (London, 1867), 4-5. Jeafferson was a barrister, having been called to the bar in 1859, although he never practised. He was a prolific author and wrote popular social histories, biographies, and literary studies. He served as an inspector for the Royal Manuscripts Commission from 1874 to 1887. In addition to his study of the bar, he also wrote about the medical profession and the clergy. *DNB,* Supplement 1901-1911, pp. 265-6.

Inns of Court, had by the eighteenth century lost most of its prestige and power and was destined to be dissolved before the end of the nineteenth century. The serjeants did not belong to any of the Inns of Court, but had their own Serjeants' Inn to which a barrister transferred upon taking rank and after having been rung out of his old Inn. The serjeants wore a special wig as a sign of their rank and had a monopoly on cases in the Court of Common Pleas until 1846. Finally, by convention, all judges had to be chosen from the serjeants, but by the eighteenth century all that remained of this custom was the form. Until 1875 when this rule was abolished, every barrister appointed to the bench who was not yet a serjeant, was made a serjeant *pro-forma* before officially entering judicial office.[15]

By the early nineteenth century, the leaders of the bar both in fact and in official precedence were the law officers of the crown, the Attorney- and Solicitor-General. These officers were political appointees and acted as legal advisers to the government in Parliament. Both law officers sat in the House of Commons, usually in a safe government seat, since they were required to be re-elected after appointment to an office under the crown. Besides being politicians, the men appointed to these posts were usually among the top barristers in the realm and often their legal careers culminated with appointment to the high court. Law officers were perfectly free until the early 1890s, to practise privately while they held their offices.[16] By tradition they gave up going the circuit, except for an occasional special retainer, and confined their legal activities to London.[17] The Attorney-General was in a special position with regard to judicial appointment. In 1850, while giving evidence before a Parliamentary inquiry, Lord John Russell agreed that 'the common practice is that the Attorney-General of the day has a sort of claim on the Chief Justiceship of Common Pleas'.[18]

Unlike the barristers, the civilian lawyers were required to study law in a university, either Oxford or Cambridge. All of the civilians held the degree of Doctor of Civil Law (D.C.L.) from one of the two universities. Upon completing their legal education, they were eligible to be admitted to the College of Advocates which was located at Doctors' Commons. Once the young advocate had been admitted, he was required to undergo a year of silence, which was a year of formal legal apprenticeship,

[15]Holdsworth, *History of English Law,* XII, 5.

[16]J.B. Atlay, *The Victorian Chancellors,* II (London, 1906), 102.

[17]Horace Twiss, *The Public and Private Life of Lord Chancellor Eldon,* I (London, 1844), 189.

[18]*Report of the Select Committee on Official Salaries,* p. 143.

during which time he acquired experience in the ecclesiastical and admiralty courts.

As with the common law and equity bar, the civilian side was divided into two branches with the advocates as the upper branch, and the proctors, who were the attorneys of the civil law courts, as the lower. The number of civilian lawyers was always very small — during the eighteenth and nineteenth centuries it never exceeded three dozen. Perhaps it was because the number of civilians was so small that that side of the legal profession never developed formal ranks as did the common lawyers; advocates did not have an equivalent to the ranks of King's Counsel or Serjeant-at-law. The civilians, as a result of their close connection with the ecclesiastical establishment, often held administrative offices in the Anglican Church and judicial offices in diocesan and other lower level ecclesiastical courts. Finally, there was an office held by a member of the civil law side of the profession which was comparable in official status, but not in political power, to that of Attorney-General, namely, the Advocate-General.

Sociological definitions of the professions often stress the significance of a professional organization. The bar has never had an organization parallel to the attorneys' Law Society or to the doctors' British Medical Association. As a result of the long history of the bar as an independent profession, its organization has centred around the four Inns of Court, which are much closer to the medieval collegiate system than to the modern professional organization. The Inns were most certainly not democratic in their organization but each was presided over by an autocratic executive committee known as the bench, which had an annually elected treasurer at its head. The benchers were chosen periodically from the distinguished members of the Inns: from the late seventeenth century, if not earlier, they were more often than not King's Counsel and other holders of royal favour, rather than well respected members of the junior bar as had previously been the case.[19] The extensive powers of the bench were challenged from time to time;[20] nevertheless, during the eighteenth century its control over the members and students of the Inns became absolute.[21]

[19] Holdsworth, 'The Rise of the Order of King's Counsel', *Law Quarterly Review* 36 (1920), 220-1.

[20] In 1821 D.W. Harvey, who had been refused a call to the bar by the benchers of the Inner Temple, appealed to the judges but his appeal was rejected. Abel-Smith and Stevens, *Lawyers and the Courts,* pp. 63-4. See also the *Second Report of the Select Committee on the Inns of Court,* PP, XVIII, 1834, which examined the circumstances associated with the Harvey Case.

[21] Holdsworth, *History of English Law,* XII, 18. In 1780 Lord Mansfield's decision in the *King vs. the Benchers of Gray's Inn* recognized the right of judges to review the

Although the Inns had served for centuries as both professional societies and as educational institutions, the seventeenth century saw the decline and decay of the latter function. The symptoms of this decline were already evident in the first half of the seventeenth century, but the crisis in education occurred, according to Holdsworth, during the Great Rebellion. The war acted as a catalyst by creating conditions appropriate for the rapid transformation of the Inns by forces which had been building in intensity for some fifty years or more.[22] During both the Commonwealth and the Restoration, attempts were made to reverse the process of educational decay, but they were uniformly unsuccessful. The judges who were active in the struggle to revive legal education in the Inns were forced to fight against the benchers, as well as the bar, whose members were ready to embrace the chance to escape from their educational obligations.[23]

As a consequence of this course of development, the eighteenth-century Inns of Court were professional clubs in which barristers could socialize with their colleagues, take meals in the great communal halls, and practise their profession in the numerous chambers within the precincts of the Inns. With the disappearance of formal legal education from the Inns, their importance in the intellectual and political life of Britain was also greatly reduced.

> The Inns of Court had ceased to hold the position in the national life which they had held from the days of Fortescue to the middle of the seventeenth century. They were ceasing to be a university, to which many young men, who never intended to make their living by the law, came, in order to get the benefit of social as well as intellectual education and training, which their common life and activities and system of teaching gave to their inmates.[24]

While the judges included in this study were at the Inns, no formal legal education was provided by the Inns nor was any attempt made to insure that prospective barristers had even a rudimentary knowledge of the law.[25] The only requirement that had to be fulfilled

decisions of the Inns. According to Mansfield, the Inns of Court 'are voluntary societies, which, for ages, have submitted to government analogous to that of other seminaries of learning. But all the power they have concerning admissions to the Bar, is delegated to them from the Judges, and, in every instance, their conduct is subject to their (the Judges') control as visitors . . .' *The English Reports,* I Douglas 354-7, XCIX, King's Bench Division (XXVIII), pp. 227-9.

[22]Holdsworth, *History of English Law,* VI, 487-90; Wilfrid R. Prest, *The Inns of Court 1590-1640* (London, 1972), pp. 124-37, 237.

[23]*Ibid.*

[24]Holdsworth, *History of English Law,* XII, 15.

[25]Reader, *Professional Men,* p. 79.

before a prospective barrister was called to the bar was that he ate twelve terms of meals in the Commons of his Inn and wait for five years after his admission to the Inn. Even these rules were not strictly enforced, and it was not until 1762 that the Inns drafted a set of common rules regulating calls to the bar. These rules, whose purpose was to encourage university men to enter the Inns and thereby ensure the gentlemanly quality of their members, [26] stated that:

> The standing for the bar be five years from admission, none to be called under the age of 21 years; that 12 terms' commons be actually kept; that masters of arts and bachelors of laws of the University of Oxford and Cambridge be dispensed with two years' standing, but not with any commons; no exception with regard to Ireland or the West Indies; no attorney or solicitor, clerk in chancery or exchequer, to be called until they have discontinued practice as such for two years.[27]

The source and effect of these rules which gave advantages to university men were undoubtedly more social than educational. Although a large number of Inns of Court men went to university, it never became a prerequisite for the bar. In addition, the provisions for the study of law at Oxford and Cambridge were at best meagre until the middle of the nineteenth century, giving a degree in civil law only. Since neither the universities nor the Inns were prepared to provide a satisfactory legal education for the future barrister, he was left to his own devices to gain sufficient training in the law to enable him to practise his chosen profession. The two most common methods were either for him to spend time in an attorney's office as an articled clerk, a system which as we shall see was increasingly frowned upon, or to attach himself to a special pleader, conveyancer, or junior barrister who for a fee of 100 guineas per year would provide the student with a practical training in the elements of the law.

Not until the middle of the nineteenth century were any steps taken to re-introduce education into the Inns of Court. In 1846 and 1847 a few legal lecturers were appointed to the four Inns, and with the urging of Richard Bethell, later Lord Chancellor Westbury, the Council on Legal Education was established in 1852 to supervise the legal education of the Inns. Despite the establishment by that body of a number of readerships, law courses, and a voluntary examination, the Royal Commission on the Inns of Court of 1854 found facilities for legal education insufficient. In spite of this public criticism, the

[26]Paul Lucas, 'Blackstone and the Reform of the Legal Profession', *English Historical Review* 77 (1962), 460.

[27]In 1793 the privileges conferred on graduates of Oxford and Cambridge were extended to graduates of the University of Dublin. *Report of the Select Committee on Legal Education,* PP.,X., 1846, p. 307.

Inns were slow to institute reform, and it was not until almost twenty years later in 1872 that a compulsory system of courses and examinations was established.[28]

The reforms in legal education had a negligible impact on the judges included in this study, since even the youngest of the group, William Ventris Field and Nathaniel Lindley, were called in 1850, by which time only the most minimal changes had been instituted. The quality of the bench throughout the years 1727-1875 was high despite the degenerate state of professional education. Nevertheless, the standardization of legal studies at the Inns and the establishment of minimal educational requirements, an integral part of the professionalization process, was essential in an age when the bar was expanding at an unprecedented rate. Reform could not guarantee brilliant or outstanding barristers and judges, nor could it assure professional success to those called to the bar, but it could, if properly organized, ensure that all barristers received a basic legal education.

The Judiciary and the Courts

By 1727 the English courts of justice, which were the product of hundreds of years of development, conflict and reorganization, had begun to be fixed in their modern form. The common law and equity courts had gained supremacy over the ecclesiastical and prerogative courts; the judges held office during good behaviour rather than during royal pleasure; and the jurisdictions of the three common law courts were almost entirely unified. During the remainder of the eighteenth and nineteenth centuries the reform of the judicial machinery of England continued, and despite the inertia of tradition which sometimes made the courts, judges and lawyers resistent to change, jurisdictions were clarified, the number of judges was increased, centralization was imposed, sinecures, fees and patronage were reduced, and court procedures were rationalized.

The judicial establishment of England in 1727 consisted of seventeen judges: the Lord Chancellor and Master of the Rolls in the Court of Chancery, two Chief Justices, one Chief Baron, six puisne judges, and three puisne barons in the three common law courts, plus a cursitor baron in the Court of Exchequer – an expert in finance, and one judge each in the Prerogative Court of Canterbury and the Court of Admiralty. By 1875, when the population of England had increased more than five-fold, the number of judges was only twenty-seven. In

---

[28]Holdsworth, *History of English Law*, XV, 237-9. See also *Report of the Select Committee on Legal Education*, PP, X, 1846; and *Report of the Commissioners appointed to inquire into Arrangements in the Inns of Court*, PP, XVIII, 1854-5.

1813. one judge, the Vice-Chancellor, was added to the Chancery; in 1841 the number of Vice-Chancellors was increased to three, and in addition, two Justices of Appeal in Chancery were appointed in 1851. Each of the three common law courts gained an additional puisne judge in 1830 and in 1868, while the cursitor baron was eliminated from the Exchequer in 1856. No additions or deletions occurred in the number of judges in civil law courts, although their jurisdictions had passed to newly established courts between 1857 and 1860. In this process, the ecclesiastical Prerogative Court was divided into the Court of Divorce and Matrimonial Cases and the Court of Probate, both of which were presided over by the same judge.[29] Finally, in November 1875, a unified Supreme Court of Judicature was established with a High Court composed of five divisions (Chancery, Common Pleas, Exchequer, Queen's Bench, and Probate, Divorce, and Admiralty) and a Court of Appeal.[30]

The reorganization which was accomplished by the Judicature Acts of 1873 and 1875 was preceded by a number of court reforms. Although they were haphazard in their goals and limited in their effectiveness, these reforms indicate the depth of dissatisfaction with the structure of the judicial system which existed both in Parliament and the profession. The goals of the reform movement can be divided into two main categories: one, a rationalization and simplification of the appeals process; and two, a professionalization of those courts and judicial offices which were outside the control of the Royal Courts.

The first step in the creation of a uniform appeals process was taken in 1830 with the restructuring of the Court of Exchequer Chamber — the appeals court for the common law courts. The process was continued in 1848 when the Court of Crown Cases Reserved was established to provide appeals for criminal cases, and in 1851 with the establishment of a permanent court for Chancery appeals.[31]

Two other appeals courts, the House of Lords and the Judicial Committee of the Privy Council, became professionalized during this era. Traditionally any peer could participate in the judicial proceedings of the Lords as a court of appeal. By the nineteenth century, however, the ability of lay peers to influence the verdict of the nation's court of final appeal was recognized as a serious problem. As a result, it was decided in the *O'Connell Case* of 1844 that lay peers would henceforth be prohibited from voting on appeals to the Lords.

[29] Joseph Haydn, *The Book of Dignities* (London, 1890), pp. 349-50.

[30] Abel-Smith and Stevens, *Lawyers and the Courts,* p. 50.

[31] *Ibid.,* p. 43 and Holdsworth, *History of English Law,* I, *passim.*

A more extensive reform occurred in the judicial machinery of the Privy Council in 1833. As a result of this change initiated by the eccentric, but ever energetic Lord Brougham, not only did the court with a newly created professional judiciary hear appeals from the rapidly expanding colonial courts, but it emerged as the appeals court for ecclesiastical and admiralty cases.[32] In colonial appeals it replaced an earlier committee made up of a motley bench of non-professionals which was satirized by Brougham in his 1828 speech.[33] The Judicial Committee also superseded the somewhat less than professional Court of Delegates, which had served as the appeals court for Doctors' Commons. The Court of Delegates was not a permanent body, but was appointed from time to time to hear specific appeals. In the eighteenth century it had included laymen on its bench, but by the nineteenth century the tribunal was composed of three common law judges and five civil law advocates; usually the most inexperienced civilian advocates were chosen because they had little other business. Not surprisingly this court, which violated all the principles of the new administrative professionalism, was abolished in 1832.[34]

The provincial court system, too, was given a permanent and professional foundation during this period. As indicated earlier, the Courts of Requests had served as small claims courts in the eighteenth and early nineteenth centuries. Until 1833 the judges in these courts were laymen appointed to hear cases under the title of commissioners. Between 1833 and the final abolition of these courts, some attempt was made to give their judiciary a professional look.[35] Finally in 1846, due to public pressure and despite the opposition of sections of the bar and some London solicitors, sixty country court circuits were established to expedite the hearing of small civil suits.[36]

---

[32] D.B. Swinfen, 'Henry Brougham and the Judicial Committee of the Privy Council', *Law Quarterly Review* 90 (1974), *passim*.

[33] As quoted in Holdsworth, *History of English Law,* XII, 298. According to Brougham, the Appeals Court in the Privy Council usually included one lawyer; 'but the rest are laymen . . . the Master of the Rolls alone is always to be seen there, of the lawyers; for the rest, one meets sometimes in company with him, an elderly and most respectable gentleman, who has formerly been an ambassador, and was a governor with much credit to himself in difficult times; and now and then a junior Lord of the Admiralty, who has been neither ambassador or lawyer, but would be exceedingly fit for both functions, only that he happened to be educated for neither. . . '.

[34] G.I.O. Duncan, *The High Court of Delegates* (Cambridge, 1971), pp. 28-30, 178-84.

[35] Winder, 'Courts of Requests', pp. 380-81, 394.

[36] Abel-Smith and Stevens, *Lawyers and the Courts,* pp. 34-6.

There was at least one revision in the jurisdiction of the courts during the decades which cannot be explained by reference to the desire for administrative efficiency. In fact according to a recent study, the abolition of the equity court of the Exchequer was the result of its abandonment by equity lawyers in the 1830s. This court, which had been in a position to relieve the pressure on the court of Chancery, was dissolved in 1841 not because it had failed to serve the public adequately, but because its structure did not suit the profession.[37]

The lack of a centrally organized judicial system until the 1870s was reflected in the physical arrangement of the courts themselves. The Royal Courts did not receive a permanent home until 1884 with the opening of G.E. Street's massive gothic structure on the Strand. Prior to the opening of this building, which housed all the divisions of the newly organized Supreme Court, the courts had been spread over the City, Westminster and Holborn, and were housed for the most part in borrowed or makeshift accommodations. Some of the courts had had permanent quarters in Westminster Hall since the Middle Ages. There was not sufficient space in that ancient hall to house the ever expanding and busy judicial establishment. Even the new courts at Westminster built by Sir John Soane in the 1820s proved insufficient. The Court of Chancery, for example, did not use the courtroom built for its use, but instead borrowed the great hall of Lincoln's Inn and lent its official headquarters to the Probate and Divorce Courts which had no permanent locations. In addition to the sites already mentioned, courts also met during the first three quarters of the nineteenth century in the London Guildhall, Doctors' Commons, Serjeants' Inn, and the Rolls House in Chancery Lane.[38]

The judges who served in these diverse surroundings were all either barristers or doctors of law, all judges since the seventeenth century having been selected from the practising bar. The head of the judicial establishment was the Lord High Chancellor, whose office had both legal and political functions. He was the first judge of the realm, the head of the Court of Chancery, a cabinet member, was always given a peerage with his office, and sat on the woolsack as speaker of the House of Lords. The Chancellor held his office for the life of the government, as did all the members of the cabinet, and an electoral defeat of the administration resulted in a loss of office.[39] He

[37]W.H. Bryson, *The Equity Side of Exchequer* (Cambridge, 1975), pp. 160-6.

[38]Holdsworth, *History of English Law*, I, 648-9.

[39]Between 1714 and 1801 the Lord Chancellor was a member of the government but his office did not depend on the life of the government. 'He was in practice as well as in theory responsible only to the King.' Brown, *Chathamites*, pp. 235-6.

appointed the other judges, often in consultation with the Prime Minister, the other judges, and especially prior to the reign of Queen Victoria, with the sovereign. There were, however, several judicial offices to which the Chancellor did not have the absolute right of appointment, namely the Chief Justice of King's Bench, the Chief Justice of Common Pleas, the Master of the Rolls, and the Lords Justices of Appeal.[40]

Throughout our period, the House of Lords stood as the court of final appeal, the functioning of which became increasingly professional as a result of the *O'Connell Case* and 1876 Appellate Jurisdiction Act. To fulfil the judicial role of the House of Lords required the periodic appointment of Law Lords. As a consequence, it was usual for several judges besides the Lord Chancellor to be created peers, most often the Chief Justice of King's Bench, and sometimes the Chief Justice of Common Pleas, the Chief Baron and the Master of the Rolls. Since 1876, a formal system of ensuring a permanent judicial presence in the Lords has existed with the establishment of the office of Lords of Appeal in Ordinary. Originally two Lords of Appeal were appointed as life peers; this was increased to four, and now stands at nine.[41]

Besides those judges who were raised to the peerage and were thereby enabled to sit in the House of Lords, the holders of three judicial offices were eligible to sit in the Commons: the Master of the Rolls, the Judge of the Court of Admiralty, and the Judge of the Prerogative Court of Canterbury. The reasons for these exceptions to the general rule that prohibited judges from sitting in the Commons may be traced to the ecclesiastical origins of the two latter offices. They were only annexed to the lay judicial machinery in 1858. The Master of the Rolls did not acquire separate jurisdiction until rather late (even in the eighteenth century he was considered a deputy of the Chancellor instead of a judge in his own right)[42] and probably for this reason was not prevented from sitting in the Commons until the Judicature Act of 1873. Since the implementation of that act, the separation of the judiciary from the House of Commons has been complete, though of course judges to this day may sit in the Lords, and the Chancellor is still a member of the Cabinet.

The nineteenth-century zeal for reform, led by such figures as Samuel Romilly, Henry Brougham, Richard Bethell and Roundell Palmer, not only affected the procedure, organization, education and

[40]Peter Archer, *The Queen's Courts* (Harmondsworth, 1963), pp. 60-1.

[41]Haydn, *Book of Dignities*, pp. 351-2; *ibid.*, pp. 86-7.

[42]Holdsworth, *History of English Law*, I, pp. 419-21.

administrative structure of the courts, but had a direct impact on the judicial bench. As a result of efforts by men such as these, the proposals for reform in the judicial machinery and legal system made by Jeremy Bentham were partially implemented. Until the 1820s, the discrepancies between the official salaries of the puisne and chief justices were small, but the actual difference in incomes was enormous. As a result of legislative action in the last quarter of the eighteenth and first half of the nineteenth century, a scale of salaries was established, and no longer could these be supplemented by the collection of fees, sales of offices, or the appointment of near relatives to sinecure offices. While the new legislation recognized the need for a salary differential between the chief and puisne judges, it ended the system by which puisnes would be earning one or two thousand pounds a year while their chiefs received fifteen or twenty thousand pounds. As part of the process of administrative rationalization, Parliament, in addition to establishing fixed judicial salaries, decreed that court fees would now go to the treasury and not to the judges, abolished most of the sinecurial offices, forbade judges to sell offices under their patronage, and established a system of pensions.[43] These reforms did not abolish judicial patronage. The Chief Justices and the Chancellor retained possession of a number of non-judicial offices attached to their courts, and the Chancellor's control of his clerical patronage remained intact. The reforms did, however, eliminate those offices to which few if any duties were attached, but carried salaries of hundreds and sometimes thousands of pounds.[44]

The business of the courts was usually confined to London, but twice a year the judges and barristers would leave their homes and courts to travel the circuit providing for the administration of royal

[43]In 1850 the salaries of the various judges were as follows: 1. Lord Chancellor £10,000 plus £4,000 as speaker of the House of Lords. 2. Master of the Rolls £7,000. 3. Vice-Chancellor of England £6,000 (office abolished in 1850). 4. 3 Vice-Chancellors £5,000 each. 5. Chief Justice of Queen's Bench £8,000. (officially £10,000 but by consent of Lord Denman the lower salary was paid). 6. Chief Justice of Common Pleas £8,000. 7. Chief Baron of the Exchequer £7,000. 8. 12 puisne judges of Q.B., C.P., and Exch. £5,000 each. 9. Judge of the Court of Admiralty £4,000. 10. Judge of the Prerogative Court of Canterbury £4,300. The above information is derived from the *Report of the Select Committee on Official Salaries,* pp. 208-209, and *Report on Judges' Salaries,* PP, XXXIII, 1850, *passim.*

[44]In 1810 the annual receipts of sinecure offices executed wholly or chiefly by Deputy, in the Law Courts of England, were £62, 462. Some of the more valuable of the sinecure offices were the Office for executing the Laws concerning Bankrupts (Chancery) £4,544 *p.a.* Chief Clerk of King's Bench £5,544 *p.a.* Filizer, Exigenter, and Clerk of Outlawries (King's Bench) £3,955 *p.a.,* Filizer for Middlesex and other counties (Common Pleas) £736 p.a. All these offices were held by the heirs or near relatives of former holders of the Chancellorship or one of the Chief Justiceships. *Report of the Select Committee on Sinecure Offices,* PP, X, 1810, pp. 43-4. *Report of the Select Committee on Sinecure Offices,* PP, VI, 1834, p. 4.

justice in the provinces. Until the reorganization of the system in 1876, there were six circuits in England, each of which was presided over by two judges of the high court and attended by the barristers who were members of the circuit.

A system of itinerant justice had existed in England since the reign of Henry II, and the assize system was established in an embryonic form as early as the reign of Edward I. Over the centuries the assizes underwent structural modifications but even in the eighteenth and nineteenth centuries their medieval origins had not been completely obscured. Strictly speaking, the judges of assizes did not derive their judicial powers on the circuit from their offices as judges of the high court, but rather by virtue of temporary writs, issued regularly, appointing them commissioners of assize. The commissioners provided for the administration of criminal cases committed for trial before the court of assize and civil cases begun in any of the three common law courts. Thus litigants in civil suits were spared the inconvenience of coming to Westminster for trial.[45]

During the course of the assize, the judges and barristers visited each of the towns on the circuit, usually the county towns, to attend to all those cases which had arisen since the previous meeting of the assize court. Not only was the session of the assize court an important legal event for the town, but also one of the most elaborate ceremonial affairs of the year. One judge, Sir John W. Huddleston, has left a long description of the ceremonial details of the assize which provides us with an idea of the scale of the pageantry and the importance of the assize in the life of a town.

> On arriving at the Station [this was written after the opening of the railway] of the Assize Town, the Judge is received by the High Sheriff, the Chaplain, & the Under Sheriff, uncovered, accompanied by 2 trumpeters, & in some Counties by Javelin men, in others by the Police or Constabulary. The Marshal presents the High Sheriff & Chaplain to the Judge.
>
> A procession is formed. . . They go to the carriage, the Trumpets are sounded as the Judge gets into the carriage, which he does first, the Sheriff & Chaplain standing on each side of the carriage door. . . The cortège then proceeds to the Lodgings.[46]

---

[45]The modern general commission of assize is actually composed of four specific commissions as follows: (1) of oyer and terminer (power to try criminal cases); (2) of gaol delivery (power to clear jails of offenders); (3) of nisi prius (power to try civil cases); (4) of the peace (all JPs are bound to be present at their county's assize). Clifford Walsh, ed., *The Dictionary of English Law,* I, (London, 1959), 167, Bryce Lyon, *A Constitutional and Legal History of Medieval England,* (New York, 1960), pp. 445-6, and Holdsworth, *History of English Law,* I, 274-85.

[46]Cambridge University Library, Pollock MMS., box 1, D/2.

The costume worn was in keeping with the importance of the occasion. The Sheriff, according to Huddleston, was dressed either in uniform or court dress, while in Cathedral and University towns the judges donned a 'scarlet robe, belt, & hood with beaver hat, full bottomed wig, & ermine mantle'[47] before going to church, which they did soon after entering the town.

Each barrister, soon after his call to the bar, picked a circuit and thereafter was restricted by tradition to practise only on that circuit, although change was possible. In addition, a barrister was allowed to take special retainers on other circuits at a higher than normal fee, which was intended to discourage or limit the practice. Until the end of the Napoleonic Wars all barristers went the circuit, but subsequently chancery barristers usually confined their practice to the equity courts and did not join a circuit.[48] The business of the assize courts provided the common law barrister with a large share of his professional income, and the quantity of business on the circuit was often the primary determinant of a successful professional year. The assizes were often the arena in which a young barrister made his name by success in an early case. The income earned in the assize courts was supplemented by that which could be earned in the quarter sessions of the county magistrates, usually held soon after the close of the assizes. The sessions were attended mainly by younger barristers and afforded them the opportunity to gain some income and experience without having to compete with the top barristers.

The session of the assize courts required the lawyers to give up the society of London for several weeks twice a year. To compensate for this, each of the six circuits, the Home, the Western, the Oxford, the Northern, the Norfolk, and the Midland, established an institution known as the bar mess.[49] These messes provided a social life and

---

[47] Ibid.

[48] Atlay, *The Victorian Chancellors*, I, 386.

[49] The English counties were divided into circuits as follows: *Home Circuit* — Essex, Hertfordshire, Kent, Surrey, Sussex, *Midland Circuit* — Derbyshire, Leicestershire, Lincolnshire, Northamptonshire, Nottinghamshire, Rutland, Warwickshire. *Norfolk Circuit* — Bedfordshire, Buckinghamshire, Cambridgeshire, Huntingdonshire, Norfolk, Suffolk. *Oxford Circuit* — Berkshire, Gloucestershire, Herefordshire, Monmouthshire, Oxfordshire, Shropshire, Staffordshire, Worcestershire. *Northern Circuit* — Cumberland, Durham, Lancashire, Northumberland, Westmoreland, Yorkshire. *Western Circuit* — Cornwall, Devon, Dorset, Hampshire, Somersetshire, Wiltshire. There were, in addition, two Welsh circuits which included the English county of Cheshire. Middlesex was not on any circuit, and cases in that county were tried by the King's Bench (civil) and by London officials (criminal) until the establishment of the Central Criminal Court in 1834.

camaraderie for the members of the circuit, and, from descriptions of the messes, were primarily concerned with entertainment, eating and drinking.[50] In addition the messes acted as guardians of the professional conduct of the members and fostered a feeling of professional brotherhood and communal spirit among the barristers.[51]

Life on the circuit had developed in an age when barristers travelled on horse-back or in carriages. While the organization and institutions of the circuit survived into the twentieth century, the coming of the railway made an impact on the system. No longer did a barrister have to leave his family for weeks at a time to travel the circuit. For those circuits near to London it was possible for the barrister to commute to the assizes on a daily or weekly basis. In fact the ease by which a London based barrister could reach an assize town by rail may have influenced the establishment of near monopolies on each of the circuits, which limited the ability of barristers who were not members from appearing as counsel in its assizes. To this end a system of special fees was implemented and somewhat later attempts were made to apply similar measures to the quarter sessions.[52]

The Gentlemen of the Bar

Earlier the organizational division of the legal profession into an upper branch, the barristers, and a lower branch, the attorneys and solicitors, was examined. The distinctions were not just a reflection of differences in occupational functions, but represented a very real social cleavage. The barrister who did not deal directly with clients and who only received fees through the medium of the attorney was considered a gentleman; the attorney was not. Direct contact with a client smacked of business, and a tradition which connected the attorney with sharp practice gave him a reputation of dishonesty. This reputation was resented by the attorneys, and one of the primary objects of their professional organization was to alter the public image of their profession, a task in which they were ultimately successful.

The barrister, and more especially the judge, had far better reputations than the attorney, but the bar was by no means free of the

---

[50]Jeafferson, *A Book About Lawyers,* II, 263.

[51]A. Polson, *Law and Lawyers: or sketches and illustrations of legal history and biography,* I, (London, 1840), 136.

[52]Abel-Smith and Stevens, *Lawyers and the Courts,* pp. 220-1; Jeafferson, *A Book About Lawyers,* I, 144-5; and J.A. Strahan, *The Bench and Bar of England,* (Edinburgh, 1919), p. 12.

stigma of participating in the subversion of justice for profit. It is in this vein that we find Dr. Thomas Arnold writing to his friend John Taylor Coleridge:

> I think if I were asked what station within possibility I would choose, as the prize of my son's well doing in life, I should say the place of an English judge. But then, in proportion to my reverence for the office of a judge, is, to speak plainly, my abhorrence of the business of an advocate. . . . I have been thinking, in much ignorance, whether there is any path to the bench except by the bar; that is, whether in conveyancing, or in any other branch of the profession, a man may make his real knowledge available, . . . without that painful necessity of being retained by an attorney to maintain a certain cause, and of knowingly suppressing the truth, for so it must sometimes happen, in order to advance your own argument.[53]

The extent to which these sentiments expressed mid-nineteenth-century public opinion can be judged by the apparent need felt by at least one barrister, Fitzjames Stephen, to defend the moral basis of his profession. In 1861 he wrote,

> To judge from the representations given by popular writers, it would appear to be the common opinion that such practices [trickery, garbling or misquoting cases, and attempts to confuse witnesses] are regarded, both by the bench and by the bar, as triumphs of ingenuity. . . . The simple truth is that advocacy is neither more or less moral than other professions. It is a practical expedient designed as the best mode of doing a very difficult thing, namely administering the law.[54]

In order to preserve its gentlemanly status and to protect and improve the reputation of the profession, the Bar Committee, and later the General Council of the Bar which superseded it, began in the late nineteenth century to formalize and codify traditional elements of the bar's ethical code.[55] The strict code of professional etiquette which emerged prohibited the formation of partnerships and advertising, discouraged social intercourse with solicitors, and forbade barristers to have direct access to clients in contentious business and from suing for fees, which were designated as an 'honorarium' and not a payment for services rendered.

---

[53] Arthur P. Stanley, *Life of Thomas Arnold D.D.,* (London, 1910), p. 299.

[54] Fitzjames Stephen, 'The Morality of Advocacy', *Cornhill Magazine* 3 (1861), 454-8.

[55] Abel-Smith and Stevens, *Lawyers and the Courts,* pp. 221-2; W.W. Bolton, *Conduct and Etiquette at the Bar,* (London, 1971), pp. 8-9.

The status of the profession was protected if not enhanced by these regulations and by the inclusion of the bar among the higher gentlemanly professions. The foundation, however, upon which the reputation and status of the bar rested, consisted of the honours which accrued to its most successful members. At the end of the eighteenth century one writer could describe the bar as the 'high road to the first situations in the state' in which 'men of good abilities and great professional fame, are frequently called to the highest offices of society'.[56] The bar was the only profession in which knighthoods were regularly bestowed and which was graced on a regular basis with peerages. In 1810 John Campbell, future Lord Chief Justice and Lord Chancellor, provided an insight into the status of the up and coming young barrister when he wrote to his brother, 'I now live on a footing of perfect equality with men of high birth, of the best education, and the most elegant manners.'[57]

[56]T. Ruggles, *The Barrister or Strictures on the Proper Education for the Bar,* II, (London, 1792), 158.
[57]John Campbell, *The Life of John Lord Campbell,* ed. Hon. Mrs. Hardcastle, I. (London, 1881), 225.

2

THE PREPARATION FOR A PROFESSION

The Inner for the rich man,
The Middle for the poor;
Lincoln for the gentleman,
Gray's Inn for the boor.[1]

Prior to his call to the bar, the future barrister had to pass through many years of general and professional education. In this chapter I consider the educational careers of the judges in secondary school, university, and the Inns of Court with the dual aim of describing the educational patterns of the judiciary and of evaluating the social implications of those patterns.

The choice available in planning the educational career of the prospective barrister was extensive and the desirable paths by no means remained constant throughout the eighteenth and nineteenth centuries. In order to aid parents in choosing the best possible course for their sons, numerous guidebooks and pamphlets were available for their edification; those with acquaintances at the bar or on the bench could benefit from personal professional advice. In order to provide a context for the data on the educational careers of the judges, I begin by examining attitudes towards the choice of the law as a suitable career, and the details of the pre-professional and professional educational programmes suggested for the future barrister.

Attitudes towards the Law and Education

The status, wealth, power and glamour of the bar, and especially of the bench, were obvious to the eighteenth- and nineteenth-century Englishman. Of all the professions, the only one in which successful practitioners were regularly advanced to the peerage was the law; and the only professionals whose grandeur surpassed that of the judges of the high court were the most famous military commanders, the Marlboroughs and Wellingtons. Those writers who propounded the advantages of entering the legal profession never tired of emphasizing the prizes which awaited the successful barrister, which included 'not only large fortunes, in acquiring which, moreover, are also gained

[1] Strahan, *The Bench and Bar of England*, p. 198.

great reputation and influence in society; but of a long series of Offices and Employments, all lucrative and dignified in proportion to their eminence'.[2]

While few would doubt that the bar and bench were, in terms of status and financial and honorific rewards, at least equal to the other higher professions, they stood apart from the army, navy, church, and top echelons of the civil service until the third quarter of the nineteenth century. Unlike the others, the law was a competitive profession even prior to the introduction of a system of entrance exams in the military and the civil services between 1855 and 1870. Besides the bar, the other higher professions were reserved for the sons of the rich and influential. Appointments were either purchased (as in the army) or made on the basis of connection and patronage (as in the civil service, navy, and the most lucrative livings in the church). Advancement required little or no proof of competence, especially if access to political influence was available.

By contrast, in the law competition acted to limit the importance of connection if it did not entirely eliminate its impact. The assurance that success was possible without connection, and that with hard work nothing was out of reach, not even the woolsack, was no doubt most encouraging to middle-class parents for whom the professional guides were written. Parents were assured that the bar was a career open to talent, and that perseverance coupled with ability and merit were qualities which would lead their sons to successful careers as barristers and perhaps judges. One late eighteenth-century guide to the law guaranteed its readers that in earlier days:

> a recommendation of protection to the great, was absolutely essential to success.
>
> Thanks to the protecting GENIUS of this flourishing and happy island; no such apology can now be admitted; a certain honourable road is now open to abilities, and merit finds it's [sic] sure reward, early in life enjoying those fruits, to which, in former days, the lucubration of twenty years scarce gave a distant possibility of access.[3]

While it was useless for these books and articles on the law to deny that connection was useful to the young lawyer, they attempted to emphasize that it was not essential for success by giving examples of famous judges who, it was claimed, reached the most exalted

---

[2]Samuel Warren, *Introduction to Law Studies,* I (London, 1845), 1.
[3]Ruggles, *The Barrister,* I, 15-17.

positions in the profession completely through their own exertions.[4]
As a consequence, the guides helped to propagate what may be called
the myth of the self-made barrister-judge, whose existence was rarely
disputed in the legal literature of the eighteenth- and nineteenth-
centuries. An evaluation of the validity of this myth must be
postponed to the next chapter; however, there can be no doubt but that
the myth had established itself in the professional imagination by the
late eighteenth century.

Connection, most of the guides insisted, could never make an
incompetent or ignorant lawyer successful, for who would be foolish
enough to entrust life, liberty, or property to a young man simply
because he was well-connected? Severe competition, which helped to
minimize the value of wealth, patronage and birth in pursuit of the
honours of the bar, was the best ally of the young barrister who had to
rely primarily on his own efforts.[5]

While the vast majority of writers on the law agreed that
competition would weed out the incompetent but well-connected,
there was a lack of consensus on the importance of luck. Some guides
propounded the view that ability would win out whatever obstacles
were placed in its path, while others insisted that perseverance and
ability had to be pushed along by Lady Luck. What was more certain
was that young men with influence were better advised to use their
connections to get a sure place in one of the other 'higher professions'
rather than wasting it on the uncertain prospects of the law. It was in
this vein that John Campbell wrote to his father in 1800, at the time
he was deciding on his profession; 'For one who can enter into any
advantageous line of life with the probability of success, I think it
would be folly to even think of becoming a lawyer, — the chance is
four in one that he fails'.[6]

Of course the uncertainty of the bar even for the well-connected
could be viewed in two diametrically opposed ways. On the positive
side it might be a source of encouragement for a family without
connections to send its son to the bar since it would seem that he would
be at no great disadvantage; conversely, it might encourage the same
parents to urge their son to pursue another profession of lower
status and eventually lesser rewards, but one in which competition
was not as stiff and in which the chances of success were better than

[4]Thomas N. Talfourd, 'On the Profession of the Bar', *The London Magazine and
Review*, 1 n.s. (March, 1825), 323.

[5]Richard L. Edgeworth, *Essays on Professional Education*, (London, 1809), pp.
283, 334-5, and Warren, *Introduction to Law Studies*, I, 6-7.

[6]Campbell, *Life* 1, 48

the 'four in one' at which Campbell rated the law. Despite all the attractions of the bar as a profession, many guidebooks suggested that parents try to direct their sons to other occupations.

The metaphor of the law as a lottery was continually emphasized in the professional guides. In an imaginary dialogue written in the 1780s we read; 'In this lottery, Policrites, the number of great prizes will ever bear a small proportion to the number of competitors.'[7] By the mid-nineteenth century the problem had, if anything, worsened according to the *Saturday Review* which warned: 'While legal business which had to be transacted by barristers had fallen off about one half since the reforms in the Common-Law and Equity procedure [in the 1830s and 1840s], we are informed that the entries at the Inns of Court have pretty nearly doubled.'[8]

Many guides warned the prospective barrister that although the layman's view of the profession was one which emphasized the wealthy and famous barrister and judge, these men represented but a small percentage of those who had been called to the bar. Success, if it were ever to come at all, lay in the distant future only. In consequence, one of the most valuable assets a young barrister could possess was 'a large stock of dignified patience, to enable him to go through the long Pythagorean probation of silence.'[9]

The briefless barrister not only appeared as a spectre in the guidebooks to the professions, but was also a frequent character, albeit a pitiable one, in Victorian literature. In the *Pickwick Papers,* Dickens humorously exposes the plight of the unknown barrister: ' "Yes, he is a very young man," replied the attorney. "He was only called the other day. Let me see — he has not been at the bar eight years yet." '[10] In addition, Thackeray, who had first-hand experience in the Inns of Court since he spent some time reading for the bar, provided the following career analysis of an eminently successful barrister: 'But a short time since he was hungry and briefless in some

[7]Edward Wynne, *Eunomus or Dialogues Concerning the Law and Constitution of England,* II (London, 1785), 258-9. In a similar vein Adam Smith wrote: "Put your son apprentice to a shoemaker, there is little doubt of his learning to make a pair of shoes: But send him to study law, it is at least twenty to one if ever he makes such proficiency as will enable him to live by the business. . . . The counsellor at law who, perhaps, at near forty years of age, begins to make something by his profession, ought to receive the retribution, not only of his own so tedious and expensive education, but of that of more than twenty others who are never likely to make anything by it." Adam Smith, *An Inquiry Into the Nature and Causes of the Wealth of Nations* (New York, 1937), p. 106.

[8]*Saturday Review* 4 (December, 1857), 507.

[9]Edgeworth, *Essays on Professional Education,* p. 355.

[10]Charles Dickens, *The Posthumous Papers of the Pickwick Club* (Harmondsworth edn., 1972), p. 518.

garrett of the Inn; lived by stealthy literature; hoped, and waited, and sickened, and no clients came; exhausted his own means and his friends' kindness; had to remonstrate humbly with duns, and to implore the patience of poor creditors. Ruin seemed to be staring him in the face, when, behold a turn of the wheel of fortune, and the lucky wretch in possession of one of those prodigious prizes which are sometimes drawn in the great lottery of the Bar.'[11]

The guidebooks stressed that the newly called barrister might well have to face the very real prospect that he could spend years reading for the bar followed by fruitless years in search of a practice. If at one end of the lottery lay a pot of gold, at the other lay unemployment and failure; writers on the professions never failed to point this out. The law was portrayed as a profession in which there were only extremes — of success and wealth, or of failure and poverty. 'There is no profession in which there are so many *bona fide* practising members, making *nothing at all* by their profession. Not the prizes, but bare subsistence cannot be obtained without the greatest difficulty.'[12]

Before enrolling as a student in one of the Inns of Court, a young man and his parents, in addition to considering the advantages and disadvantages of the law, had to decide whether the intended lawyer had the physical and mental qualities which the guidebooks insisted were absolute prerequisites for success. According to Samuel Warren, himself a successful barrister, four mental attributes were essential to any barrister hoping to reach the heights of his profession, namely, a good memory, quick mind, fixed attention, and the ability to detect falsehoods.[13] Other guidebooks agreed that these were among the qualities necessary to the great lawyers though all were not essential to one content with moderate success. Interestingly enough, the one physical requirement deemed essential for success at the bar, namely stamina or a good constitution, received as much, if not more emphasis, than the mental attributes. Almost every book tried to impress on its readers the stresses which the practice of law, especially at the bar, could place on the body, and implored those of less than sturdy constitution to give up the idea of entering the law and to choose another profession.[14]

In his description of his student days at the Middle Temple in the early nineteenth century, John Taylor Coleridge adds credence to the

[11]William Thackeray, *The History of Pendennis* (Harmondsworth edn., 1972), p. 31.

[12]Thomson, *The Choice of a Profession,* pp. 95-6.

[13]Warren, *Introduction to Law Studies,* I, 68-9.

[14]Ruggles, *The Barrister,* I, 7.

emphasis on the importance of a good constitution. He provides us with a glimpse of the typical day of legal study which is enough to exhaust even the fittest of men.

> My life here is, I assure you, sufficiently laborious. Patteson calls and lights my candle soon after six regularly and then lights a fire, which we have always laid in one of our rooms overnight. We read till breakfast, and afterwards till about half-past ten; then go to the Office and sit till between three and four. We then return to smarten a little for a walk to the West, generally on some commission. We walk in this way at a good round pace till half-past five, and repair half famished to a coffee-house in Fleet Street. Here we sit for about an hour, home again for about as long, and then back to our pens and ink till between nine and ten. Then we shut our Law for the day and come home to read generally as long as we can keep our eyes open, which is seldom more than an hour.[15]

Once a parent had decided that his son should enter upon a career at the bar, there was no lack of advice on how best to educate his child for that profession. At the secondary school level the most attractive form of education for the future barrister, at least by the mid-nineteenth century, was seen as the public school.[16] Here a boy learned to participate and interact with his schoolfellows and acquire traits that were believed useful later in his career. Despite the real weaknesses of the public school education, it was considered superior to private tuition which did not inculcate the value of sociability. In addition, some writers saw private tuition as a source of pernicious influences especially on younger sons of wealthy families.

> At home, the sons of rich parents often find in grooms and coachmen worse and more dangerous companions, than any that could be found among the most idle and mischievous schoolboys; the younger sons of opulent parents, who are frequently intended for the law, are peculiarly subject to acquire in this manner, even under parental eye, tastes and notions, which destroy in a few months, perhaps in a few days, the precious labour of years, and all future hope of professional application and eminence. If the boy learns from the coachman, that the characteristic of a gentleman is to drive four in hand, he will look with admiration and perhaps envy upon his elder brother, on whom this glorious privilege devolves by birthright, or is entailed by family settlement, he will lament his hard fate in being condemned to college studies, and the drudgery of the law.[17]

[15]Bernard J.S. Lord Coleridge, *The Story of a Devonshire House,* (London, 1905), pp. 205-6.

[16]*Ibid.,* p. 24 and Thomson, *The Choice of a Profession, passim.*

[17]Edgeworth, *Essays on Professional Education,* p. 306. This guide, published in

University education had never been a prerequisite for the barrister, though it was for the civil advocates before the merging of the two branches of the profession in the late 1850s. Despite the fact that attendance at the universities was voluntary, most guidebooks to the professions and every work on the legal profession stressed the need for a university education for the prospective barrister. Probably the most influential discussion on the importance of a university education for a barrister, prior to the practical training at the Inns of Court, was the address delivered by Sir William Blackstone in 1758 on his becoming Vinerian Professor. Blackstone's address, *A Discourse on the Study of Law,* was issued both as a separate pamphlet and also as an introduction to his monumental series of lectures on the law, *Commentaries on the Laws of England.* In this address the great jurist, who served successively as judge of the courts of Common Pleas and King's Bench, presents us with a complete discussion of who should go to the Inns of Court, what constitutes a well-rounded study for the bar, and what type of legal study should be avoided. At this juncture it is the latter issues that are of primary interest. As for the first point, it will be sufficient to note that Blackstone was greatly concerned with encouraging the sons of the gentry and aristocracy to attend the Inns. He favoured this policy, not because he believed that they would necessarily practise law, but because their position in society, especially that of first sons, required them to have a basic knowledge of the laws of England.

Blackstone's first concern was that the barrister should be a well-educated man with at least an introduction to the subjects of a liberal education. He felt that not only did the lawyers avoid the universities but by the same token the universities avoided the teaching of law. This state of affairs required a remedy which, according to Blackstone, necessitated 'making academical education a previous step to the profession of the common law, and at the same time making the rudiments of the law a part of academical education'.[18] Blackstone's address, according to Professor Paul Lucas, strongly influenced the Inns of Court decision in 1762 to favour university graduates. That regulation conferred upon graduates of Oxford and Cambridge the right of being called to the bar in three years instead of the statutory five.[19] A number of later writers on legal education commended the Inns for this decision. By encouraging prospective barristers to attend

1809 before even the earliest public school reforms, still recommends public over private tuition.

[18]Blackstone, *Discourse on the Study of the Law,* p. 29.

[19]Paul Lucas, 'Blackstone and the Reform of the Legal Profession', *passim.*

university prior to enrolling in one of the Inns of Court, the benchers were seen to be serving the interests of the profession and of the nation. These writers agreed with Blackstone that a liberal and classical university background was essential for the barrister, since it was desirable that members of that profession should not be merely legal technicians but gentlemen.[20]

Second, the great jurist insisted that practical study of the law during a student's residence at the Inns did not provide the barrister with a sufficient knowledge of the law. Practical study must be combined with theory, which should be found in a properly constituted university course on the elements of English law. It was essential that the law student first be instructed in the 'elements and first principles' of his intended profession and only after that should he begin to study the practical side of the law.[21] Third, according to Blackstone, not only does the time spent at the university provide the student with a knowledge of the law and a general education but it also allows a few more years for maturation within the confines of the university before he ventures into London to study at the Inns of Court, where he 'is transplanted on a sudden into the midst of allurements to pleasure, without any restraint or check but what his own prudence can suggest.'[22]

Finally, Blackstone saw the institution of a university education as a prerequisite to admission to the Inns of Court as a method of social control. A general fear that socially undesirable men were being called to the bar is apparent in those guides written in the second half of the eighteenth and first decade of the nineteenth century. These men, to whom Blackstone referred as 'obscure and illiterate men,'[23] seemed to threaten the gentlemanly character of the bar which could only be preserved by restricting the entry of undesirable elements into the Inns and thereby into the profession. At the same time these writers, including Blackstone, believed it essential to encourage gentlemen to become barristers. Since there were no examinations or formal apprenticeship at the Inns of Court, the addition of university attendance to the established route to the bar would, it was believed, ensure the gentlemanly status of the barrister.[24]

---

[20] Polson, *Law and Lawyers,* I, 5, and Wynne, *Dialogues Concerning the Law and Constitution of England,* II, 20.

[21] Blackstone, *Discourse on the Study of the Law,* pp. 27-9.

[22] *Ibid.,* pp. 27-8.

[23] *Ibid.,* p. 29.

[24] Edgeworth, *Essays on Professional Education,* p. 315, and Wynne, *Dialogues Concerning the Law and Constitution of England,* II, 251-2.

In addition to advocating the university as a prerequisite to the bar, Blackstone also led the attack on the eighteenth-century trend for young men aspiring to the bar to spend some time as clerks in an attorney's office. In the first place, much as university attendance would encourage a more gentlemanly barrister, so attendance in an attorney's office would have the opposite effect. This result was inevitable if the current practice continued, according to Blackstone; 'for (as few persons of birth, or fortune, or even of scholastic education, will submit to the drudgery of servitude and the labour of copying the trash of an office) should this infatuation prevail to any considerable degree, we must rarely expect to see a gentleman of distinction or learning at the bar.'[25]

Blackstone and a number of other legal writers also questioned the value of law as taught in an attorney's office. The strong prejudice against the attorney was still prevalent in the late eighteenth and early nineteenth centuries and members of the lower branch were considered by members of the upper branch as little more than ignorant thieves. Thus one writer on the law concluded that a young man could learn no law from an attorney since the latter knew none, and the clerk only acquired bad habits with 'a probable loss of every sentiment of decency, morality, and religion, together with health'.[26] While Blackstone did admit that a number of distinguished barristers and judges had been trained by attorneys (this included Lord Hardwicke, the most important Lord Chancellor of the eighteenth century, who had retired from the bench two years before Blackstone's address was written), these men he insisted were the exceptions to the rule, and their success in the law had been in spite of and not as a result of their early training.[27] All the guidebooks agreed that parents should be wary not to allow their sons to follow this course of legal education, for its only result would be to teach them not law but the 'mechanical part of business.'[28]

Since pupilage with an attorney was held in low regard by the middle of the eighteenth century, law students had to find another system by which to acquire the professional knowledge essential to their careers. As a consequence of the decay of the educational functions of the Inns of Court, students logically began to turn to qualified practitioners for their training. The usual course, throughout

[25]Blackstone, *Discourse on the Study of the Law*, p. 29.

[26]Ruggles, *The Barrister*, I, 29-30. For another view see Smollett's comments on what is learned from an attorney, *Humphry Clinker*, p. 205.

[27]Blackstone, *Discourse on the Study of the Law*, p. 28.

[28]*Ibid.*, and Polson, *Law and Lawyers*, II, 29-31.

most of our period, was for the law student to learn at least the practical side of the law in the office of a special pleader, conveyancer, equity draftsman, or junior barrister. No formal syllabus existed and so the student who wanted to learn the principles of the law had to rely on advice provided by established barristers.

Examples of courses of study suggested by experienced members of the profession can be seen in two letters. The first, written by Lord Kenyon after his appointment as Chief Justice of King's Bench (1788-1802), provides us with a reading list for a law student of the late eighteenth century. The first task, according to Kenyon, is to read Blackstone's *Commentaries* carefully and then to reread it once or twice more if possible. Then the young student is advised to read Serjeant Hawkins's abridgement of *Coke on Littleton*, and once this had been completed, to proceed with the 'arduous task' of reading the complete version of *Coke on Littleton*. Next he should turn to modern court reporters, including the works of Sir J. Burrow, Mr. Douglas, Mr. Cowper, and the term reports. For an introduction to equity law, Kenyon suggests the first volume of Equity Cases, Mr. Cox's edition of Peere Williams, Hawkins's Reports in the time of Lord Talbot, and *Precedents in Chancery*. If the young man intends being called to the bar after the completion of this course of reading, then Kenyon suggests that he enlist himself in the office of an able special pleader under whose guidance he can get practical experience in his chosen profession by which to supplement the knowledge gleaned from the suggested literature.[29]

The second set of letters was written by Lord Cottenham to Lord Brougham in November 1841 soon after the end of the former's first term as Lord Chancellor. Cottenham advises Brougham on an appropriate course of legal apprenticeship for someone intending to be called to the chancery bar. He suggests that the best mode of preparation is for the prospective chancery barrister to spend two years under the supervision of a conveyancer, and afterwards another two years with an equity draftsman. Cottenham also concedes that although he was trained by a special pleader, this form of pupilage is in most cases not as satisfactory as that with a conveyancer or equity draftsman, since busy special pleaders have little time for students, and those who have but a small practice cannot be of much use to the student. If, however, the student does find a good special pleader with whom to study, he should not throw the chance away but spend one or

[29]Hon. George T. Kenyon, *The Life of Lloyd, First Lord Kenyon, Lord Chief Justice of England* (London, 1873), pp. 397-8. Lord Eldon proposed an almost identical course of study to a law student who hoped to practise at the Chancery bar, in a letter written in 1807. Holdsworth, *History of English Law*, XII, 87.

preferably two years with that practitioner and then an additional two years with a draftsman or conveyancer.[30]

School, University, and Inn of Court

As indicated in the professional guidebooks, the choice of a suitable school was most important for the future barrister. In order to facilitate an examination of the education of the judges, all schools which had a minimum of two judicial alumni are individually recognized in Table 1 (below). In addition those schools that only counted one judge among their old boys are grouped into five categories: miscellaneous public schools based on membership in the Headmasters' Conference;[31] miscellaneous grammar schools; other schools/at home: these include private and dissenting academies and private tuition at home; foreign schools; and those which are unknown. In all cases, if an individual attended more than one institution, his educational classification is based on the school last attended.

Table 1: Schools attended by future judges

School	1727-1760	1760-1790	1790-1820	1820-1850	1850-1875	Total
Eton	5	1	6	6	8	26(13%)
Westminster	5	4	0	3	3	15(7%)
Charterhouse	0	2	2	3	1	8(4%)
Harrow	0	0	3	3	1	7(3%)
Winchester	0	1	0	2	3	6(3%)
St. Paul's	0	0	1	3	2	6(3%)
Litchfield G.S.	4	0	0	0	0	4(2%)
Manchester G.S.	0	2	0	1	0	3(1%)
Ruthin G.S.	0	2	1	0	0	3(1%)
Reading G.S.	0	0	0	3	0	3(1%)
Merchant Taylors	0	1	0	0	1	2(1%)
Rugby	0	0	0	2	0	2(1%)
King's School, Canterbury	0	1	1	0	0	2(1%)

(continued)

[30]D.M.S. Watson Library, University College, London, Brougham MSS, 28.747 and 28.748.

[31]Membership in the Headmasters' Conference was chosen as the criterion for classifying a school as a public school. Despite the fact that this is anachronistic for the eighteenth and most of the nineteenth centuries, it was chosen as the only available criterion. In fact it affects the classification of only 5 schools in all.

Table 1 (continued)

School	1727-1760	1760-1790	1790-1820	1820-1850	1850-1875	Total
Palace School, Enfield	0	0	0	0	2	2(1%)
Edinburgh G.S.	0	0	0	1	1	2(1%)
Tonbridge G.S.	0	1	0	1	0	2(1%)
Newcastle G.S.	0	0	2	0	0	2(1%)
Miscellaneous Public Schools	0	0	1	1	3	5(2%)
Miscellaneous Grammar Schools	3	1	5	5	7	21(10%)
Other School/ at home	5	5	3	4	12	29(14%)
Foreign	0	0	1	0	0	1
Unknown	22	11	3	6	15	57(27%)
Total	44	32	29	44	59	208

The school careers of the judges spanned the period from 1690 to 1840. As a result of enormous changes in education and in the history of individual schools during these years, generalizations concerning the secondary education of members of the judiciary must be treated with caution. In addition, the analysis of the data on the educational choices of the members of the judiciary is further complicated by the lack of comparative evidence prior to the nineteenth century.

Only a handful of judges attended school after the initiation of the educational reforms of the first half of the nineteenth century usually associated with Dr. Thomas Arnold. Nevertheless, even in the eighteenth century the 'great public schools' had began to be recognized as the élite of the endowed schools. These schools included the seven national boarding schools, Eton, Westminster, Charterhouse, Winchester, Harrow, Rugby, and Shrewsbury — and the two day schools, St. Paul's and Merchant Taylors, which had only gained formal recognition of their élite status in the *Public Schools Commission* which issued its report in 1864. The Commission was headed by the Earl of Clarendon, whose name was bestowed collectively upon the nine élite public schools.

These schools provided education for more than one third of all the judges appointed between 1727 and 1875, and two schools between them, Eton and Westminster, accounted for 20% of the total. Six of the 'great public schools' dominated the secondary education of the members of the judiciary: Eton with 26 judicial alumni, Westminster 15, Charterhouse 8, Harrow 7, and Winchester and St. Paul's 6 each. Only one of the schools, Shrewsbury, was not represented at all, while Rugby and Merchant Taylors each had 2 old boys on the bench during this period.

The availability of printed school registers for most of the 'great public schools' means that few if any of the judges in the unknown category attended these élite institutions. For the other schools, the data can provide only a picture of the minimum number of judges who attended a particular institution. The data available for the periods 1727-60, 1760-90, and 1850-75 particularly suffer from a high percentage of missing details. Evidently the 57 judges (27%) for whom there is no data on secondary education could significantly alter the patterns described here.

The next largest category after the public schools is the grammar schools which had limited endowments and provided education for members of the middle classes in the localities. In total, 27 grammar schools educated 39 (19%) of the men appointed to the bench between 1727 and 1875, and seven of these schools accounted for 19 judges, almost half of the grammar school contingent: Litchfield, Manchester, Ruthin, Reading, Edinburgh, Tonbridge, and Newcastle. Strangely enough, Litchfield Grammar School had all four of the judges among its old boys, Richard Lloyd, William Noel, Thomas Parker, and John Willes, appointed to the bench between 1727 and 1760. In addition, Litchfield's most famous alumnus during this era, Dr. Samuel Johnson, also had connections with the legal profession.

Unfortunately the comparative data on the educational patterns in other professional élite groups is very limited. There is no information for the eighteenth century; for the nineteenth there is similar data for the medical profession, the Anglican episcopal bench, and foreign office clerks, while in the twentieth century there are two surveys of the judicial bench. Among the élite of the medical profession (fellows of the Royal Colleges of Physicians and Surgeons) appointed between 1800 and 1889, of the physicians 13% attended public schools and 19% attended grammar schools, while for surgeons the figures were 2% and 7% respectively.[32] The Anglican bishops had a

[32]M. Jeanne Peterson, *The Medical Profession in Mid-Victorian London* (Berkeley, 1978), pp. 50-1.

far higher percentage in public schools than did the judges, with 75% of all bishops holding office between 1860 and 1960 having attended one of these élite institutions, 61% for the period 1860-99.[33] The foreign office clerks, who were not even a professional élite, also included a higher percentage of public school boys than did the judges. Of those clerks appointed between 1824 and 1857, 52% had attended a public school and 32% had been to either Eton or Harrow.[34]

The twentieth-century judiciary was also more public school oriented than were its eighteenth- and nineteenth-century predecessors. Of the judges sitting on the bench in 1941, approximately 80% had attended one of the public schools; by 1956, 71% had done so, and a random sample of the judiciary in 1969 indicated that 71% were public school old boys. [35] The eighteenth- and nineteenth-century judiciary, then, had only a moderately exclusive education — considerably inferior to that of the nineteenth-century clerical élite, the foreign service, and their own twentieth-century successors.

Similarities notwithstanding, the secondary education patterns followed by the judiciary were not constant during the 148 years encompassed by this study. Unquestionably the judges appointed between 1790 and 1850 received, on average, a more élitist education than those raised to the bench before 1790 and after 1850. Of the men in the 1790-1820 group, 41% attended a Clarendon school, 48% a public school, and 28% a grammar school, while of those receiving an appointment in the years 1820-50, 50% attended a Clarendon school, 52% a public school, and 25% a grammar school. The percentages in both periods are significantly higher than the averages for the entire 148 year time period: Clarendon Schools 35%, all public schools 38%, and grammar schools 19%. The public and grammar school totals during the years 1790-1820 account for slightly more than three-quarters of the judges in each group and the size of the unknown category is much smaller than during the three other periods. In fact it seems possible that the superior quality of the data for the years 1790 and 1850 is another reflection of the more distinguished and therefore better documented educational careers of the judges appointed during those years.

A university degree has never been a prerequisite for admission to the Inns of Court or to the bar in England. Nevertheless, by the

[33]D.H.J. Morgan, 'The Social and Educational Background of Anglican Bishops — Continuity and Changes', *British Journal of Sociology* 20 (1969), 298.

[34]Ray Jones, *The Nineteenth Century Foreign Office, An Administrative History* (London, 1971), p. 63.

[35]Abel-Smith and Stevens, *Lawyers and the Courts,* p. 299, and Henry Cecil, *The English Judge* (London, 1972), pp. 34-6.

eighteenth century, university attendance had become a regular part of the educational careers of the judges of England; almost three-quarters of the judiciary attended university during the period of this study. In order to provide a more detailed description of the patterns of university attendance, the judges in each period have been divided into six categories: Oxford, Cambridge, University of Dublin, other universities in the United Kingdom, foreign universities, and no university. If an individual attended more than one university or college, then he is categorized on the basis of the institution from which he received his bachelor's degree. Also included in the university attendance data are men who matriculated but never received a degree, but these instances are infrequent and only account for 5% of those judges who attended a university.

The preponderance of Oxford and Cambridge graduates is overwhelming, only dropping below 90% in the period 1850-75. This is not surprising considering that until the 1820s and 1830s with the founding of University College and King's College, London, and the University of Durham, Oxford and Cambridge were the only universities in England and Wales. There were of course other universities in Scotland and Ireland, including Trinity College, Dublin, and the Universities of Glasgow, Edinburgh, St. Andrew's, and Aberdeen — but by and large students at these institutions were local residents, while the judiciary was naturally dominated by Englishmen.

The pattern remains quite stable throughout the entire 148 year period with two exceptions. First there is an evident rise in the percentage of judges from Cambridge and a fall in those from Oxford during the first four periods. Second, the Oxbridge contingent constituted a smaller percentage of graduates between 1850 and 1875, than in earlier periods. This was not simply a consequence of the greater choice available but also as a reflection of changes in social and geographical recruitment patterns. The increasing importance of Dublin and the other United Kingdom universities may well indicate an increase in the number of Irish and non-Anglicans on the bench during the last period.[36] Whether or not this pattern of increasing educational, religious, and geographical diversification continued in the late nineteenth and early twentieth century, is a question which must await further research. However, a number of

[36]These suppositions are confirmed by evidence included in Chapter 3. The influx of Irishmen was a mid-nineteenth-century phenomenon. The non-Anglican contingent was largely composed of dissenters including Scottish Presbyterians and Unitarians, but also two Roman Catholics, one of whom later converted to Anglicanism and one Jew.

surveys of the judiciary during the period 1940-63 reveal that by the mid-twentieth century the patterns had been reversed. Not only did Oxford and Cambridge together account for up to ninety per cent of all university graduates on the bench, but Oxford had regained its previous position of dominance.[37]

Table 2: Universities attended by future judges

		Oxford	Cambridge	Dublin	Other U.K.	Foreign	Total	No University
1727-	No.	18	12	0	1	0	31	13
60	%	41	27	0	3	0	70	30
1760-	No.	10	12	0	1	0	23	9
90	%	31	37	0	3	0	72	28
1790-	No.	10	9	0	1	0	20	9
1820	%	33	32	0	3	0	69	31
1820-	No.	8	24	0	2	0	34	10
50	%	18	54	0	4	0	77	23
1850-	No.	9	17	6	7	4	43	16
75	%	15	29	10	12	7	73	27
Total	No.	55	74	6	12	4	151	57
	%	26	36	3	6	2	73	27

Once again comparative data for other professions is scarce. The two élite groups for which data is available, the Fellows of the Royal Colleges of Physicians and of Surgeons and the Anglican bishops, stand at opposite ends of the scale. Of the fellows of the College of Physicians, 30% between 1800 and 1849 and 24% between 1850 and 1889 had received a B.A. before embarking on medical studies, while for fellows of the College of Surgeons 2% and 13% had earned a B.A. degree in these two periods.[38] Among the bishops, for whom university was almost an absolute necessity, 96% were graduates during the years 1860-79 and 90% for 1880-99.[39] The foreign office clerks, despite the fact that they were not an élite group, were members of

[37] Abel-Smith and Stevens, *Lawyers and the Courts,* p. 299; Cecil, *The English Judge,* pp. 36-7; Anthony Sampson, *Anatomy of Britain Today* (New York, 1965), p. 170.

[38] Peterson, *Medical Profession,* pp. 50-1.

[39] Morgan, 'The Social and Educational Background of Anglican Bishops', p. 298.

an extremely high status profession. However, they included many fewer university men than either the bishops or the judiciary, with 62% in 1824-57, 31% in 1857-71, and 47% in 1871-1907.[40].

The members of the judiciary may be seen as typical of the student bodies at the universities of Oxford and Cambridge, which had considerable numbers of students from the landed classes in the eighteenth century but which by the nineteenth were becoming more and more middle-class institutions.[41] On this basis, one might have expected to find that the judges' colleges constituted an essentially random sample in both universities. On the contrary, however; the judges showed very definite tastes in colleges. This can probably be explained as a social phenomenon. Thus we find that at Cambridge 44% of the judges matriculated at Trinity College, 'in which most wealthy or aristocratic students tended to congregate',[42] and the percentage at Trinity was highest in the last two periods — 62% in 1820-50 and 75% in 1850-75. As will be seen, the judges did not come from aristocratic origins or from families of enormous wealth. Their families did, however, represent the high status professions; perhaps this was another key to the great gates of Trinity. Only one other Cambridge college could claim more than 10% of the judges as students: that was Trinity Hall, which has long had a reputation as the home of canon lawyers. Trinity Hall students accounted for 17% of the Cambridge total. Judicial alumni of this college were particularly numerous in the periods 1727-60 (almost one third) and 1760-90 (almost one half). In addition to these two leading foundations, three other colleges each had more than 5% of the Cambridge men on the bench: St. John's with 8% and Caius and King's with 7% each. Together these five colleges accounted for 83% of the Cambridge educated judges.

At Oxford the collegiate concentration of the judges was much less significant. Only one college was able to claim more than 10% of the Oxford judicial contingent and that was the aristocratic Christ Church with 20% of the judges. The 55 judges at Oxford attended 14 of the 20 colleges. Both St. John's and New College had 5 judges (9%) as members; Trinity, University College, Wadham, Queen's, and Balliol had 4 (7%) each; and Corpus Christi and Exeter 3 (5%) each.

[40]Jones, *Nineteenth Century Foreign Office*, p. 64.

[41]Hester Jenkins and David Caradog Jones, 'Social Class of Cambridge Alumni', *British Journal of Sociology*, (1950), 99, as quoted in Sheldon Rothblatt, *The Revolution of the Dons* (New York, 1968), p. 87. Lawrence Stone, 'The Size and Composition of the Oxford Student Body 1580-1909', in *The University in Society*, I, (Princeton, 1974), 37-56, 66-7, 93, 102.

[42]Rothblatt, *Revolution of the Dons*, p. 235.

The young men who were in later years to sit on the judicial bench were not content merely to reside for three years at the university and at the end receive their pass degree with a minimum effort. Their university records were as a group outstanding and abound with honours degrees. Of the 149 university graduates, 41 or 28% received first class honours. This total becomes even more impressive when it is realized that the honours system at Oxford and Cambridge had not really begun in earnest until the end of the eighteenth or beginning of the nineteenth century.[43] As a result, there was little chance for judges in the periods 1727-60 and 1760-90 to obtain an honours degree, and the possibility was limited for the men appointed between 1790 and 1820. Of the 96 university men who were raised to the bench between 1790 and 1875, 39 or 41% received a first class degree. Firsts were received by 20% of the judges in the 1790-1820 group, 35% in the 1820-50 group, and 52% in the 1850-75 group. Of the total of 40 firsts, 16 were in mathematics, 6 in classics, 13 were double firsts in mathematics and classics, and 5 were in other subjects.

Having completed his secondary and university education, if he chose to follow that educational path, the prospective barrister was ready to enter one of the four Inns of Court. In Table 3 the judges have been divided into five categories according to their Inn affiliation. The fifth category 'No Inn' is reserved for those civilian advocates who sat

Table 3: Inns of Court affiliation

		Middle Temple	Inner Temple	Lincoln's Inn	Gray's Inn	No Inn
1727-60	No.	17	14	11	1	1
	%	39	32	25	2	2
1760-90	No.	12	9	8	0	3
	%	37	28	25	0	9
1790-1820	No.	8	5	13	2	1
	%	28	17	45	7	3
1820-50	No.	11	10	18	4	1
	%	25	23	41	9	2
1850-75	No.	19	17	17	6	0
	%	32	29	29	10	0
Total	No.	67	55	67	13	6
	%	32	26	32	6	3

[43]V.H.H. Green, *The Universities* (Harmondsworth, 1969), *passim.*

on the bench and were never called to the bar at one of the Inns, a practice which continued until the fusion of the common law and ecclesiastical law benches in the 1850s.

Throughout the eighteenth and nineteenth centuries there were three major Inns of Court and a minor one. The two Temples and Lincoln's Inn each accounted for just under one third of the 208 judges, while Gray's Inn had an overall contribution of 6% and only once, between 1850 and 1875, were as many as 10% of the judges appointed from that Inn. To explain these recruitment patterns as well as some of the short term fluctuations in the percentage of judges originating from the four Inns, it is necessary to examine the comparative size of the Inns. Since no definitive information is available on the number of barristers called by each of the Inns, we must be content with the records of admission for the years between 1700 and 1799. These show that 16,042 students were admitted to the Inns, of whom 38% were enrolled at the Middle Temple, 26% at Lincoln's Inn, 24% at the Inner Temple, and 11% at Gray's Inn.[44]

These percentages closely mirror the proportion of the judges appointed from each of the Inns, with Lincoln's Inn being slightly over-represented and Gray's Inn somewhat under-represented. The number of judges appointed from a particular Inn sometimes even reflected periodic fluctuations in the admissions to the Inn. For example, the contribution of Lincoln's Inn to the bench was particularly high during the periods 1790-1820 and 1820-50, 45% and 41% respectively. As expected, during the years 1770-90, at which time these judges were law students, 40% of all admissions were at Lincoln's Inn.[45]

The overall impression that one gets from examining the educational careers of the judges is that those appointed between 1790 and 1850 (who were educated for the most part between 1760 and 1820) had a somewhat more exclusive education than those in the first two periods and especially those in the last. As has been noted, the concentration of judges in the public schools and at Oxbridge which existed in the third and fourth periods seemed to be breaking down in the last period, as was the supremacy of the prestigious Lincoln's Inn among the Inns of Court. Whether or not this trend is indicative of a change in the social composition of the judiciary must be left to later chapters.

---

[44]Paul Lucas, 'A Collective Biography of Students and Barristers of Lincoln's Inn 1680-1804: A Study in the "Aristocratic Resurgence" of the Eighteenth Century', *Journal of Modern History* 46 (1974), 245.

[45]*Ibid.*

Before concluding, it may be useful to establish, at least in general terms, what the education and pre-bar preparation would cost the intended lawyer. Secondary education could be fairly inexpensive for those willing to live at home, though as we have seen a substantial number of judges attended the more expensive public boarding schools. If parents chose to send their son to a public or grammar school as a boarder, for even his last four years, they could immediately count on an expenditure of £300-£500 in the early nineteenth century.[46] Charterhouse in 1805, for example, was estimated, according to James Parke, later baron of the Exchequer, to cost £70 a year for tuition and board, plus a 12 guinea registration fee.[47] Professor F.M.L. Thompson writes that costs at Eton and Harrow, again in the early part of the century, could range from £175-£250 per annum.[48] During the rest of the century, the range of school fees seems to have remained fairly constant, though they may have dropped slightly.

If the future barrister decided to continue his education in university, as did the majority of judges, he would have to add another £100 a year to his budget at the end of the eighteenth century. By the first third of the nineteenth century the estimated cost of a year at university had increased to £150-£200 if a student pared his expenses to the minimum.[49]

By the time the prospective barrister left university to enter an Inn of Court, he may already have expended between £800 and £1,600 on his education and he was still faced with a minimum of three more years before he could expect to earn a guinea from his profession. Furthermore, the financial burdens of his education were not yet at an end. By the middle of the nineteenth century, the law student could expect to spend an average of £400 for three years, including a £35 entrance fee to his Inn, £100 security deposit which was eventually returned, £200 for two years pupilage with a special pleader, conveyancer, or equity draftsman, £100-£200 for his library, and £5-£7 per annum for the minimum meals in commons.[50] In addition, the

---

[46]Rothblatt, *Revolution of the Dons,* pp. 56-8, and F.M.L. Thompson, *English Landed Society in the Nineteenth Century* (London, 1963), p. 84.

[47]Ridley (Blagdon) MSS. deposited in the Northumberland Record Office. ZRI 31/2/10 quoted by permission of the Rt. Hon. Viscount Ridley TD DL, Blagdon Hall, Seaton Burn, Northumberland.

[48]Thompson, *English Landed Society in the Nineteenth Century,* p. 84.

[49]Rothblatt, *Revolution of the Dons,* pp. 66-7.

[50]Thomson, *Choice of a Profession,* pp. 99-100, and Warren, *Introduction to Law Studies,* I, 73-74.

law student had the expense of room and board in London for three or four years which was estimated in 1857 to be some £600 for the entire period, though it would have been less costly earlier.[51] Lloyd Kenyon, for example, paid £15 12s a year for his accommodation in Bell Yard, right across the street from the Temple.[52] It would be safe to estimate that school, university, and the Inns of Court would cost the future barrister and his parents up until the day he was called to the bar, between £1,200 and £2,600 over a period of ten years or so.

A more personal insight into the scale of costs, primarily at the Inns of Court, can be gathered from the biographies of members of the eighteenth- and nineteenth-century judiciary. For example, John Taylor Coleridge was able to attend Oxford, finish his residence in London, and obtain his call to the bar only by borrowing £100 from his father.[53] Likewise Roundell Palmer, the future Lord Chancellor under the title of Lord Selborne, was aided by the money invested in his name by his uncle.[54] Henry Bickersteth, later Lord Langdale, was given £200 by his brother to cover the costs of his being called to the bar.[55] A number of future judges were not so lucky, and some like John Campbell had to work as newspaper reporters to earn the money needed to supplement the funds received from relatives.[56] Others, such as John Rolt, later a Lord Justice of Appeal, had no familial support to rely on and had to make their own way. Rolt was able to cover his expenses by obtaining the secretaryship to two schools for £100 per annum and a minor ecclesiastical court office which brought in another £50, and finally by putting his meager savings into jeopardy by borrowing £200 on a life assurance policy he held.[57]

The education of a son for the bar was a long process for the young man and a costly investment for his parents. In addition, the call to the bar as we shall see did not signal the beginning of the young barrister's self-sufficiency, but may have actually deepened his dependence on

[51]Thomson, *The Choice of a Profession,* pp. 18-19.

[52]Kenyon, *The Life of Lloyd, First Lord Kenyon,* p. 15.

[53]Coleridge, *Story of a Devonshire House,* p. 192.

[54]Roundell Palmer, Earl of Selbourne, *Memorials, Family and Personal,* I, (London, 1896), 198-9.

[55]Thomas D. Hardy, *Memoirs of the Right Honourable Henry Lord Langdale* (London, 1852), pp. 279-81.

[56]In a letter to his brother, John Campbell writes that he has earned £105 as a reporter for the *Morning Chronicle,* £100 from Tidd, the famous special pleader, for looking after his office and this was supplemented by £100 from his brother. This total of £305 was estimated by Campbell to last from March 1805 until his expected call to the bar in November 1806. Campbell, *Life,* p. 164.

[57]John Rolt, *The Memoirs of the Right Honourable Sir John Rolt, 1804-1871,* (London, 1939), pp. 42-6.

outside assistance. The long years of education and the hundreds and thousands of pounds of expense for that education did not, as parents and sons had to be aware, guarantee professional success, but were merely the price of admission to the lottery of the bar.

3

BEGINNING A CAREER

The opening years of a barrister's career were crucial to his later progress. While ability in the courtroom was the most important ingredient of success, it was not the only one. An examination of the judges' early careers will enable us to assess the importance of social and occupational origins, pre-bar employment, family and regional connections, and parental wealth as factors in the promotion of the prospective barrister.

Social Origins

The character and status of an occupation are often determined or at least influenced by the social origins of its members. Changes in social composition may reflect a variety of transformations in society, the economy, or in the structure of particular occupations. There are indications in the limited research available at present on the nineteenth-century professions that by and large changing patterns of social recruitment were directly related to the professionalization process, as well as to a fundamental restructuring of English society.

An evaluation of the origins of the judges of England should provide an indication of the nature and extent of the social revolution which the bench was undergoing in the eighteenth and nineteenth centuries. In Table 4, the members of the judiciary have been divided into fifteen categories, according to their father's principal occupations or sources of income.[1]

The most striking change in Table 4 is the rapid and continuous decline in the contribution of the landed classes to the English

---

[1] Recent work in social history includes a growing number of examinations of the social origins of various occupational and social groups. These studies of social origins are often derived from occupational, educational, or regional directories which list fathers' occupations using vague terminology, such as esquire or gentleman. For the eighteenth and nineteenth centuries, these titles actually hinder the analysis of social origins. While they indicate middle- or upper-class origins in the loosest sense of these descriptions, they blur the very real social and economic distinctions between members of the landed gentry, the various professions, and the mercantile and entrepreneurial classes. It is impossible to know with any precision the exact meaning of these titles; an esquire for example could be a landowner, a professional, or a merchant, though for convenience researchers often immediately classify gentlemen and esquires as landowners. See Lawrence Stone, 'The Size and Composition of the Oxford Student Body', pp. 48 and 66-7.

Table 4: Socio-occupational origins of the judges 1727-1875

Father's Occupation	1727-1760 No.	%	1760-1790 No.	%	1790-1820 No.	%	1820-1850 No.	%	1850-1875 No.	%	Total No.	%
Landowners	20[a]	45	8[b]	26	5[c]	17	7	16	5	8	45	21
Barristers	4[d]	9	7[e]	22	1	3	5[f]	11	9[g]	15	26	13
Clergymen	5[h]	11	5[i]	16	3[j]	10	6	14	4[k]	7	23	11
Military Officers	0	0	0	0	2	7	0	0	7	12	9	4
Govt. Officials/Civil Service	0	0	0	0	1	3	0	0	3	5	4	2
Doctors	0	0	2	6	3	10	5	11	3	5	13	6
Solicitors/Conveyancers	2	5	2	6	1	3	5	11	4	7	14	7
Teachers	0	0	0	0	1	3	0	0	1	2	2	1
Misc. Professionals	0	0	2	6	0	0	2	4	1	2	5	2
Total Professional	11	25	18	56	12	41	23	52	32	54	96	46
Businessmen	0	0	0	0	3	10	2	4	1	2	6	3
Large Merchants	1	2	2	6	3	10	3[l]	7	7[m]	12	14	7
Misc. Merchants	2	5	2	6	2	7	3	7	9	15	19	9
W. Indies Proprietors	0	0	0	0	0	0	2	4	1	2	3	1
Total Merchants and Proprietors	3	7	2	6	5	17	8	18	17	29	35	16
Artisans	1	2	0	0	2	7	2	4	0	0	5	2
Unknown	9	20	4	12	2	7	2	4	4	7	21	10
Total	44		32		29		44		59		208	

Note: a includes 7 baronets and peers; b includes one baronet; c includes 1 baronet and 1 peer; d includes 1 Welsh judge; e includes 3 royal judges and 1 Scots judge; f includes 1 royal judge; g includes 2 royal judges, 1 Welsh judge, 1 Canadian judge and 1 Solicitor-General; h includes 2 bishops; i includes 1 bishop; j includes 1 bishop; k includes 1 admiral and 1 general; l includes 2 baronets; m includes 2 baronets.

judiciary.[2] This decline is even more significant when one realizes that of the 18 judges whose fathers were landowners in the earliest period, more than one third were from titled families (baronetcies or peerages), while of the 25 landed judges in the last four periods only 3 had fathers who were titled. Over the 148 year period covered in this study, there was a decline of over 75% in the proportion of judges of landed origins. In addition, those landed families whose sons were appointed to the bench after the earliest period were primarily from the middling and lesser gentry owning several hundred to one or two thousand acres. The influence of these families rarely extended beyond the locality, and while in quite a few cases they were justices of the peace, only a handful could claim control of a parliamentary seat.

The professional group which accounted for 25% of the judges in the first period filled the vacuum created by the decline of the landowning contingent among the judges. The percentage of judges from professional families almost doubled from the first period to the second, and from then until 1875 it never dropped below 41% of the total. No one profession dominated the social origins of the judges, and even if barristers and solicitors are combined, less than 20% came from legal families. The judges from professional origins were almost exclusively the sons of lawyers, clergymen, doctors, and military and naval officers; the other professions accounted for a mere 5% of the total.

In the period 1790-1820 the merchant/proprietor group began its steady rise, equalling the landowning percentage in the third period and accounting for a quarter of the judges in the last period. The rise of the merchant and business group in the third period (together they account for 28% of the total) occurs concurrently with the opening phases of the industrial revolution. Although the judges in the third period were appointed to the bench between 1790 and 1820, if we estimate an average pre-judicial career, measured from the beginning of residence at one of the Inns of Court, to be 25 years, then these judges entered the profession between 1765 and 1795 during Britain's 'take-off'.

[2]The extent of landowning origins among the judges in the eighteenth and nineteenth centuries can be compared to data on landed origins among barristers and advocates in the sixteenth and seventeenth centuries. In 1519, of the 49 practising barristers who can be identified, 29 or almost 60% were of landed origins. Similarly of the 372 barristers called to the bar of the Middle Temple between 1599 and 1642, 77% were sons of landowners, while landed origins were attributed to 49.5% of the 200 civilian lawyers practising during the same period. Ives, 'Some Aspects of the Legal Profession in the Fifteenth and Sixteenth Centuries', p. 79, and Brian P. Levack, *The Civil Lawyers in England 1603-1641, A Political Study,* (Oxford, 1973), pp. 10-11.

Few judges were the sons of men who could be described as members of the eighteenth-century 'working trades' or the nineteenth-century working classes. Even the aristocracy of the working men, the artisans, accounted for a mere 2% of the judiciary, and only in the third period did they constitute more than 5% of the total. The infrequency with which the sons of artisans achieved eminence in the legal profession is clear evidence that despite changes in social composition, the bench remained an almost exclusively middle and upper class preserve.

The eighteenth- and nineteenth-century judiciary was not a profession dominated by eldest sons. In no period did firstborns constitute a majority of those appointed to the bench, and of those judges whose family position is known (85%) just in excess of one third were first sons, while just under one third each were second sons, or third and younger sons. By comparison with other samples of members of the legal profession these totals are strikingly low. For example, a similar analysis of serjeants-at-law in the fifteenth century showed that 75% of the serjeants were first sons.[3] Comparable results were obtained in analyses of the family position of Toulousian advocates in the eighteenth century (70% were first sons)[4] and Inns of Court entrants in the early seventeenth century (60% were first sons or heirs).[5]

The percentage of eldest sons fluctuated between 1727 and 1875, first falling from 39% in the period 1727-60 to 19% in 1760-90, then rising and levelling off to 28% in 1790-1820 and 29% in 1820-50, and finally reaching a peak of 41% between 1850 and 1875. This pattern conforms in part to that found among Lincoln's Inn barristers by Professor Lucas, although the changes were more moderate for the judges.[6] He has attributed the decline and subsequent increase in the number of eldest sons at this Inn to a rise in the social status of the bar and renewed educational and political interest among the gentry. The

[3]Ives, 'Some Aspects of the Legal Profession in the Fifteenth and Sixteenth Centuries', pp. 138-9.

[4]See the original version of Lenard Berlanstein's Ph.D. thesis on the advocates of Toulouse, Johns Hopkins University, 1973, pp. 98-9, now published in a revised version as *The Barristers of Toulouse in the Eighteenth Century (1740-1793)* (Baltimore, 1975).

[5]Prest, *Inns of Court,* p. 32.

[6]Lucas, 'A Collective Biography of Students and Barristers of Lincoln's Inn', pp. 248-51. While Lucas's claim to have discovered an aristocratic resurgence at Lincoln's Inn must remain suspect due to his use of the titles 'gentleman' and 'esquire' as proof of landed origins, there is no reason not to accept his evidence concerning a rise in the percentage of first sons.

large increase in the percentage of first sons among the judges, allowing for 25-30 years between a man's call to the bar and his elevation to the bench, occurred among those barristers who began their professional careers between 1825 and 1850. If these patterns are an accurate reflection of the practising bar, then they may well be explained by reference to conditions of employment in the other gentlemanly professions, in the social composition of the bench, and in the social and administrative changes in the nation at large.

While there is much that remains unknown about the conditions in the professions in the first half of the nineteenth century, it seems possible that relative to the increase in the middle-class population there was a decrease in opportunity in the most prestigious and least strenuous of the higher professions. The number of men needed in the services undoubtedly shrank as a result of the lull in major international conflicts between 1815 and 1854. Many of the most desirable sinecures were disappearing during the post-war years as a result of the administrative housecleaning begun in the late eighteenth century. The church could not absorb the overflow and it too was to undergo an era of reform in the 1830s. Conditions like these may have made competition at the bar less of a deterrent than it had been in the late eighteenth century. Furthermore, the decline in the landed and the rise in the professional and mercantile contingent on the bench may also help to provide an explanation. The members of the urban middle classes usually did not have the connections or patronage necessary to place their sons in the most desirable non-competitive upper professions, so little was sacrificed by trying their luck at the bar.

The judges appointed during the years 1727-60 were the most socially exclusive group, who included the highest percentage of landed men and of those with titles. During the last four periods, 1760-1875, the judiciary was composed primarily of the sons of the upper middle classes of England and increasingly of those from urban origins. The landowners among them were from the middle ranks of landed society — between the great wealth, power, and landholdings of the territorial nobility and the wealthiest of the landed gentry on the one hand, and the yeoman farmers and small owner occupiers on the other. The professional element was composed mainly of members of the gentlemanly professions, and later on of substantial foreign and domestic merchants and bankers.

This characterization of the judiciary lays to rest what I have called the 'myth of the self-made barrister/judge' prevalent in the professional guidebooks of the eighteenth and nineteenth centuries and which is sometimes found in scholarly studies in the twentieth.[7] Of course not all contemporary commentators misrepresented the profession's composition — in fact one summed it up almost exactly, describing the members of the bar as belonging 'to respectable families — to that minor aristocracy which is interposed in England, between the patrician gentry and the middle or tradesman classes'.[8] Likewise a French visitor wrote in the early nineteenth century that English barristers were 'generally the younger sons of rich landowners, bishops, barristers, bankers, and merchants'.[9] Despite the possible overstatement, this assessment is not too far from the actual situation in the first third of the nineteenth century.

The bar, as we have seen, was too expensive an occupation for a poor man and too much of a risk for the very wealthy or well-connected. The rewards, however, were large enough to attract the most able elements of the middle classes. The bar could be the most glorious path to fame and fortune — or it could be a professional dead end. During the first half of the nineteenth century increasingly large numbers of young men entered the lottery which they hoped would enable them to try for the big prize, a seat on the bench. It is to the early years of that quest that we must now turn.

Expenses and Income

In Chapter 2 it was estimated that the education of a barrister at the secondary level, in university, and at the Inns of Court could cost his parents from £1,200 to £2,600. The real expense, according to the guidebooks, began when a barrister was called to the bar and started to practise his chosen profession. A young barrister had to keep a set of chambers, usually in or near the precincts of his Inn, which in some cases also served as his living quarters. He had to have a clerk, he had to go the circuit twice a year, he had to begin or augment a legal library, and he had to find a place for himself in legal and professional society.

The cost of his chambers and living quarters is difficult to estimate, though a few examples may provide an idea of the possible expense. In 1804 John Campbell wrote to his brother that he had just leased a set of chambers which cost £32 per annum including taxes,

[7]For example see John Vincent, *The Formation of the British Liberal Party* (Harmondsworth, 1972), p. 78.

[8]Polson, *Law and Lawyers*, I, 145.

[9]M. Cottu, *On the Administration of Criminal Justice in England and the Spirit of English Government* (London, 1822), p. 142.

and that he had to purchase all the furnishings of the chambers, which were valued at £20.[10] Sixteen years later, Thomas N. Talfourd rented a set of chambers for four years for the sum of £55 per annum.[11] Another guess coming from the 1820s, was that a set of chambers cost the contemporary barrister from £50 to £70 per annum.[12]

Probably the largest expense for the barrister was the bi-annual going of the circuit, which removed the common law bar from the London courts to the courts of the assizes. During each of these assizes, which lasted approximately six weeks, the barrister would have to pay for his transport, board and lodging, and social life. The rules of the bar required barristers to travel either by horse or private coach, and prohibited them from finding accommodation in local inns, the most inexpensive lodgings. These restrictions were formulated to protect the dignity of the bar, but their result was to raise the expenses of the young barrister needlessly, thereby making it more difficult for those of limited means to pursue a career at the bar. Most of the guidebooks seemed to agree that the young barrister, even if he pared his circuit expenses to the minimum, could not travel the circuit in the middle of the nineteenth century for much under £90-£100 per circuit, or £180-£200 per annum.[13]

The cost of beginning a professional library was estimated at from £100-£200, while the yearly expense for its upkeep was rated at £15-£20.[14] The fledgling barrister's library probably included the standard reference works of jurisprudence, foremost among which were Blackstone's *Commentaries* and Coke's *Institutes,* and perhaps a legal dictionary as well. In addition, he would require works on procedure in the civil or common law courts, on pleadings and precedents, and on more specialized topics such as criminal law, commercial law, conveyancing and the law of real property, or probate law, depending on his interests. Finally, he would need a set of law reports, new volumes of which were issued every few years, and perhaps a subscription to one of the several professional periodicals, such as the *Law Journal* or the *Law Times.*

In addition to the cost of his profession, the young barrister had a number of everyday expenses which could not be kept below another

[10]Campbell, *Life,* I, 151.

[11]Robert S. Newdick, 'Sir Thomas Noon Talfourd D.C.L.', an unpublished manuscript in the Berkshire County Library, p. 45.

[12]Cottu, *On the Administration of Criminal Justice in England,* pp. 141-2.

[13]*Ibid.,* and Warren, *Introduction to Law Studies,* I, 73-4.

[14]Thomson, *The Choice of a Profession,* pp. 99-101.

£100-£200 annually. The household needs, including food, alcohol, coal, candles, laundry, and perhaps part-time domestic help and rent, if he had an apartment as well as chambers, could cost a minimum of £80-£100. Lastly, as a gentleman he would have the additional expenses of a life style which was appropriate to his social and professional position, such as dress, transport, and entertainment, that accounted for another £20-£50 or more per annum.[15]

The estimates on the total expenses of the novice barrister vary widely, though most of the guidebooks seem to agree that £250-£300 per annum was the absolute minimum, and that few barristers were able to keep their expenditures even at this level. If we take our estimates of £50 for chambers, £180 for the two circuits, and £30 for a library, we already exceed the £250 figure, without having included the expenses of a clerk, food, or social life. A contemporary estimate by John Campbell in the first decade of the nineteenth century proposes £400 as a reasonable sum. John Taylor Coleridge in 1817 lists his yearly expenses at a time when he was still a special pleader, as £200, which, if we add in the cost of going the circuit (a task not required of a pleader), would bring his outlay close to the £400 a year figure.[16] Finally, we have an estimate in *The Complete Book of Trades* in 1842 which proposes that anyone planning to begin a career at the bar must have access to a minimum of £1,000-£1,500, a sum which was said to suffice only with the most careful planning.[17] Thus we find that the young barrister had entered a profession in which competition was fierce, early income was unlikely, and which required a yearly expenditure of approximately £400 or more — a sum equal to the yearly income of many middle-class Englishmen in the eighteenth and nineteenth centuries.

Having been called to the bar, the young barrister could do little more than enter his newly acquired chambers and wait for a knock on his door which would signal the arrival of his first brief, usually marked by the lowest possible fee — 1 guinea. The young barrister's wait was often long. Unless he was lucky enough to have connections with a firm of solicitors, what was to attract a brief to an untried practitioner? So hundreds, if not thousands of barristers were condemned to the confines of their chambers spurred on only by the hope that today would be their lucky day when they would be

[15]J.A. Banks, *Prosperity and Parenthood* (London, 1954), pp. 32-69 and pp. 86-102.

[16]Campbell, *Life*, I, 206, and Bodleian Library, Oxford University, Coleridge MSS. d, 128, p. 84.

[17]Banks, *Prosperity and Parenthood*, p. 175.

entrusted with the case that would lift them out of obscurity. Years might elapse before a barrister could fully support himself on his professional earnings, and even the luckiest and most able barristers were usually unable to support themselves from their fees during the first few years.[18] One guidebook sums up the newly called barrister's prospects most pessimistically by saying that 'his chances of success *at all* are very remote, and his hopes of a remunerative income within the first ten years rationally small; during that period, unless he has some other means of exerting his powers, he must live on his own resources or those of his friends'.[19] In a similar vein young Henry Bickersteth, later Master of the Rolls and a peer, wrote to his parents in 1811 that although his immediate prospects were not rosy, most successful barristers only gained prosperity 'by very slow degrees'. Bickersteth continued by noting 'that many men who are now making great fortunes were sometimes two or three years without getting any business, and sometimes eight or ten years hardly able to maintain themselves, . . .'.[20]

Details of the incomes of fledgling barristers provide striking evidence of their inability to support themselves on professional fees alone. I have been able to discover the exact or approximate earnings of eight judges and two very successful barristers during their first two years of practice. The barristers, although never appointed to the bench, were among the top income earners in the profession. Lloyd Kenyon earned £17 0s. 6d his first year at the bar, 1757, £21 in his second year, and by 1764, his seventh year at the bar, he was earning £80 per annum. Charles Yorke, the son of the Lord Chancellor, earned £121 his first year of practice and £201 his second year. George Jessel, who later in his career would earn £30,000 in one year, had an income of 52 guineas in his first year and 346 guineas in his second. John Dunning, who had the largest income of any lawyer of his day, earned £13 3s. his first year at the bar and £48 3s. the following one. The first year's earnings of two of the nineteenth century's Lord Chancellors were for Richard Bethell, 100 guineas and for Roundell Palmer, £165. Another Lord Chancellor, John Campbell, earned 41 and a half guineas for his first seven months at the bar. Finally, there were Charles Pratt who had practically no income for a number of years and almost left the bar out of desperation; William Murray, later Lord Mansfield, who held only one brief during his first two years; and Samuel Romilly, later

[18]*Ibid.*, p. 174.

[19]Thomson, *Choice of a Profession*, p. 19.

[20]Hardy, *Memoirs of the Right Honourable Henry, Lord Langdale*, I, 279.

Solicitor-General, who had a negligible income during his first three years of practice. Thus we see that even among these men, all of whom would eventually be top income earners in the profession, none was able to support himself during his first year at the bar solely on his professional income.

Fledgling barristers were compelled to receive at least part of their support from sources other than the bar, but at the time of their call they were already beyond the age when they could reasonably rely on their parents. Only 18% were under 24 when they were called to the bar. Approximately 50% in each of the five periods were between 24 and 29 years old, while 21% were 30 or older when they were called. Thus on average they were men in their mid-twenties, who needed to find additional sources of income to supplement the money earned from their profession or provided by friends or relatives.[21]

One of the most common ways for fledgling barristers to earn the necessary additional income was to be elected to a university fellowship.[22] While sometimes there was stiff competition for the fellowships, they provided a sizeable income to their holders without requiring the performance of any real duties. The only drawback was that fellows were not allowed to marry, but with the limited income of most young barristers, this was not a step which could be contemplated for a number of years. The income of these fellowships could be as high as £200-£400 per annum, and this alone could provide the barrister with at least a limited degree of financial independence.[23] Richard Bethell, the future Lord Chancellor, was a Vinerian Scholar (the Oxford law scholarship) for which he received £300 per annum, while at the same time he served as an academic coach for well-to-do students, for which he received an additional sum of several hundred pounds per year.[24] Fellowships were used by judges appointed in all five periods as a supplementary or even primary source of income; a total of 30 judges or 20% of the university graduates held fellowships. In fact the widespread use of fellowships as a means of support by young professionals during their early careers became an issue in the university reorganization in the late nineteenth century.[25]

[21] For the problems associated with the need for financial aid in the early years of a legal career see Shadwell vs. Shadwell (1860) 9 C.B. (N.S.) 159.

[22] Thirty judges (14%) held university fellowships during their careers at the bar. They are divided by period as follows: 1727-1760 - 2 (5%), 1760-1790 - 4 (13%), 1790-1820 - 9 (31%), 1820-1850 - 8 (18%), 1850-1875 - 7 (12%).

[23] Banks, *Prosperity and Parenthood,* pp. 181-2.

[24] Thomas A. Nash, *The Life of Richard Lord Westbury* (London, 1888), pp. 27-9.

[25] Banks, *Prosperity and Parenthood,* pp. 181-2.

The other most frequent non-legal occupation for the judges, during their years as law students or soon after their call, was journalism. Some confined themselves to reporting significant court cases from Westminster and the assizes in newspapers such as *The Times* and the *Morning Chronicle,* or in professional journals. Others wrote articles and reviews on subjects other than the law for major English periodicals. John Taylor Coleridge was a frequent contributor to the *British Critic* and *Quarterly Review,* while his son, John Duke Coleridge, wrote book reviews and articles for the *London Guardian* which gave him an income of £200 yearly.[26] Thomas Talfourd served as a drama critic for the *New Monthly Review* among his other journalistic endeavours.[27] Likewise, Roundell Palmer, as a result of a most successful interview with Thomas Barnes, editor of *The Times,* became a regular contributor from 1840 to 1843 during which time he wrote a number of leading articles.[28] Although journalism was important in the early careers of a number of judges, it was only a secondary occupation, and many of them abandoned it when, as was almost inevitable, writing began to interfere with their practice at the bar.

Often the law student or barrister could find sources of additional income within the legal profession. Some of these positions were reserved for the period before the prospective barrister was called to the bar, while others, such as writing law reports or legal textbooks, could be pursued concurrently with a career at the bar. For example, John Campbell, who was called to the bar in 1806, earned £60 as a law reporter in 1808 and he expected his income from that source to increase to £150 or even £200 in 1809.[29]

The most popular form of pre-bar legal employment among the judges was special pleading. Forty, or 20% of the 208 judges, spent part of their careers in this capacity. The work required of a pleader was ideally suited to the prospective barrister, and the income was often large enough to allow the practitioner to accumulate savings which could aid him in his early years at the bar. For example, Charles Abbott, later Lord Chief Justice of King's Bench, practised for seven years as a special pleader, and during his last year he earned £1,000.[30]

[26]Coleridge, *Story of a Devonshire House,* p. 210, and Ernest H. Coleridge, *Life and Correspondence of John Duke Lord Coleridge, Lord Chief Justice of England* (London, 1904), p. 205.

[27]Newdick, 'Sir Thomas Noon Talfourd, D.C.L.', p. 83.

[28]Earl of Selbourne, *Memorials, Family and Personal,* I, 103.

[29]Campbell, *Life,* I, 231.

[30]John Campbell, *Lives of the Lord Chancellors and Keepers of the Great Seal of England,* IV, 5th edn. (London, 1868), p. 278.

Table 5: Judges' legal activities other than the bar

	1727-1760		1760-1790		1790-1820		1820-1850		1850-1875		Total	
	No.	%	No.	%	No.	%	No.	%	No.	%	No.	%
Scots bar	0	0	1	3	0	0	1	2	0	0	2	1
Solicitor	0	0	0	0	0	0	0	0	1	2	1	1
Special Pleader	0	0	3	9	4	14	9	20	8	14	24	12
Special Pleader & Solicitor	0	0	1	3	0	0	1	2	1	2	3	1
Law Reporter & Author	7	16	4	12	1	3	7	16	10	17	29	14
Special Pleader & Reporter	0	0	1	3	3	10	2	4	4	7	10	5
Special Pleader & Solicitor & Reporter	0	0	0	0	0	0	0	0	3	5	3	1
Solicitor's clerk	2	4	2	6	2	7	2	4	3	5	11	5
None or unknown	35	79	20	62	19	66	22	50	29	49	125	60

Just over one third of the judges were employed during their early careers in legal occupations other than that of counsel. Even if we exclude those who served merely as solicitors' clerks or apprentices, more for the sake of learning than for making money, a full 34% were employed as solicitors, special pleaders, Scots advocates, law reporters, or a combination of these. The percentage of those so employed rose during the five periods, so that of those judges appointed between 1727 and 1760, only 20% had held one or more of these positions, while of those serving between 1850 and 1875, 51% had done so. The steady rise may have been a result of an increase in the opportunities for legal work for the law student and young barrister, especially in the realm of law reporting and special pleading. In addition, it is possible that for social or economic reasons, the judges in the later periods were able to depend on a lesser amount of direct parental support during their first years at the bar.

These employment opportunities provided a means for the sons of the less affluent members of the professional and commercial classes to contribute at least partially to their own support. Furthermore, these occupations were a source of knowledge and experience which would be most useful to a barrister in his professional life. Finally, it afforded the prospective barrister an opportunity to make his name known to established members of the legal profession; this was essential if success was ever to be achieved.

Connection and the Bar

The term 'connection' as used in this study has two aspects which are often, but not necessarily, found in conjunction with each other. The first is monetary. A young man who came from a family which was affluent and who could be assured of ample financial support during the early years of his career, both as a student and as a novice barrister, had a great advantage over less financially secure competitors at the bar. The young man of ample means often had the benefit of the most prestigious education, which was a means of introducing him to the 'right people' who could be of advantage later in life. In one recent study of the public schools and the middle classes, the function of the school as a source of connection and influence was made explicit. 'Public School education was valued by many parents as a means of securing their sons' material advancement in the world, and the method enjoined was to make useful social connections among one's schoolfellows.'[31]

[31]Frank Musgrove, 'Middle-Class Education and Employment in the Nineteenth Century', *Economic History Review* 12 (1959), 101-2.

Wealth also provided the fledgling barrister with financial independence. There was no necessity to worry about monetary support during the early years at the bar, which were so often barren of clients and bleak of future prospects. Having the financial means to wait provided the sons of wealthy parents with an advantage over those men whose parents had limited resources. Members of this latter group could not afford the luxury of waiting for an opportunity to show their mettle, and therefore could be deprived of pursuing a career in the law.

The second aspect of connection is more pronounced. A young barrister's family could be in a position to give him a helping hand in his profession as well as giving him the necessary financial support. His father, brother, uncle, or cousin might already be a member of the legal profession, in which case they could introduce him to individuals who might be able to direct clients to his door. Or he might be connected to members of other professions who could send him their business and encourage their acquaintances to do likewise. In much the same way and perhaps to an even greater extent, the son of a merchant or businessman might have been able to begin to build his practice from clients in a particular business or from a particular locality. The barrister from a gentry family was often in great demand at the assize held near to his home because of the influence of his family in the locality. Finally, any young man whose family had the ear of influential men in government could often rely on a push in the right direction early in his career.

Some of the writers of the professional guidebooks recognized the importance of wealth and connection in promoting a successful career at the bar. One of them wrote in 1867 that although some men of 'plebeian rank' had been appointed to the High Court, these represented only occasional exceptions to the general mode of judicial appointments. Such appointments, he continued,

> are made to sustain a theory (fruitful of disappointment in the lower grades of our great middle rank) which teaches ambitious boys to regard the bar as the profession in which men of ability and courage, unsupported by private means or connection, have many chances of winning fame and power. A more fallacious or disastrous theory cannot be imagined. If legal biography tells aught plainly it asserts in the plainest terms that the bar is the worst possible profession for young men who start in life without either fortune or strong friends, and are dependent solely upon their own talents and energy.[32]

[32] Jeafferson, *A Book About Lawyers,* I, 331.

64

These sentiments were wholeheartedly endorsed by Walter Bagehot, himself a barrister, in an essay on the legal profession written three years later, in which he stated that no one should go to the bar 'unless he has some particular "connection", or unless he has money enough to keep him in idleness for years'.[33]

In spite of the aforementioned opinions, the importance of connection in achieving professional success should not be over-estimated. Alone it could not assure a barrister's professional eminence or his appointment to the bench. Since competition was intense, connection could help smooth the way for a young barrister by helping him to attract a few early cases. However, if the young barrister was not able to prove his ability consistently in the courtroom, no amount of connection could guarantee him a steady stream of clients.

By and large the judges sprang from exactly those social and occupational groups which could provide them with the greatest assistance. Judicial biography abounds with examples of the importance of connection in the opening stages of a legal career. The multifarious nature of the connection useful to the young barrister may be illustrated by several examples from the early careers of the judges. Philip Yorke, later Lord Hardwicke, was the heir of an important and prosperous attorney in Dover, with extensive con-nections both in Dover and throughout Kent. As a result, Philip was the recipient of many briefs as soon as he had been called to the bar. In addition, he had the fortune of being introduced to Lord Macclesfield, Lord Chief Justice and later Lord Chancellor, by a fellow attorney's clerk, who was Macclesfield's nephew. As a result, Yorke gained the favour of the Chief Justice, who did his best to assist the young barrister's professional advancement.[34]

William De Grey, later Lord Walsingham, was the son of a prosperous Norfolk landowner. His father was acquainted with Thomas Coke, Lord Leicester, whose help he requested in furthering the career of his son. Leicester told De Grey in July 1746 that he could offer nothing definite to his son but: '[I] shall however introduce Mr. De Grey to Mr. Pelham [recently named 1st Lord of the Treasury] as soon as the hurry is a little over, & don't doubt but from the opinion he has of you as well as for my sake he'll serve him when he can.'[35]

[33] As quoted in Holdsworth, *History of English Law,* XV, 2421.

[34] Philip C. Yorke, *Life and Correspondence of Philip Yorke, Earl of Hardwicke,* (Cambridge, 1913), I, 57, and Holdsworth, *History of English Law,* XII, 238-40.

[35] Norfolk Record Office, Walsingham MSS., XIII/1.

There can be little doubt that this connection was most useful to the young barrister, who received appointments to two government places in quick succession. We find from De Grey's account book that in October 1746 he began collecting £150 per annum as Collector of First Fruits and Tenths and in the following February another £100 per year as treasury counsel.[36]

Charles Christopher Pepys, later Lord Cottenham, was said to have made but slow progress at the bar after his call in 1804. At least one judicial biographer, however, doubts the truth of this assertion. Pepys's father was a Master in Chancery, and with such a powerful office in the Court of Chancery he was in an excellent position to aid the career of his son who was at the Chancery bar. The son was a success within five years of his call to the bar, as a letter from his father to Hannah More asserts. 'The success of my second son at the Chancery Bar has been most rapid, and highly gratifying to me.'[37]

Finally, there is the case of Roundell Palmer who early in his career, which began in 1837, received a steady supply of business from the City. The source of this business is described by Palmer in his memoirs:

> To the great City House of Messrs. Freshfield, solicitors to the Bank of England, who were at the head of their branch of the profession, I was indebted for my first opportunity; as long as I remained at the junior Bar, they gave me from that time a steady support, and were my principal clients. My Uncle Hornsley, whose position in the City and in the Bank made his recommendation influential, had (I have no doubt) spoken a word in favour; the head of the house also had been my Uncle Ralph's friend, and they were accustomed to send him business when at the Bar. My university successes would never by themselves, have procured me a brief.[38]

One of the most significant types of connection for the judges in their early years at the bar was influence in the locality. In order to assess the importance of local connection, it will be worthwhile to examine the geographical origins and circuit affiliations of the judges. In Table 6 the judges are divided according to their county of origin. In a majority of cases this is the county of birth, sometimes it is the county of longest residence by their family, and finally in some cases it is the county in which their fathers resided at the time they entered the Inns of Court.

[36]Walsingham MSS., XIII/2.

[37]J.B. Atlay, *The Victorian Chancellors,* I (London, 1906), p. 385.

[38]Earl of Selbourne, *Memorials, Family and Personal,* I, 246-7.

Table 6: Judges' counties of origin, 1727-1875

	Total No.	1727-1760	1760-1790	1790-1820	1820-1850	1850-1875
Bedfordshire	2	0	1	0	1	0
Berkshire	3	0	1	0	1	1
Buckinghamshire	4	4	0	0	0	0
Cambridgeshire	0	0	0	0	0	0
Cheshire	1	0	0	0	1	0
Cornwall	1	0	1	0	0	0
Cumberland	1	0	1	0	0	0
Derby	1	1	0	0	0	0
Devonshire	9	1	1	1	3	3
Dorset	5	2	0	0	2	1
Durham	1	0	0	0	1	0
Essex	5	2	1	0	2	0
Gloucestershire	2	2	0	0	0	0
Hampshire	4	0	0	2	1	1
Herefordshire	3	3	0	0	0	0
Hertfordshire	1	1	0	0	0	0
Huntingdonshire	1	1	0	0	0	0
Kent	4	3	0	1	0	0
Lancashire	8	1	2	0	2	3
Leicestershire	3	1	0	0	0	2
Lincolnshire	1	0	1	0	0	0
Middlesex	59	8	8	6	15	22
Monmouthshire	2	0	0	1	1	0
Norfolk	6	0	2	0	2	2
Northamptonshire	1	0	0	1	0	0
Northumberland	4	0	0	2	1	1
Nottinghamshire	0	0	0	0	0	0
Oxfordshire	6	1	1	0	2	2
Rutland	0	0	0	0	0	0
Shropshire	1	1	0	0	0	0
Somersetshire	5	0	1	4	0	0
Staffordshire	5	4	1	0	0	0
Suffolk	3	0	0	0	1	2
Surrey	3	0	0	0	1	2

(continued)

Table 6 *continued*

	Total No.	1727- 1760	1760- 1790	1790- 1820	1820- 1850	1850- 1875
Sussex	2	1	0	0	0	1
Warwickshire	2	0	1	0	0	1
Westmoreland	4	0	1	1	2	0
Wiltshíre	2	2	0	0	0	0
Worcestershire	1	0	0	0	0	1
Yorkshire	8	2	2	3	1	0
Wales	7	1	2	2	0	2
Scotland	11	1	2	3	2	3
Ireland	8	0	0	1	0	7
Foreign	4	0	0	0	2	2
Unknown	4	1	2	1	0	0
Total	208	44	32	29	44	59

In general, the number of judges from a particular county was proportional to that county's population, though this is by no means true in every case.[39] The most outstanding exception was that of Middlesex and London, which accounted for 29% of the judges. The dominance of London and Middlesex is not all that surprising since they were the centre of mercantile and professional England, housing the Bank, Royal Exchange, the largest port, the Banking institutions of the City, the Royal Colleges of Physicians and Surgeons, the Law Society, Parliament, all government offices, and of course the Inns of Court, and the courts of justice. It is no wonder that the sons of the metropolis, who were raised close to the heart of the law, were represented in the highest positions of the profession in greater proportion than their provincial counterparts.

There were other very pronounced patterns of regional distribution of the judges. With the exception of Middlesex, the judiciary was dominated by men from the western half of England. The best represented regions were the Southwest, the Northwest — dominated by Lancashire — and the Western Midlands, including Staffordshire, Oxfordshire, and Berkshire. The only region to have a sizeable

---

[39]For data on county by county population in the years 1701, 1755, 1781, 1801, and 1831 see Phyllis Deane and W.A. Cole, *British Economic Growth 1688-1959* (Cambridge, 1969), p. 103.

representation in the Southeast, again excepting the capital, was East Anglia. On the other hand, the industrial midland counties produced very few judges, as did the Northeast with the exception of Yorkshire, and the counties surrounding East Anglia, such as Lincolnshire, Cambridgeshire, and Hertfordshire. Scotland, Wales, and Ireland accounted for 12% of the judges.

The appointment of judges of Irish extraction to the bench was a rather late development. Of the total of 8 Irish judges, 7 were appointed between the years 1850 and 1875. The men, none of whom were Catholics, belonged to the generation born in the years just preceding or following the Act of Union between Great Britain and Ireland. Just as Scotsmen went south after 1707, so it seems that Irishmen began crossing to England in search of professional success after 1801. This development clearly confirms earlier suggestions about an increasing Irish presence on the bench based on the rise in the number of judges who studied at Trinity College, Dublin, in the last period.

Despite the fact that the law was essentially a London based profession, regional associations are not absent.[40] Most striking is the similarity between the geographical origins and the circuit affiliations of the judges during their pre-judicial careers. The dominant circuits, the Northern with 34 judges (16%), the Home with 24 judges (12%), and the Western with 20 judges (10%), correspond to the three areas which produced the most judges — Lancaster and Yorkshire, the London region, and the Southwest. The Oxford circuit which was slightly smaller, (16 judges (8%)) corresponds to the Western Midlands, which produced a large number of judges, while the small Midland circuit which had 6 judges (3%), corresponds to the industrial Midlands which produced very few judges. Only in the case of the Norfolk circuit with 3 judges (1%), which corresponds to East Anglia and the surrounding counties, was there a discrepancy between the proportion of judges belonging to a circuit and the percentages of judges who hailed from that region.[41]

---

[40]This discussion of circuit affiliation only deals with 45% of the judges since almost 30% of them did not go on English circuits during their pre-judicial career. This group includes chancery barristers, barristers who went on one of the Welsh circuits, and the civil advocates of Doctor's Commons. In addition, the circuit affiliations of another 23% are unknown. The percentages for each circuit are calculated on the basis of all 208 judges, not just those who went on one of the six circuits.

[41]There is no indication that barristers from any one circuit had a greater chance for judicial appointment than barristers from any of the other circuits. The size of a circuit's judicial affiliation in any one of the five periods was directly proportional to the size of that circuit's bar 20 to 30 years previously, as recorded in the *Law List*.

Local connection seems to have been of particular importance for barristers who went the circuit. Of the 114 barristers who were of English origins (excluding those from Cheshire, which was on the Welsh circuit, and Middlesex, which was not attached to any of them), 49 were members of one of the six English circuits.[42] Of these, 37 (76%) joined one which included their home county, while the remaining 12 (24%) joined a non-local circuit. This markedly strong preference for their home assizes, despite the equivocal nature of the quantitative evidence, does suggest the existence of a regional bias in the selection of circuits. Undoubtedly the realization that friends and family could provide them with briefs at the assizes or quarter sessions in their home county influenced the barristers' choices.

In a letter written in 1820 by John Taylor Coleridge to his friend and benefactor, John May, we see the extent to which connection determined the distribution of briefs — in this case on the Western circuit:

> the next thing is my progress, with which I am on the whole well satisfied: a rapid rise to *general* business of the whole circuit is out of the question I think: business among the juniors (I mean among those who have any at all) is divided by counties among the men who have interest, or attend the sessions in them; that one set have briefs in Wilts, another in Dorset, and so on. In this way I think I am getting a place in my own county [Devon], and fortunately for me, there is more business in it than in any other on the circuit.[43]

There were judges who served between 1727 and 1875 who began their careers without the benefit of connection of any kind, and in spite of this disadvantage rose to the top of their profession. Others had the benefit of a few hundred or few thousand pounds to help them through the difficult early years at the bar. Still others were from families of modest connections in the locality — the professions, or commerce — who could provide them with business in the early stages of their careers. Finally, a few judges had had extensive and influential connections which could give them a powerful boost up the professional ladder. However, despite the fact that the majority of judges had the advantage of some connection when they entered their profession, few, as we shall see below (pp. 78-96), were appointed to the judiciary without first having proven their ability in the fierce competition of the courtroom.

[42] Although Middlesex was not included in any circuit, its location gave it an affinity with the home circuit. Not surprisingly judges born in Middlesex joined the home circuit more frequently than any other.

[43] Bodleian Library, Coleridge MSS., c.289, p. 81.

The cost of education, uncertainty of success, intensity of competition, lack of early remuneration, and the value of connection helped to ensure that the judiciary remained the preserve of the landed, professional, and commercial classes, and prevented it from becoming a path of vertical mobility for individuals from the lower middle and artisan classes. These factors created an almost impenetrable barrier for individuals who came from those social and occupational groups ranking below the level of members of the lower professions and the small merchants. Undoubtedly a successful career in the law was for the members of these two latter groups a means of upward social mobility, but they could only avail themselves of the opportunity because, in most cases, they had already achieved a position in society which could act as a springboard for their sons who wanted to become barristers.

For the sons of higher professionals, the landed gentry, and the large merchants, entry into the law was really an example of horizontal mobility. In the case of the sons of large merchants and successful businessmen, the object was to acquire a social standing equivalent to the economic achievements of their fathers. On the other hand, the sons of members of those higher professions which had a gentlemanly status but a relatively small income, for example clergymen and military officers, may have seen a career at the bar as providing the best opportunity of combining gentlemanly status with the possibility of acquiring substantial wealth.

Here we have the key to the great popularity of the law as a profession and an explanation of why, despite overcrowding and the uncertainty of success, young men by the thousands continued to enter the bar during the eighteenth and nineteenth centuries. The law was one of the few occupations in which the twin goal of reputation and fortune seemed within the grasp of talented practitioners.

As well as providing a means of mobility into the upper strata of the middle class, the law was perhaps the most important path to the pinnacle of socio-economic achievement in Britain. For the small group of barristers who were appointed to the judiciary, little was beyond their reach. Describing the members of the English bar in 1835, Alexis de Tocqueville wrote,

> 'lawyers belong to the people by birth and interest, and to the aristocracy by habit and taste; they may be looked upon as the connecting link between the two great classes of society'.[44]

[44] Although Tocqueville refers to lawyers as 'belonging to the people', as we have seen this terminology can only be used in the most restricted sense. Tocqueville, *Democracy in America*, I, 286.

Success at the bar and judicial appointment meant gaining admittance to the most exclusive circles in English society. The purchase of a great landed estate, acquisition of a peerage, and the establishment of a great family were opportunities open to members of the judiciary. Finally, as the careers of Lords Hardwicke and Eldon so aptly illustrate, appointment to high judicial office could be accompanied by the acquisition of enormous political power.

4

PROGRESS, PROMOTION, AND POLITICS

The newly called barrister, faced with years of struggle for a secure place within his profession, invariably looks upon the relative calm and repose of the judiciary as his ultimate goal. For the eighteenth- and nineteenth-century barrister, appointment to the High Court meant the acquisition of economic security, of increased prestige and influence, and sometimes of political power. The competition for a seat on the bench was intense, and the road to that goal was long and hazardous. Even with the advantages of connection, the path was not clear and the future judge had to tread his way warily. His ascent was marked by many opportunities for the receipt of professional and non-professional offices and honours, some of which served as stepping stones to his final goal. As a result, the successful barrister was inevitably faced with difficult and often critical career choices in his quest for high judicial office.

Careers in Mid-Course

During the eighteenth and nineteenth centuries, there were no regulations concerning the minimum number of years which had to elapse between a barrister's call to the bar and his appointment to the bench. This is reflected in the disparity in the lengths of pre-judicial careers and in the age at which barristers were appointed to judicial posts in those centuries. Six were barristers for 10 years or less before they were raised to the bench, while two practised for more than 46 years; six were under the age of 40 at the time of their appointment, while six others were over the age of 70. Overall, there was a considerable lengthening of pre-judicial careers and a rise in the average age at the time of judicial appointment during the period under investigation. Between the periods 1727-1760 and 1850-1875, the mean length of pre-judicial careers increased from 24.3 to 29.2 years, and the average age of appointment rose from 43.9 to 56.7 years.

The precise reasons for the lengthening of the pre-judicial careers and the consequent rise in the average age of judicial appointment are difficult to ascertain, although we may make several tentative explanatory suggestions. As we shall see,[1] incomes rose dramatically between 1727 and 1875. Perhaps this encouraged barristers in the late eighteenth and nineteenth centuries to remain at the bar for a

[1]Below, pp. 105-11.

longer time than their mid-eighteenth-century predecessors, in order to take advantage of the higher income. Furthermore, the increasing competition in the profession may have resulted in a more demanding and therefore more extensive pre-judicial career, which prevented young barristers from rising as quickly to the top of the profession as they had done earlier. Finally, there was a general rise between 1727 and 1875 in the age at which judges left office; this may have resulted from an increase in life expectancy during the eighteenth and nineteenth centuries. In turn, this would have tended to raise the age at which their successors were appointed, and would therefore have increased the length of their pre-judicial careers.

There was no single pre-judicial career pattern followed by all or by even a majority of the judges during our period, and in consequence, the formulation of one or more model career lines is impossible. All that can be done here is to chart the frequency with which certain professional ranks and offices were held by the judges during their careers at the bar. In this way it will be possible to indicate in the most general terms some of the avenues of advancement open to the eighteenth- and nineteenth-century English barrister.

Until today, the listing of the initials QC (Queen's Counsel) after a barrister's name indicates that he has achieved a considerable measure of success and stature in the law. This rank allows a barrister to wear a silk gown instead of a stuff one, marks him as a leader of the profession, and confers upon him certain rights and duties which have already been mentioned. Although it was not until the reign of Queen Victoria that this rank gained the significance which it now possesses, it was among the more important steps on the professional ladder throughout our period. Between 1727 and 1875 we find a substantial increase in the number of judges who had been QCs or holders of Patents of Precedence. The distribution of these ranks in each period is as follows:

1727-1760, 18 (41%); 1760-1790, 19 (59%); 1790-1820, 17 (59%); 1820-1850, 25 (59%); 1850-1875, 50 (85%); 1727-1875, 129 (62%).

Another position which usually indicated the rise of a barrister to professional prominence was that of recorder. This office, which existed in some boroughs throughout the eighteenth and nineteenth centuries, was extended to all boroughs by the Municipal Corporations Act in 1835. The recorder, a part-time judge, had duties similar to those of the JPs, and it was often a barrister's first judicial experience. In most cases the men selected by the boroughs to fill these positions were practising barristers who had already gained professional recognition and who often had some connection with the boroughs. Between 1727 and 1875, 41 judges or 20% of the total served as recorders. The percentage of men who served in each of the five periods is as follows:

1727-1760, 16%; 1760-1790, 22%; 1790-1820, 28%; 1820-1850, 25%; and 1850-1875, 15%.

The successful eighteenth- and nineteenth-century barrister was also eligible for a variety of professional offices, of which some were government appointments, some corporate, and some ecclesiastical. These middle ranking positions can be divided into nine distinct categories, whose criteria for selection ranged from merit and reputation, to connection and patronage, to rewards for political services. Appointment to these offices represented, above all, the rise of a barrister from the mass of practitioners up the ladder of professional advancement and achievement. A total of 75 judges (36%) served in one or more of these capacities during the early years of their careers, and they are divided as follows: Law Officers to members of the Royal Family, other than the Monarch — 23 men (11%); Counsel to government departments, especially the Treasury and Admiralty — 18 men (9%); Judges of lower courts, i.e. the Bankruptcy and the Palace Court of Westminster — 10 men (5%); Counsel to the universities — 9 men (4%); Vicar General to the Archbishop of Canterbury — 6 men (3%); Officers of the Counties of Durham and Lancashire — 6 men (3%); Counsel to the Charter Companies, such as the East India Company — 4 men (2%); Chancellors of the English dioceses — 4 men (2%); and Masters in Chancery — 2 men (1%).

The largest of the categories, the Law Officers to the Royal Family, exhibits very distinct periodic fluctuations, which reflect domestic peace or strife within the monarchy. In times when inter-generational conflict was rife, owing to the presence of an adult heir to the throne, as in the 1720s, 1740s, and between the 1780s and 1790s, or in the case of marital conflicts, such as existed between the Prince Regent and Princess Caroline, the royal family's need for legal advisers increased enormously. Often by serving as a legal adviser to royalty, a barrister was able to enhance his professional reputation, as well as securing the gratitude (or abhorrence) of powerful political figures. This was the fate of the six men who incurred royal and ministerial disfavour by acting as advisers and law officers to Princess and later Queen Caroline during her unhappy and stormy career, but who were eventually all raised to the bench when their allies came to power after the death of George IV.[2]

[2]Queen Caroline's six legal advisers were Henry Brougham, Thomas Denman, Stephen Lushington, Nicholas C. Tindal, Thomas Wilde, and John Williams. Of these

Three other offices, namely those of Solicitor- and Attorney-General to the crown and the judges of the Welsh circuits, were of even greater significance in contributing to the career prospects of members. The two law officers of the crown ranked at the head of the practising bar, and were almost invariably appointed to the highest judicial offices. Usually the Solicitor-General was promoted to fill the place of the Attorney-General upon the latter's retirement, death, or advancement to the judiciary. Altogether 63 judges (30%) served either as Solicitor- or Attorney-General, or both, during their careers at the bar.

The Welsh judges ranked below the judges of the Royal and Ecclesiastical Courts, and in contradistinction to the latter were not debarred from practising as advocates by their judicial appointments. The men who filled these positions were either top barristers who were given a place on the Welsh bench (usually as Chief Justice) for a few years before promotion to a senior judgeship in the Royal Courts, or they were barristers of the second rank who were never to rise above this level. The separate Welsh judiciary was abolished in 1830 and therefore played no part in the career histories of the royal judges appointed after 1820.

There was, of course, no necessity for a barrister to have held any of these offices prior to his elevation to the bench. Quite a few judges, especially in the eighteenth century, spent their entire pre-judicial careers as successful barristers, who appeared in Westminster and on the circuit without any rank or office. By the same token, there were barristers who held professional ranks and offices, but were for one reason or another never appointed to the bench. Nevertheless the receipt of ranks and offices was usually an indication of a barrister's professional success, and they were often important components in the careers of the judges, especially those who sat in the highest judicial offices.

For the ambitious barrister who had pretensions to these high judicial positions, a career in politics was often a means of securing appointment to the legal offices which have just been surveyed, especially to the Attorney- or Solicitor-Generalships, whose holders were invariably MPs. All the parties and factions that dominated the parliamentary scene in the eighteenth and nineteenth centuries were anxious to secure the services of able members of the bar.[3]

six men, two were later to become Lord Chancellors and two others Chief Justices.

[3]Lewis Namier, *The Structure of Politics at the Accession of George III* (London, 1957), p. 43.

Table 7: Law officers and Welsh judges among the judges of the High Court

	1727-1760 No.	%	1760-1790 No.	%	1790-1820 No.	%	1820-1850 No.	%	1850-1875 No.	%	Total No.	%
Solicitor-General	4	9	1	3	0	0	3	7	5	8	13	6
Attorney-General *	3	7	4	12	2	7	6	14	3	5	18	9
S.G. & A.G.	3	7	4	12	4	13	2	5	10	17	23	11
Welsh Judges	5	11	1	3	4	13	0	0	0	0	10	5
S.G. & Welsh J.	0	0	0	0	4	13	0	0	0	0	4	2
A.G. & Welsh J.	0	0	1	3	0	0	0	0	0	0	1	0
S.G. & A.G. & Welsh J.	1	2	1	3	2	7	1	2	0	0	5	2
No Office	28	64	20	62	13	46	32	73	41	69	134	65

* Eleven of the men classed as having served as Attorney-General actually served as King's Advocate or as Admiralty Advocate, the Crown's representatives respectively in the Prerogative Court of Canterbury and the Court of Admiralty. The status of these men on the civil side of the profession seems comparable to that of the Attorney-General on the common law side and therefore I have grouped them together.

Politics was seen by many if not most barrister-MPs as a road and a very important one at that to professional eminence; nevertheless politics remained a secondary consideration to the demands of the profession. An indication of the importance attached to this order of priorities is provided by a letter written by the Whig leader, Earl Grey, to the young Henry Brougham in 1810. Brougham had sounded Grey out on the feasibility of combining a career at the bar with one in the Commons. Grey encouraged the young barrister to accept a seat at Camelford which he had been offered by the Duke of Bedford (this had been the result of Lord Holland's influence), but at the same time he cautioned Brougham to form and declare 'your intention to adhere to your profession and your intention to attend Parliament as constantly as your legal avocations would permit but not beyond that point.'[4]

For many barristers, the choice of whether or not to enter Parliament was a difficult one. The final decision may often have been the result not of deep-rooted interest in political affairs, but rather of the purely practical considerations of the most effective way to advance a career at the bar.[5] If this was in fact a frequent pattern, then an entry in the diary of Thomas Talfourd during the year 1841 epitomizes the reasoning of the barrister concerning a seat in the Commons. Talfourd, who had just decided to retire from politics, assessed the possible advantages and disadvantages of his choice.

> I have looked out on the plain of life — saw the two paths diverging from this spot — one a Parliamentary life, full of bustle, care, weariness, excitement, and [illeg.], but with the chance of eminence, and the certainty of a kind of éclat— the other a more Professional life with meals of [illeg.] and with *the*

[4]Henry Lord Brougham, *The Life and Times of Henry Lord Brougham,* I, 497-8.

[5]In his study of the Commons in the nineteenth and twentieth centuries, W.L. Guttsman makes a similar point when he writes, 'Among the group of professional men in the political elite, we find the counterpart of the status-seeking businessmen in the legal careerist who held legal office and sat in the cabinet by virtue of office, or for personal rather than political reasons. These men came almost entirely from the new middle class and entered the House of Commons mostly at a fairly advanced age. Before their election to Parliament they rarely show a deep interest in political issues, nor do they have any hobbies or interests outside their work at the bar.' W.L. Guttsman, *The British Political Elite* (London, 1963), p. 177. Furthermore according to Sir Richard Pares, entry into Parliament was for many eighteenth-century barristers, and we may assume for nineteenth-century lawyers as well, merely a useful means to advance one's career, but one which took away too much time from business. Pares writes: 'Some of these parliamentary lawyers grudged the price of their preferment, tried to extort the maximum of promotion in exchange for the minimum of debating, and evidently looked upon the professional rivalries as the reality, their House of Commons careers as a disagreeable farce.' Richard Pares, *King George III and the Politicians* (Oxford, 1967), pp. 22-3.

certainty (for so I regard it) of never being higher than I am, and maybe retiring some 14 years hence with some £20,000 to a country life of contemplation & literary leisure. I have now chosen the latter, — and I believe better path.[6]

Just over half the judges who were appointed between 1727 and 1875 chose the Parliamentary course. Of the judges appointed between 1727 and 1760, 25 or 57% sat in Parliament; from 1760-1790, 16 judges or 50% were MPs; from 1790-1820, 17 judges or 59% were MPs; from 1820-1850, 23 judges or 52% were MPs; and from 1850-1875, 32 judges or 53% were MPs. Thus in total, of the 208 men appointed to the bench between 1727 and 1875, 113 sat in the House of Commons during their pre-judicial careers.

Undoubtedly a seat in Parliament was one of the most frequent non-professional adjuncts to a career at the bar, at least for men destined for the bench. The question of whether in fact service in the House of Commons actually boosted a man's chances of receiving a judicial appointment, which was one of the common assumptions both inside the profession and among the educated public, must be deferred at the moment, since it can only be evaluated properly in the context of a complete analysis of the appointment process.

Selection and Appointment

No single authority was responsible for choosing all the judges of the Royal and Civil Courts of England. The power of judicial appointment was divided between several officials, the most important of whom was the Lord Chancellor. The Chancellor appointed the Lord Chief Baron, the Vice-Chancellors, the puisne judges of the three Common Law Courts, the judges of the Bankruptcy Court, the County Court judges, and the Welsh judges. The Chancellor himself was appointed by the Prime Minister, and the latter also appointed the Chief Justices of King's Bench and Common Pleas, the Master of the Rolls, and the Lords Justices of Appeal in consultation with the Chancellor. The Dean of the Arches and Judge of the Prerogative Court of Canterbury were appointed by the Archbishop of Canterbury as were all the judges of the lesser courts in the Province of Canterbury. Finally, the Judge of the Court of Admiralty was appointed in the eighteenth and nineteenth centuries by a letter patent from the

---

[6]Berkshire County Library, Diaries of Thomas N. Talfourd, I, 143. Talfourd served as M.P. for Reading from 1835 to 1841. His retirement from politics lasted for 6 years, until 1847, when he was elected once again as M.P. for Reading, a post which he held until his appointment to the bench in 1849.

Crown.[7] In fact, regardless of which official actually chose the judges, the government and the Sovereign (the latter until the reign of Victoria) were consulted and their judgements influenced judicial appointments.

In most cases, the criteria for appointment included an evaluation of the functions of the judicial position to be filled, and of the characteristics which would be most desirable for that situation. Naturally, there was no single formula which could be used to determine the most suitable candidate for every seat on the bench. A particular barrister might have been the best possible appointee for one judicial position and the worst for another.

One question which I will try to answer in this examination of the process of judicial selection is which qualities — intellectual, personal, professional and political — were considered to be most desirable for each category of judicial office. In order to facilitate this evaluation, the judiciary has been divided into four groups as follows: 1) the puisne judges and barons of the Common Law Courts and the Vice-Chancellors; 2) the Chief Baron of the Exchequer, the Master of the Rolls, and the Lords Justices of Appeal; 3) the Lord Chancellor, the Chief Justice of King's Bench, and the Chief Justice of Common Pleas; 4) the Judge of the Prerogative Court of Canterbury and the Judge of the Court of Admiralty.

The judges in the first three groups all served in the Royal Courts. The divisions are based on patterns of recruitment and selection, size of the emoluments, status within the judicial hierarchy, and political influence and power of the judges in each category. The two judicial offices included in group 4 belonged to the system of Civil Law Courts. Until the late 1850s, the holders of these positions were separated from the rest of the judiciary by training, career patterns, as well as by the method of judicial selection. While the organization of the judiciary and the selection process were more fluid than these divisions might suggest, they do provide the most useful means of comparison for the entire period 1727-1875.

By far the largest of the four categories is that of the puisnes and Vice-Chancellors. In total, 141 judges or 68% of the total spent at least part of their judicial careers in one of these positions. This was the lowest rung in the hierarchy of the judges of the Royal and Civil Law Courts. Most of the judges in this category never sat in the House

---

[7]F.L. Wiswall Jr., *The Development of Admiralty Jurisdiction and Practice Since 1800* (Cambridge, 1970), p. 4.

of Commons, and political involvement and partisanship was by no means an essential criterion for appointment. However, there is no doubt that political services could prove to be a determining factor when choosing between two evenly matched candidates for appointment to a puisne judgeship or Vice-Chancellorship. This becomes evident in a letter from Lord Chelmsford to Lord Cairns concerning the selection of a new baron for the Court of Exchequer.

> I may say that if another vacancy had occurred upon the Bench during my term of office I had made up my mind to make Cleasby a Judge & I believe that the selection would be satisfactory to the Profession. I have the highest opinion of Grove but I do not know what reason you have for putting him above Cleasby as a Lawyer. I have had few opportunities of judging of his qualifications in this respect but from what I have seen of him I should not be disposed to rank him before Cleasby who I have always taken to be a well read Lawyer — upon the whole if I were myself called upon to make the choice I should prefer Cleasby, & I quite agree that if the scales hang equally between him & Grove, his services to the party act to incline them in his favour.[8]

Not surprisingly, politics did become the decisive factor and Cleasby was appointed to fill the vacancy.

Most of the judges in this first category had been successful members of the bar, but few if any had been among the most sought after or the most highly paid members of the profession. In most cases, an appointee to a puisne judgeship was a respected member of the bar but not necessarily a leader of the profession. In this regard Lord John Russell, the Prime Minister, gave the following answer to a question on the professional prominence of barristers named as puisne judges. 'I do not think it is necessary for the office of Puisne Judge, that a man should be at all the head of his profession in point of practice.'[9]

One of the clearest statements on the merits of a barrister about to be appointed to a puisne judgeship is contained in a letter from Lord Eldon to the Prince Regent in 1818 in which John Richardson was proposed to fill a vacancy in the Court of Common Pleas.

> Mr. Richardson was educated at Harrow, and afterwards at Oxford, where he greatly distinguished himself. For his principles as to State & Church I believe him to be perfectly sound: as a lawyer I think I am well informed when he is represented to me as exceedingly learned in the law. He is, as the times require, firm.

---

[8]Public Record Office, Cairns MSS., PRO 30/51/9, letter 12.

[9]*Report of the Select Committee on Official Salaries,* p. 144.

He has not quite the size and bulk of person, and strength of
voice, which Lord Coke would have required of a Judge.[10]

Of course the Chancellor could not be intimately acquainted with
every barrister in Westminster Hall, and often inquired of the Chiefs
and sometimes of well respected puisnes, which barristers in their
estimation would be suitable appointees for a judicial vacancy. There
was often extensive communication between the Chancellor and the
other judges before an appointment was made, and almost always he
consulted the Chief of a court before appointing a new puisne judge to
that court.

In the vast majority of cases, puisne judges were chosen from
barristers of proven professional ability. Ability in the law could mean
many things, including a barrister's income at the bar, a high
proportion of successful cases, the receipt of professional offices and
ranks, scholarship in the law, or fame. Often it was a combination of
all or most of these characteristics which led to a judicial appointment,
but sometimes a barrister was selected solely on account of his
outstanding legal scholarship. Probably the most famous instance of
this was the appointment in 1859 of Colin Blackburn to the Queen's
Bench by Lord Campbell. The appointment was made as a result of
Blackburn's learning in the law, and in spite of his lack of success in
court. Not unexpectedly Campbell was attacked by the profession for
appointing him over the heads of more prominent barristers, many
of whom were Queen's Counsels.[11]

In rare instances, barristers who could claim none of the criteria of
success were chosen to fill a judicial vacancy in preference to more
qualified men solely on the basis of connection. Five such cases have
been discovered among the appointees to puisne judgeships. The
earliest occurred in 1754 when Henry Bathurst, son of Lord Bathurst,
was named to the Common Pleas as a result of his father's influence
and despite the opposition of Lord Hardwicke, who favoured John
Wilmot whom he called 'the fittest man I know'.[12] In 1775 Beaumont
Hotham, who was a supporter of the Duke of Portland, was
appointed a Baron of the Exchequer by Lord North. In exchange for
the appointment, Portland named a man favourable to the government
to replace Hotham as MP for Wigan.[13] The next instance also took
place during the North Ministry, in 1780, when John Heath was

[10] A. Aspinall, ed., *The Letters of King George IV, 1812-1830*, II (Cambridge, 1938),
261.

[11] Campbell, *Life*, pp. 272-3, and *DNB*, Supplement I, 203.

[12] *History of Parliament*, 1715-1754, I, 446.

[13] *Ibid.*, 1754-1790, II, 641.

named to a seat in the Common Pleas by his friend Lord Thurlow, despite his lack of qualifications.[14] The final two examples both occurred during Eldon's tenure as Chancellor. In 1824 George Bankes, who 'does not appear to have achieved any remarkable professional success,' was appointed Cursitor Baron of the Exchequer by Eldon, whose daughter had married Bankes's brother several years before.[15] Similarly, John Vaughan was appointed a Baron of the Exchequer in 1827 because of the influence of his brother, Dr. Henry Halford, the royal physician. As a result of the circumstances which surrounded his promotion, Vaughan was known in the profession as 'judge by prescription'.[16]

These five examples notwithstanding, the profession jealously guarded the judiciary from being given over to well-connected but unsuccessful barristers. Members of the bar were sure to register their disapproval when such appointments were made, and though this did not always prevent them, it did assure that they occurred only infrequently between 1727 and 1827. They disappeared almost entirely after that period.[17]

Barristers who had risen to the top of their profession, especially those who were appointed Attorney- or Solicitor-General, did not as a rule receive appointments as puisne judges or as Vice-Chancellors. The law officers were leaders in the profession, and these lower judicial offices were not considered suitable to their dignity. This was

[14]*DNB*, XXV, 334.

[15]*Ibid.*, III, 120.

[16]Edward Foss, *Biographia Juridica* (London, 1870), p. 668.

[17]Later judicial appointments were not free of criticism. Two of the most prominent examples in the second half of the nineteenth century, while having occurred after 1875, nevertheless require some comment. Lord Halsbury's appointments while Lord Chancellor (1885-86, 1886-92, 1895-1905) have been attacked as less than judicious, but Professor Heuston has revised this assessment. See R.F.V. Heuston, *Lives of the Lord Chancellors, 1885-1940* (Oxford, 1964), pp. 36, 65. Another appointment which elicited an unfavourable reaction was that of Alfred Thesiger in 1877 as Lord Justice of Appeal by Lord Cairns. Thesiger's father was Lord Chelmsford, the former Lord Chancellor. The propriety of this appointment was questioned by his contemporaries and by at least one modern scholar. See Vincent, *The Formation of the British Liberal Party*, p. 83. Professor Vincent inadvertently called Thesiger Frederic (his father's name) instead of Alfred. There seems to be reason at least to reconsider this long-standing criticism. At the time of his appointment, Thesiger was earning approximately £10,000 a year, which made him one of the leading income earners at the bar despite his being only 39. The *Law Times* felt compelled in 1877 to defend that appointment against attacks. *Law Times*, 69, 23 October 1880, p. 433, and *ibid.*, 63, 3 November 1877, p. 1. In addition, a letter from Chelmsford to Cairns written prior to the appointment indicates that the Chancellor wanted to make the appointment despite Chelmsford's lack of enthusiasm. In response to a suggestion that he might be chosen as Lord Justice, Alfred is quoted as having replied that he preferred 'a speedy elevation to the dignified position of an Appellate Judge to the longer & more troubled course of political life'. Upon which his father commented: 'I confess that I am disappointed at this direction of his aims. . . '. Cairns MSS., PRO 30/51/9 letter 16.

the view of Lord John Russell who told the Select Committee on Official Salaries in 1850 that 'the opinion of the Bar, which has, of course, a great deal of influence, is against the Attorney-General taking the office of Puisne Judge; in fact, in more than one instance I have been told so'.[18] In total, only three Attorneys-General and six Solicitors-General were appointed puisne judges or Vice-Chancellors, and this was usually due to special circumstances. For example, Robert Monsey Rolfe, during his tenure of office as Solicitor-General, was appointed a Baron of the Exchequer in 1839. Despite the fact that he was a law officer, he gratefully accepted the offer because his private practice had almost vanished after his appointment, and he feared that the loss of office would mean his utter impoverishment.[19]

In another instance, William Baliol Brett, the Solicitor-General, accepted an appointment as a puisne judge in the Common Pleas in 1868, because he believed that his advancement to higher judicial offices was blocked. Since Lord Cairns had just been appointed Lord Chancellor at the relatively young age of 49 and since John B. Karslake, the Attorney-General, who like Brett was a common law barrister, had precedence for a future senior appointment, Brett decided, according to letters written to Cairns in 1868 and 1876, that he would accept the puisne judgeship. He indicated his desire in this correspondence to make his way up the judicial ranks by means of 'translation', which he did, eventually becoming Master of the Rolls in 1883 and Viscount Esher in 1897.[20]

Of course not all barristers felt that appointment to the bench in a junior judicial capacity was necessarily an honour to be accepted at once. Between 1727 and 1875, at least twelve barristers who were offered appointments as puisne judges refused to accept the nomination.[21] In most cases they were relatively young men who either had hopes of higher judicial office in the future and were therefore loath to accept an inferior office, or who had considerable

[18]*Report of the Select Committee on Official Salaries,* p. 143.

[19]Atlay, *The Victorian Chancellors,* II, 59, 63-4.

[20]Cairns MSS, PRO 30/51/10 letters 15 and 18. On translation see p. 91.

[21]Included in this number were James Wallace, Lloyd Kenyon, Henry Dampier, Joseph Littledale, John Richardson, Edward B. Sugden, John Campbell, Henry Bickersteth, William Horne, Lord William Courtnay, Frederick Pollock, and George Mellish. See Fortescue, *The Correspondence of George III,* II (London, 1927), 152; Kenyon, *The Life of Lloyd, First Lord Kenyon,* p. 52; *Parliamentary Debates,* second series, XIII (1825), c. 635; Cottu, *Administration of Criminal Justice in England,* p. 139; *ibid; DNB,* XIX, 153; Holdsworth, *History of English Law,* XV, 406; Hardy, *Memoirs of the Right Honourable Henry Lord Langdale,* p. 389; *ibid.;* Pollock MSS., Box 4; *DNB,* XIII, 221.

incomes at the bar which they would have had to relinquish in favour of lower judicial salaries. However, rejection of even a puisne judgeship during the eighteenth and nineteenth centuries was an infrequent occurrence.

The three judicial positions included in the second category — the Master of the Rolls, the Chief Baron, and the Lords Justices of Appeal — were held by 41 different men between 1727 and 1875. These three offices form an intermediate group between the puisnes on the one hand and the Chiefs and Chancellor on the other. The Master of the Rolls and the Lords Justices were appointed by the Prime Minister, while the Chief Baron was selected directly by the Chancellor; sometimes these judges were provided with peerages (though this was not done as a matter of course); and they usually went to barristers who had sat in Parliament.

More than three-quarters of the men who filled these three offices had been members of Parliament during their careers. One of the offices, that of the Master of the Rolls, was in fact the only judicial position in the Common Law or Equity Courts which allowed an incumbent also to sit as an MP. Not surprisingly, the appointees to that office were frequently important politicians whom the government wanted to keep in the Commons but at the same time honour with a judicial appointment. In fact, only one Master of the Rolls in our period never sat in the Commons; that was Lord Langdale. Similarly, a majority of the men who were appointed to the other two positions in the second category had been MPs during their pre-judicial careers, including 7 of the 10 Lords Justices of Appeal and 11 of the 16 Lord Chief Barons.

Since these offices were of a higher status than that of puisne judge, there was no objection to the Solicitor- or Attorney-General being offered or accepting them. When one of these posts became vacant, the law officers were often given first preference in filling them, though they did not have the right to claim any of these positions as their due. In 1834 John Campbell, then the Attorney-General, wrote to the Chancellor (Brougham), insisting that his office entitled him to succeed John Leach as Master of the Rolls. In rejecting his demand, Brougham replied: 'I am very sorry you should fancy there is any breach of precedent in passing you over, for I venture to say no one ever supposed Attorney-General had any claim to the Rolls, as he is allowed to have his 'pillow', the Common Pleas.'[22]

In total, of the 36 Attorneys-General who became judges between 1727 and 1875, 10 were initially appointed to one of the judicial

[22] Brougham, *The Life and Times of Henry Lord Brougham,* III, 427.

positions included in the second category (4 as Chief Barons of the Exchequer, 4 as Masters of the Rolls, and 2 as Lords Justices of Appeal).

Although these offices, as we have seen, were not considered below the dignity of a law officer of the crown, in fact Attorneys- and Solicitors-General were not always eager to accept an appointment to them. For example, in 1754 when a vacancy occurred in the office of the Master of the Rolls, the Duke of Newcastle suggested to Lord Hardwicke that William Murray be given first option in accepting the office. This step would have taken some strain off Murray, whose health was weak (according to the Duke), it would have kept him in the Commons to support the government, and it would have provided him with an office which was 'a very honourable station, consistent with his seat'.[23] Murray, however, did not concur with the last part of the Duke's assessment and rejected the Rolls as not being of sufficient dignity.[24] Similarly, in 1777, both the Attorney-General (Thurlow) and the Solicitor-General (Wedderburn) rejected the suggestion that one of them should accept the office of Lord Chief Baron. The Solicitor's specific objections were that the office was not sufficiently remunerative, that it was not held in high enough esteem, and that it did not immediately confer a peerage upon its holder.[25]

In practice these intermediate offices were often filled after consultations between the Lord Chancellor and the Prime Minister, although with regard to the Master of the Rolls and later with the Lords Justices of Appeal the Prime Minister had the final word. In 1788, for example, when Lord Kenyon left the Rolls to become Lord Mansfield's replacement as Chief Justice of King's Bench, Richard Pepper Arden was named Master of the Rolls. Although Arden was Attorney-General at the time and therefore a perfectly acceptable candidate, his appointment was opposed by Lord Thurlow, the Chancellor, for personal reasons. In the end, however, the wishes of the Prime Minister, William Pitt, prevailed and Thurlow had to name Arden to the office despite his objections.[26] The Prime Minister could not, however, always enforce his opinions with regard to the choice of men to fill the Rolls. In 1827, during the negotiations to form his ministry, Canning proposed that William Plunket be named Master of

[23] Harris, *The Life of Lord Chancellor Hardwicke,* III, 11-12.

[24] Yorke, *The Life and Correspondence of Philip Yorke,* III, 279. Dudley Ryder, later Chief Justice of King's Bench and Murray's predecessor in that post, also rejected an appointment as the Master of the Rolls because he was not granted a salary increase. *History of Parliament, 1715-1754,* II, 397.

[25] J.W. Norton-Kyshe, *The Law and Privileges Relating to the Attorney-General and Solicitor-General of England* (London, 1897), p. 11.

[26] Holdsworth, *History of English Law,* XII, 320.

the Rolls. Much to his surprise, the fact that Plunket was an Irish barrister and not an English one made him unacceptable to the English bar, and as a result Canning was forced to withdraw the nomination.[27]

Here, as in the case of the puisnes, judicial selection on the basis of connection existed, but its importance was minimal. Only two men who were appointed to these middle ranking judgeships could be said to have entered the judiciary by means of connection, and in both cases they served as Chief Barons of the Exchequer. This office, it seems, was considered the personal property of the Chancellor who had great freedom in bestowing it. As Lord Brougham wrote in 1834, 'everyone knows that the Chief Baron of the Exchequer is the peculiar patronage of the Great Seal'.[28] This being the case, it is not surprising that it was in this office in particular that connection sometimes became an important criterion for appointment.

In 1783 Archibald MacDonald, the Attorney-General, was appointed to fill the office of Chief Baron. Such a selection was by all tradition perfectly proper, except for the fact that MacDonald's rise to prominence in the profession had been 'due partly to his own abilities, legal and social, and more especially to his marriage to the daughter of the Earl of Gower'.[29] The second case came during the Chancellorship of Lord Eldon, who, as we have seen earlier, was not backward in advancing his friends and relations to the bench. William Alexander, an equity barrister who had a respectable practice in the Court of Chancery, was appointed a Master in Chancery in 1809 by Eldon, with whom he had become friendly. In 1824 Richard Richards, the Chief Baron, died in office and Alexander was named by Eldon to fill the vacancy. According to Foss this selection, which smacked of favouritism, came as a surprise, and was not appreciated by the profession.[30] In the end, however, Alexander turned out to be a good Chief Baron, especially in dealing with the equity side of Exchequer.

These two examples of judges who became Chief Barons as the result of connection, were by no means representative of the men appointed to the three judicial positions included in the second category. Among the individuals who held these offices during their judicial careers, we find such outstanding barristers and judges as Lord Kenyon, Lord Lyndhurst, Lord Abinger, Lord Cranworth, Sir

[27] DNB, XIV, 446.

[28] Brougham, *Life and Times of Henry Lord Brougham,* III, 427.

[29] Holdsworth, *History of English Law,* XIII, 556.

[30] *Ibid.,* pp. 557-8, and Edward Foss, *The Judges of England* (London, 1864), p. 74.

William Grant, and Sir George Jessel. As this illustrious list indicates, professional success and ability were the most important criteria used in choosing men to fill the offices of Master of the Rolls, Lord Chief Baron, and Lords Justices of Appeal.

We now come to the third category which includes the three judicial offices which form the pinnacle of the legal profession in England: the Lord Chancellor, the Chief Justice of King's Bench, and the Chief Justice of Common Pleas. The men who held these three positions had the highest incomes, the most prestige, and the greatest power of all the judges. Peerages were liberally bestowed upon these men: of the 47 senior judges, 27 were created peers. Many were intimately involved in politics and the affairs of state, and only a few confined their activities solely to their professional affairs.

Over 90% of the men who filled these senior judicial offices sat in the Commons, and only 3 of them had never been elected to Parliament. There is little doubt that political service assisted a barrister in securing appointment to the highest offices in the profession. In 1850 Lord John Russell made plain the connection between politics and judicial appointments. According to his understanding of the situation, many able lawyers entered the political arena to further their professional career and help them towards appointment to high judicial office. While service in the Commons and especially in the law offices was not sufficient to merit advancement to the head of the judiciary, it was a consideration in making appointments. Russell agreed that it was common practice for the government 'to require the assistance of the first lawyers in the House of Commons, and afterwards to promote them to the highest situations on the Bench'.[31]

The vast majority of the men who served as Chief Justice of the Courts of the King's Bench and Common Pleas entered Parliament well after they had established themselves as leading members of the legal profession; they were generally in their early forties upon entry into the Commons. More than 80% served either as Solicitor-General or Attorney-General or both prior to their appointment to the bench, and in most cases their election as MPs anticipated their appointment as a law officer of the crown by several years. Among the men who subsequently became Chief Justice of the King's Bench, the average length of time that elapsed between their entry into Parliament and their appointment as law officers was 3 years, while for the Chief Justices of Common Pleas the average was 6 years. The judicial post which was most frequently bestowed upon the Attorney-General was that of Chief Justice of Common Pleas, a pattern which was followed

[31] *Report of the Select Committee on Official Salaries*, p. 145.

in the careers of eleven of the 36 Attorneys-General included in this study.[32]

While there was an evidently close connection between the offices of the Chief Justices and a career in politics, it was the office of Chancellor which was the most political of the judicial posts. This was a natural consequence of the character of the office. Since the beginning of the eighteenth century the Chancellor has been the only judge who holds his place during royal favour, and he is also the only judge who is a permanent member of the cabinet. All the men who occupied the woolsack between 1727 and 1875 served in Parliament prior to their appointment to the judiciary. While all the Lord Chancellors were political men, a distinct division existed between the parliamentary careers of those men appointed before 1832 and those appointed after that date. Members of the pre-1832 group entered the Commons at a younger age, averaging 33 years, and they waited for a longer time before being appointed as a law officer — approximately 6½ years. After 1832 the future Chancellors entered Parliament at the age of 45 years and they waited for just under 5 years before receiving an appointment as a law officer. Thus with regard to the age of entry into the Commons, the post-1832 Chancellors followed a pattern similar to that found among the Chief Justices. They entered Parliament only after having made their name in the law. Their pre-1832 predecessors on the other hand assumed their seats in Parliament after only a few years at the bar, and while entry invariably occurred after they had gained some success at the bar, in a number of cases it preceded the establishment of a large and secure practice.

The future Chancellors were usually loyal party men who were by and large outstanding lawyers. Politics often played an important part in their careers, but was in most cases secondary to professional concerns. Not surprisingly, the usual pattern was sometimes broken by a man whose rise to the Chancellorship was particularly punctuated by political involvement. The careers of some of the Lord Chancellors not only serve as fascinating examples of the part that partisan politics could play in a barrister's career, but they also indicate the variety of ways in which political involvement could influence appointments to the highest judicial offices. The careers of two of the men who occupied the woolsack during this period, Alexander Wedderburn and Henry Brougham, are especially illustrative in these respects.

[32]This confirms the traditional view of the existence of a claim by the Attorney-General upon the Chief Justiceship of the Common Pleas. See above; p. 84, n.22.

Wedderburn, a Scotsman by birth, came to London in 1757 after a short and unsuccessful career at the Scots bar. During his early years at the English bar he benefited from his connection with Lord Bute, who helped him secure a seat in Parliament in 1761. He was made a King's Counsel in 1763, an honour which was the result of his political services rather than of his professional eminence.[33] In 1769 he abandoned the government and joined John Wilkes and the opposition. He was given a seat in Shropshire by Lord Clive, to replace the one he surrendered when he became a member of the opposition. Throughout 1769 and 1770, he spoke against the Ministry, although he refused Chatham's overtures to join the Whigs in 1770. He roundly opposed North in the Commons, but some observers have seen his actions as less than principled. It has even been suggested that he attacked the Ministry's policies 'for the purpose of compelling Lord North to purchase his support'.[34] He actually joined the North administration in January 1771, when he was appointed Solicitor-General. He supported North throughout the American war and climbed the professional ladder steadily. In 1778 he succeeded Thurlow as Attorney-General, and finally in 1780, after extended negotiations, he was appointed Chief Justice of the Court of Common Pleas and was raised to the peerage as Lord Loughborough.[35] He continued to play a central role in party politics after his appointment as Chief Justice. In 1783 he allied himself with the Fox-North coalition, and after its fall he continued to be a supporter of Fox. He acted as a partisan of the Prince of Wales throughout the 1780s, and supported him in the regency controversy, in the hope of becoming the Prince's Lord Chancellor.[36] That office eluded him with the King's recovery of his sanity. However, Thurlow's dismissal in 1792 provided Lord Loughborough with his opportunity. He left the Prince of Wales and pledged his support to George III and Pitt, and thus received the coveted appointment to the woolsack.

Although it may be possible to ascribe Wedderburn's numerous political conversions to the fluid structure of political factions in the late eighteenth century, his ability to change his ideological colours in accordance with opportunities for professional advancement was remarkable.[37] Party and politics were for Wedderburn merely a

[33] Holdsworth, *History of English Law,* XII, 570.

[34] *DNB,* XX, 1044.

[35] For a discussion of the negotiations which eventually led to Wedderburn's appointment as Chief Justice, see below p. 93.

[36] Holdsworth, *History of English Law,* XII, 572-3.

[37] The rather harsh view of Wedderburn's political career provided here is not universally accepted. In the *History of Parliament* series, the notice of Wedderburn's

means to an end, high legal office, and he treated Parliament as a very useful stepping stone in his rise to the woolsack.

In sharp contradistinction to Wedderburn's lack of political principles and his willingness to serve any master who could advance his interests was the independent and strongly ideological political career of Henry Brougham. Brougham was the scion of a Westmorland landed gentleman, but like Wedderburn, he was born and educated in Scotland and also practised for a few years at the Scots bar. Brougham sat in the House of Commons from 1810-12 and then from 1815-30 at which time he was appointed Lord Chancellor.

Although he was a member of the Whig party, Brougham was an independent in politics. This independence prevented him from gaining official leadership of the party although he was, for all practical purposes, its leader in the Commons. During the period when he was without a seat in Parliament he became associated with Princess Caroline, and in 1820 he was appointed her Attorney-General. In that capacity he, along with Thomas Denman, led her defence against the charges of adultery by George IV. As a result of their successful defence of the Queen, Brougham and Denman incurred the hostility of the King and the Lord Chancellor, Lord Eldon, who was prone to allow his personal and political prejudices to dictate professional policy.[38] Consequently Brougham and Denman had to wait many years until they received the professional ranks which were their due. The 1820s saw a rise in Brougham's income and position at the bar owing to his success in defending the Queen.

By 1827 Brougham was one of the most influential politicians in the realm. He was a powerful and persuasive speaker, and in addition had influence over *The Times* which gave special coverage to all his speeches and pronouncements.[39] As a leader of the Whigs he played an important role in bringing about the formation of the Canning ministry in 1827. Brougham hoped that his efforts would be rewarded with the Attorney-Generalship, but his long-time adversary, the King, prevented his appointment, and the post went instead to James

career indicates that his switch to North in 1771 was one made by many of Grenville's supporters after his death in 1770. Also his defection from Fox in 1792 is explained by his opposition to the Revolution in France. Despite these explanations of Wedderburn's behaviour, the fact remains that his political career as a whole gives the strong impression of a man whose primary interest was personal professional advancement divorced from any devotion to principle or loyalty. *History of Parliament* 1754-1790, II, 614-15.

[38]Jeafferson, *A Book About Lawyers,* I, 7-8.

[39]Chester W. New, *The Life of Henry Brougham to 1830* (Oxford, 1961), p. 141.

Scarlett.[40] Several months later, in July 1827, Brougham was offered the position of Chief Baron of the Exchequer as a consolation, but this he refused since it would have removed him from the source of his political influence in the Commons.[41]

From 1827 to 1830 Brougham remained in the Commons without office, and continued to maintain his independent course. Finally in 1830 after refusing to become Attorney-General and having his request to be appointed Master of the Rolls rejected (this would have given him a judicial seat and allowed him to retain his dominance in the Commons which, to some politicians, was an intolerable combination) he accepted the office of Lord Chancellor and was created Baron Brougham and Vaux.[42] Although his acceptance of the office of Lord Chancellor resulted in his removal from the Commons, Brougham was willing to give up his seat in the House in order to assure the success of Lord Grey's ministry and because it provided him with the power to realize the proposals of legal reform which he had suggested in his famous speech in 1828.[43]

Throughout our period, it was recognized that politics was a factor which could influence not only initial appointments to the bench, but also the career prospects of sitting judges. In making appointments to the highest judicial posts, every government was faced with a choice between two procedures. Either they could select men who were still practising at the bar, or they could elevate men who had already served in lower judicial offices in the Royal and Ecclesiastical Courts. During the eighteenth and nineteenth centuries there was strong opposition to the latter process, which was known as 'translation'. These objections derived from the fact that there existed a great disparity in incomes, prestige and power between the puisne judges and the Chiefs. These differences caused some members of the profession, as well as outside observers, to fear that a judge who held one of the lower judicial positions might try to secure his rise to a higher position by putting his office at the disposal of the government, thereby gaining ministerial favour. Despite objections, 'translation' was commonly practised in the eighteenth and nineteenth centuries, with almost half the appointees to the offices of Lord Chancellor and Chief Justice having been advanced from inferior positions.

[40]*Ibid.*, pp. 315-16.

[41]A. Aspinall, *Lord Brougham and the Whig Party* (Manchester, 1927), p. 152.

[42]New, *Life of Henry Brougham,* p.416. According to New, Lord Grey was willing to appoint Brougham the Master of the Rolls and thereby let him keep his seat in the Commons but opposition by the King and Althorp prevented the appointment.

[43]Holdsworth, *History of English Law,* XIII, 639. Holdsworth also suggests that Brougham's opposition to radicalism may have been a cause for his willingness in 1830 to leave the Commons. In this way Brougham escaped having to compromise with the democratic sentiment which was developing in that House.

In this connection, Stephen Lushington, later Judge of the Court of Admiralty, declared in a Commons debate on judicial salaries in 1825, that translation 'was detrimental at once to the respectability of the judges and to the pure administration of justice, that judges should be accustomed to look for preferment to the ministers of the crown'.[44] Of course this issue was not one-sided. It could be argued that since the intellectual and emotional qualities which made for a superior advocate were not necessarily attributes which were desirable in a judge, a man's mettle should be tested in an inferior post before he was appointed to the top of the judiciary.[45] This was a debate which it was difficult if not impossible to resolve, and it continued unabated throughout our period.

One of the most fascinating examples of translation was in the career of Robert Monsey Rolfe. We met Rolfe earlier in this chapter as the Solicitor-General who as a result of his loss of business was forced to accept an appointment as a puisne baron in the Court of Exchequer. After 11 years in this position, during which time he was a commissioner of the Great Seal, in 1850 he was appointed Vice-Chancellor to fill the vacancy left by Launcelot Shadwell. At the time of this appointment, his abilities as a judge were acknowledged by the unusual step of granting a peerage to a Vice-Chancellor. The next year Rolfe, now Lord Cranworth, was appointed one of the first two Lords Justices. Finally, in 1852, he was appointed Lord Chancellor in Lord Aberdeen's ministry. Thus we find that a barrister whose appointment as a Baron of the Exchequer was critized by some who felt him unqualified was able to rise to the head of the judicial system by proving his ability on the bench.[46]

As is perhaps to be expected, the leading members of the English bar and therefore the leading candidates for the top judicial positions were often *prima donnas*. Since this was a factor which sometimes affected the process of judicial appointment, it is worth some attention. In certain periods there was an over-abundance of candidates for the top judicial posts, and as a result either older judges had to step down to make way for younger men, or the younger men had to be willing to accept lower judicial appointments for a few years until a vacancy occurred higher up.[47] The resolution of such a conflict often

[44]*Parliamentary Debates*, XIII, 2nd series, April-July 1825, pp. 618-23.

[45]This argument appears in a recent book on the judiciary written by a former county court judge. Henry Cecil, *The English Judge* (London, 1972), p. 78.

[46]Holdsworth, *History of English Law*, XVI, 58-60.

[47]As was seen earlier, this was in fact the reason for William Baliol Brett's acceptance of a puisne judgeship during his tenure of office as Solicitor-General.

required long and intricate negotiations, which even after much discussion did not necessarily result in the desired consequences.

In 1777 the American War was already in progress and the Attorney- and Solicitor-General (respectively Edward Thurlow and Alexander Wedderburn) were two of the strongest supporters of the colonial policies of the King and Lord North. It was decided that these two men, who were in addition very able lawyers, should be rewarded for their support by elevation to the judiciary. Thurlow replaced Lord Bathurst on the woolsack, and it was proposed that Wedderburn should become Chief Baron, but as we have seen he declined the honour. As a result Lord North began a lengthy process of negotiation, (March and April 1778) with the approval of George III, to secure the resignation of the Chief Justice, William De Grey, in favour of Wedderburn. De Grey agreed on condition that he be granted a peerage. However since Thurlow would receive a peerage upon assuming the office of Lord Chancellor, and it was intended to make Wedderburn a peer at the time of his appointment as Chief Justice, Lord North refused to accede to De Grey's demand, believing that it was impossible to create three legal peers at once. In the end the negotiations failed, and Wedderburn was named Attorney-General after having refused to become the Master of the Rolls.[48] He remained Attorney-General until De Grey's resignation from the bench for reasons of health in 1780. Wedderburn then succeeded to the office of Chief Justice of Common Pleas and was advanced to the peerage as Lord Loughborough, while De Grey was created Lord Walsingham a few months later.

As has become apparent, a barrister's chances for appointment to one of the three top judicial offices were increased by his service in the Commons. However political considerations rarely outweighed professional talent. The vast majority of Chancellors and Chief Justices were eminently qualified for their offices, regardless of their political partisanship. In fact, the careers of many of the Chief Justices and Chancellors demonstrate that skill in politics and in the courtroom were by no means mutually exclusive talents. Lords Hardwicke, Mansfield, Eldon, Denman and Westbury, among many others, proved their ability both in politics and in the law. Their careers provide ample evidence that the existence of political criteria in judicial selection need not prevent the most able barristers from being appointed to the highest positions on the bench.

[48] Sir John Fortescue, ed., *The Correspondence of George III,* IV, 65-161. Care must be taken in the use of this source as a result of the poor editing. See L.B. Namier, *Additions and Corrections to Sir John Fortescue's Correspondence of George III,* I (Manchester, 1937).

The last of the four judicial categories consists of the 14 men who served as judges in the two civil law courts, the Prerogative Court of Canterbury and the Court of Admiralty. Unfortunately the details of the method of judicial appointment in these courts are obscure and no correspondence relating to the appointment of any of the judges who sat in them has been discovered.

The problem of judicial selection in the civil law courts was different from those of the Royal Courts. The judges who sat in the latter courts were chosen from among hundreds of barristers who specialized in many types of law, practised in any one of the many common law and equity courts, and went on one of the six English or two Welsh circuits. The judges of the civil law courts, on the contrary, were chosen from the small group of advocates, never exceeding a few dozen members, all of whom practised in Doctors' Commons. The civil law advocates formed a kind of professional family, and blood relationships were not uncommon. As a result, candidates for appointment as judges in the civil law courts were all very well known by the members of the profession, and this facilitated the process of selection.

Over half the judges appointed to the civil law courts between 1727 and 1875 were members of Parliament, 9 of the 14 judges having served in the Commons. Several played an important role in the politics of their day, notably George Lee, George Hay, and Stephen Lushington, but in most cases political connection did not influence the selection process in these courts to any marked extent.

On the other hand the positions of Admiralty Advocate and King's Advocate (officers who ranked as the civil law equivalents of the law officers of the crown) seem to have been important stepping stones to judicial appointments in the Prerogative and Admiralty Courts. In total, 11 of the 14 civil law judges, or 79%, served in one of these two offices during their pre-judicial careers.

Despite the fact that family connection may at times have helped influence appointments to these courts, professional ability and reputation seem to be by far the most important criteria. The legal prowess of these men is manifest in the many significant contributions they made to the development of probate, divorce, and international law. 'And though the small number of advocates, and their collegiate life in Doctors' Commons, helped to give their meeting the character-istics of a little family party, let us not forget it was a talented little family.'[49]

[49]Holdsworth, *History of English Law,* XII, 50.

There can be no doubt from the foregoing discussion that politics has played a role in the process of judicial selection in Britain. However before concluding this examination it may be useful to try and assess the global impact of political factors on appointments to the bench. Although just over half the judges sat in the Commons prior to their appointments, these MP judges do not represent a cross-section of the judiciary. In their ranks, the senior judges are proportionately much more heavily represented than are the inferior judges. Thus of the 113 judges who sat in the Commons, 50 eventually served as Chancellor, as Chief Justice, or as Chief Baron. On the other hand, of the 95 men who never sat in the Commons, 82 served in lower judicial offices while only 13 were ever appointed Chancellor or Chief.

The fact that a barrister who sat in the Commons was subsequently appointed to the bench is not sufficient to prove that the appointment was based on political considerations. In order to analyse in more detail the part played by politics in the appointment process, I have examined the political histories of those 103 judges appointed to the bench between 1820 and 1875, by which time a party system had begun to emerge from the fluid factions of the late eighteenth century. To this end I have divided the judges according to the judicial offices held — whether they sat in Parliament, whether they had political histories outside of Parliament, and finally whether or not they were appointed by the party which they supported.[50]

Not surprisingly, all the Chancellors and Chief Justices had been MPs, and were appointed by their own parties. Of the group which includes the Chief Barons, Lords Justices of Appeal, and Master of the Rolls, only two of the 14 men never sat in Parliament, and one of the 12 MPs was appointed to the bench by the opposing party. Finally, among the 71 men who served in the lower judicial posts of puisne judge and Vice-Chancellor between 1820 and 1875, 26 were MPs, 8 owed their allegiance to one of the major political parties but never held a seat in the Commons, and 37 seem to have been non-political. Of the MPs in this group, five, almost 20%, were appointed to the bench by their political opponents. Furthermore, of the eight judges who had political attachments but who were never MPs, three were selected by the opposing party, so that of the judges in this third group a total of 44 or 63% were either non-political or were appointed by the opposition.

[50]On partisanship in judicial appointments see Vincent, *Formation of the British Liberal Party,* p. 79. The problem concerning the exact date of judicial appointments noted by Professor Vincent is solved by the use of *Haydn's Book of Dignities,* which provides precise details. As a result, it is a relatively simple task to chart which party was in power at the time of any particular appointment to the bench.

On the basis of this analysis, there seems to be no justification for the claim put forward by Harold Laski, that 'it is probable that political influence has been a factor to which undue importance has been attached in the selection of English judges'.[51] Politics has most assuredly influenced the course of judicial selection, but there is no indication that it has dominated that process.

As the pre-judicial careers of Lords Loughborough and Brougham indicate, a barrister's involvement in politics could be a two-edged sword. If he were a faithful party man and if his party managed to gain and hold power during the crucial years of the barrister's career, then his political connections could often be turned to professional advantage. If, however, he was independent or an adherent to a party which was out of power for a long time (such as the Whigs in the late eighteenth and early nineteenth centuries), then his chances of appointment to the highest judicial stations might be diminished.

The criteria for appointments to the bench throughout the period 1727-1875 varied according to the status of the judicial office. The higher a judge stood in the judicial hierarchy of the Royal Courts, the more important political considerations became as a criterion for appointment. Yet despite the importance of politics, politically active but incompetent barristers were rarely appointed to the bench. In addition the highest offices were primarily reserved for barristers who were the most successful advocates, many of whom served as law officers of the crown during their pre-judicial careers. Sometimes connection may have been a decisive factor in the selection of one man from among several equally talented candidates, but rarely was it able to secure a judicial post for a man who had not proved his ability as an advocate in the courts.

Politics and the Bench

Not surprisingly, political partisanship which was frequently a component of the judges' pre-judicial careers, also exerted an influence on their attitudes and actions on the bench. While the ideal of judicial independence has been an integral part of British political rhetoric since the Glorious Revolution, if not before, the judiciary was

---

[51] Harold J. Laski, 'The Technique of Judicial Appointment', in *Studies in Law and Politics* (New York, 1968), p. 170. On the other hand it is difficult to accept fully the claim made by John Brooke that: 'It was not the practice during this period [1754-1790] to appoint judges because of their parliamentary interest, and in fact, the majority of men who were raised to the bench never sat in the House of Commons'. John Brooke, *The House of Commons 1754-1790: Introductory Survey* (Oxford, 1968), p. 187. In fact, in our second period 1760-90, which corresponds closely to the years considered by Brooke, exactly 50% of the judges had previously sat in the House of Commons.

not completely separated from politics during our period.[52] This was the result of a number of circumstances inherent in the English legal and political system. First, the Chancellor serves both as the head of the legal establishment and as a member of the cabinet. Second, while judges were by and large excluded from the House of Commons, they were most necessary as members of the House of Lords if that body was to fulfil its function as a court of final appeal.

During the eighteenth century and the first third of the nineteenth, at least, the men who filled the highest judicial offices were also leading political figures. For example in this period two Chief Justices of the King's Bench were members of the cabinet during their tenure in that office. Lord Mansfield sat in the cabinet from the late 1750s until 1763, while Lord Ellenborough's appointment to a seat in the 'Ministry of all Talents' in 1806, at the insistence of Lord Sidmouth, resulted in a major political furor, which excluded forever all members of the judiciary, with the exception of the Chancellor, from the cabinet.[53]

Naturally the most political of the judicial offices during this period, or any other, was that of Lord Chancellor. The most powerful Chancellors not only oversaw the functioning of the Court of Chancery and the legal system in general, but they were intimately involved with all the important affairs of state. One has only to read a biography of Lord Hardwicke or Lord Eldon to realize the power of the Chancellor during much of our period. Hardwicke served as one of the most important pillars of both the Walpole and Pelham administrations. Holdsworth wrote: 'As a minister of State he exercised a steadying, harmonizing influence, which was felt and valued by all the ministries of which he was a member.'[54] His greatest services were as a mediator during the life of the Pelham ministry. The practice of employing the Lord Chancellor as a negotiator and intermediary continued into succeeding reigns. Several ministries in the late eighteenth and early nineteenth centuries were formed through the efforts of either the incumbent Chancellor or the man selected to hold

[52] On the seventeenth-century background to the struggle for judicial independence see W.J. Jones, *Politics and the Bench* (London, 1971) and G.W. Keeton, 'The Judiciary and the Constitutional Struggle 1660-88', *Journal of the Society of the Public Teachers of Law,* VII (1962), 56-68. Security of tenure and salary was provided for the judges of the High Court in 1761 by Act of Parliament, 1 George III, c. 23. Based on suggestions offered by George III in his first speech from the throne, it established the principle that the patents of the judges are not terminated by the death of the monarch. For two eighteenth-century statements on the nature and importance of judicial independence see Adam Smith, *The Wealth of Nations,* p. 681 and Blackstone, *Commentaries,* I, 259-60.

[53] Holdsworth, *History of English Law,* XII, 473, and XIII, 502-3.

[54] *Ibid.,* XII, 247.

that post in the new administration.[55] Perhaps the fact that during the eighteenth century the Chancellor, although a member of the cabinet, fulfilled a function as the King's adviser which absolved him of ministerial responsibility, made him the logical choice as negotiator. He sat as a member of the cabinet, but his office was not dependent upon the fortunes of his colleagues. As a result, the Chancellor was 'regarded (and usually regarded himself) as standing somewhat outside the parties, and as a semi-professional officer he might hope to serve in the new Ministry as well as the old, and so to represent the element of continuity'.[56]

The Chancellor's freedom from ministerial control also allowed him to set out on his own independent political course. At times, however, this independence could be carried to an extreme which aroused such indignation that the cabinet could force his removal.

Such was the case with Lord Thurlow, who served as Chancellor between 1778 and 1792, with only a short interruption in 1783. Thurlow had always been an independent spirit, and depended on his friendship with George III to protect his office. In 1792 his opposition to Pitt's policies resulted in a political explosion, and the Prime Minister demanded and obtained his dismissal. The causes of his dismissal were described by Lord Camden, a former Lord Chancellor and associate of Pitt's father, the Earl of Chatham, as follows:

> You will be surprised (if you have not yet learned it from the paper) when I tell you the Chancellor is out, his behaviour in the House & in the Cabinet has been to the last degree provoking. Either opposing or not helping but his opposition to a finance bill of Mr. Pitt's which is a subject properly of his own departure, produced at last the coup de grace. Pitt could bear it no longer, & acquainted the king with great firmness that it was impossible to go with the Chancellor any longer, and he without any *apparent* difficulty consented to part with him.[57]

Thurlow's fall from power at the insistence of Pitt and the dismissal of his immediate successor Lord Loughborough by Addington in 1801, in favour of Eldon, signalled the end of an era. With the development of the cabinet in its modern form and the acceptance of the notion of collective responsibility, it became impossible for a Chancellor to remain in office if he did not have the confidence of the Prime Minister.[58] The Chancellor was now a full-fledged member of the government; he rose with it and fell with it.

[55]Richard Pares, *King George III and the Politicians* (Oxford, 1970), p. 109.
[56]*Ibid.*, p. 110.
[57]Camden MSS., U840 C3/24.
[58]Holdsworth, *History of English Law,* X, 642-3.

This change did not mean that the Lord Chancellor immediately lost the prominent place he had held previously in the political life of the nation. In fact, during Lord Eldon's long tenure on the woolsack (1801-6 and 1807-27), he put the office of Lord Chancellor fully at the service of the Tory party. Progress in the profession was determined by political opinions. Professional honours and offices in the gift of the government were reserved for its supporters, while its opponents were denied professional recognition, such as the title of King's Counsel, on the basis of their politics only.

With the accession of Queen Victoria a noticeable decline began in the political power and involvement of the Lord Chancellor. As a result, by the 1870s his influence over affairs of state had become limited, for the most part, to issues pertaining to the administration of justice. Thus we see between 1727 and 1875 the weakening of the connection between the legal profession and party politics. The receipt of honours became more dependent upon professional qualifications and achievements than upon political involvement. At times the de-politicization of the legal profession had been applied to appointments to the bench. The law has never been completely divorced from political life, and members of the legal profession continue to sit in both Houses of Parliament; however, especially from the 1830s, the political aspects of judicial office were de-emphasized.

On the Seat of Judgement

As we have seen, the judges were a vital component of the political and social establishment. They were charged with administering a system of law whose primary function was the protection of property. That system was supported by a sanguinary criminal code in which the death penalty without benefit of clergy was applied to an ever lengthening list of crimes.[59] The thief, poacher, forger, 'black', and highwayman were liable to the ultimate penalty as were those who participated in riots which resulted in the destruction of grain stores, machinery, or turnpikes. Individuals indicted for these crimes, and for many others as well, would have to face the judges at the next meeting of the assizes, or sometimes at a special commission appointed to deal with widespread riots.

Certainly the judges, as seen from below, would have appeared very differently from the way they do in much of this study. In place of

[59]Leon Radzinowicz, *A History of English Criminal Law and its Administration from 1750* (New York, 1948), I, especially chapter 1.

their educational and professional achievements, their large fortunes and fine houses, one would find other accoutrements — the black cap, the gallows and gibbet, or the convict ship on its way to distant parts. The assize judges were often the most immediate and accessible representatives of the ruling classes in the provinces, and were perceived as persecutors of the poor and defenders of the interests of the rich and powerful. An indication of the attitude of the mob towards the judges is provided in a letter written in August 1749 from the Western Circuit by Charles Pratt, the future Lord Chancellor, to his fiancée, describing riots which broke out in protest against the erection of turnpikes. Sailors had been brought in to quell the disturbance which resulted in '5 or 6 dead and 30 arrested'.[60] The situation, according to Pratt, remained tense; the rioters were hoping to: 'intercept the Judge, who is coming as they apprehend to hang their companions. This intelligence had determined Mr. Henley [later the Earl of Northington] and myself to go to Bath and from there to ride into Bristol tomorrow, if we find all this secure.'[61]

The hanging judge was certainly a very real character in the popular imagination and even in the literature of the eighteenth century.[62] Nor were such unfavourable images of the judiciary limited to the lower classes. One can hardly imagine a more mordant description of a judge than that written by Percy Bysshe Shelley in 'The Mask of Anarchy'.

> Next came Fraud, and he had on,
> Like Eldon, an ermined gown;
> His big tears, for he wept well,
> Turned into mill-stones as they fell.
>
> And the little children, who
> Round his feet played to and fro,
> Thinking every tear a gem,
> Had their brains knocked out by them.[63]

The populace was quick to make known its feelings towards the judiciary — sometimes wrath, sometimes acclaim — in London as well as in the provinces. When the mob stormed through London during the Gordon Riots, one of their main targets was William, Earl of Mansfield, Lord Chief Justice of King's Bench. After burning down his house in Bloomsbury, the crowd, so they story goes, began a march towards Hampstead and Mansfield's estate of Kenwood.

---

[60]Kent Record Office, Camden MSS., U840 C1/30.

[61]*Ibid*.

[62]E.P. Thompson, *Whigs and Hunters* (London, 1975), p. 211-12.

[63]Percy Bysshe Shelley, *Poetical Works* (Oxford, 1970), p. 338.

Providentially, however, they stopped for refreshment at the Spaniard's Inn, a few hundred yards from the Kenwood park, and were delayed there long enough for the troops to arrive and prevent them from attacking Mansfield's country house. On the other hand, Thomas Erskine, the most successful advocate of his day, became the object of the crowd's adoration for his exhausting and successful defence of Thomas Hardy in 1794. According to Holdsworth, 'Hardy's acquittal was the signal for an outburst of enthusiasm from the spectators and crowds which thronged the streets, and the streets could not be cleared till Erskine went out and addressed the crowd and asked them to depart peaceably'.[64]

Any assessment of the attitudes of the judges towards the judged during our period must grapple with the recent revisions of the traditional interpretation of eighteenth-century criminal law administration. In particular, the work of Edward Thompson and Douglas Hay has suggested that the criminal law in the pre-reform era was one of the ruling élite's most powerful weapons in its preservation of social tranquillity and of its own position.[65] It was the death penalty or its threat which stood at the centre of the eighteenth-century criminal law — a law which has been described as one of the 'chief ideological instruments' of the ruling classes.[66]

The fact that this system, which enshrined the sanctity of private property as one of its basic principles, had a pervasive class dimension is not new, nor is it surprising. In recent studies examination of the relationship between law and class in eighteenth-century England has suggested that the legal system and its ideological underpinnings, which supposedly guaranteed equality before the law to all, were liable to manipulation by members of the ruling élite in support of their self-interest, sometimes individual and sometimes collective.[67] This is not the place for a comprehensive examination of the debate about the system of eighteenth-century criminal justice and its wider social implications. However, it is necessary to consider, albeit briefly, the role of the judiciary in the administration of criminal justice and its attitudes towards the judged.

It would be meaningless to base this discussion on an exercise in ethical bookkeeping with pluses awarded to 'good' judges and minuses to 'bad' ones. There were those members of the judiciary who

[64]Holdsworth, *History of English Law,* XIII, 586.

[65]Thompson, *Whigs and Hunters, passim.* and Douglas Hay, 'Property Authority and the Criminal Law', in Hay, Linebaugh, *et al. Albion's Fatal Tree* (London, 1977), pp. 17-63.

[66]Hay, 'Property, Authority and the Criminal Law', p. 26.

[67]*Ibid.,* p. 48 and Thompson, *Whigs and Hunters,* pp. 188-9, and chapters 9 and 10.

attempted to mitigate from the bench the most dreadful consequences of the pre-reform criminal law, and there were those to whom mercy was anathema. Nevertheless, one suspects that both groups of judges agreed on the basic principle which underlay the criminal law — the sanctity of private property. The judges were, as we have seen, recruited almost entirely from the middle and upper middle classes, and their social attitudes reflected those of their peers. Even those few men who came from artisan origins were upwardly mobile, and undoubtedly adopted the values of their colleagues. Of equal significance was the fact that many of the judges were very wealthy men and substantial property owners, and so the protection of private property was perhaps as much a matter of self-interest as it was of principle. The judges were an essential part of the establishment of eighteenth- and nineteenth-century England, and Tocqueville recognized this when he wrote: 'Lawyers belong . . . to the aristocracy by habit and taste.'[68] In regard to the natural consequences of the 'aristocratic character' of the profession he said: 'I do not, then assert that *all* members of the legal profession are at *all* times the friends of order and the opponents of innovation, but merely that most of them are usually so. In a community in which lawyers are allowed to occupy without opposition the high station which naturally belongs to them, their general spirit will be eminently conservative and anti-democratic.'[69]

As a result of their social background and of their professional socialization and training, the judges were inculcated with the ideology of the propertied classes. They may have disagreed among themselves about the efficacy and utility of the harsh eighteenth-century criminal code, but this was a difference concerning means and not ends. Even while the severity of the law was mitigated during the era of reform, the class bias of the judges remained as a kind of social myopia. Moreover, the ideal of equal justice for all often existed more as a theory than as a reality with regard to members of the working classes, both individually and collectively.

Court decisions often favoured the interests of employers over those of employees; for example, the refusal of the judges to outlaw the relay system in factories.[70] In addition, the structure of the law and the expense of litigation meant that certain remedies were unavailable to members of the working classes. As Mr. Pelling has indicated, even

[68] Tocqueville, *Democracy in America,* I. 286.

[69] *Ibid.*, pp. 284-5.

[70] W.L. Burn, *The Age of Equipoise* (London, 1968), p. 148.

after the reform in the law of divorce enacted in 1857, the costs were prohibitive.[71] In fact the reality of the situation had in effect not changed for the working classes since Dickens wrote his famous dialogue about the law of divorce in *Hard Times* in 1854. Stephen Blackpool begs his employer, Mr. Bounderby, to advise him about the possibility of securing a divorce.

> 'Now, a' God's name', said Stephen Blackpool, 'show me, the law to help me!' . . .
> 'Now I tell you what!' said Mr. Bounderby, putting his hands in his pockets. 'There *is* such a law.' . . . 'But it's not for you at all. It costs a mint of money.'[72]

But perhaps even more important than legal discrimination on a personal level in the nineteenth century was the attitude of the courts and judges towards the institutionalized representatives of the working classes — the trades unions.[73] It was here that the social myopia of the judiciary was at its worst. Five months after the sentencing of the Tolpuddle martyrs to seven years' transportation, members of the Cordwainers' Society of Cambridge, indicted for the taking of oaths, were tried on the Norfolk Circuit before John B. Bosanquet. In his address to the jury Mr. Justice Bosanquet made his attitude towards union activity patently clear.

> I have no hesitation whatever in saying, that confederacies like that which appears to have existed in the present case are as decidedly in contravention of the law of the land as they are pregnant with mischief to the community and to the working classes themselves. It is for the sake of those who belong to associations like that of the late Cordwainers' Society of Cambridge, that I now declare, that all who engage in associations, the members of which, in consequence of being so, take any oaths not required by law, are guilty of an offence against the statute, which if clearly proved, would, upon conviction, be in every case followed by exemplary punishment.[74]

In fact the trial was a mere formality, since the union had already been dissolved and the prosecution declined to present any evidence.

[71] Henry Pelling, *Popular Politics and Society in Late Victorian England* (London, 1968), p. 65.

[72] Charles Dickens, *Hard Times* (Harmondsworth edn., 1969), p. 113.

[73] Pelling, *Popular Politics and Society,* chapter 4. Pelling writes: 'the judges of the higher courts . . . usually had little understanding of the mode of life and the ways of thinking of the wage-earning class,' p. 63.

[74] *Rex v. Dixon* (1834), 6 Car. & P. 602.

Nevertheless, Bosanquet evidently felt that it was his obligation to use this opportunity to warn the working classes about the consequences of any further breaches of the law in this regard. The taking of oaths was, in his view, not only a threat to the community at large, but also to the working classes.

Almost twenty-five years later in another case concerning a trades union, Baron Bramwell provides a further example of judicial short-sightedness. He explained to the men about to be sentenced that

> for more than forty years the best men in this country, the men who you admire most, have been engaged in removing restraints from trade, commerce, industry and labour. There is now no monopoly in this land. There is no class legislation. There is no law that gives one set of men an advantage for their own particular benefit. Now, you know that as well as I do. But, strange to say, you men are trying to legislate among yourselves in a contrary direction . . . and create a sort of corporate guilds which were useful in times gone by, I dare say, but are quite otherwise in these enlightened times.[75]

These judicial attitudes, while they may offend modern sensibilities, do not add up to a conscious conspiracy to deprive the working classes of their rights or of their lives. The behaviour of the judges was a logical reponse within the parameters of social and economic ideology which neither comprehended the needs or conditions of the working classes nor was comprehensible to those classes. For Bosanquet and Bramwell, as much as for Blackstone, the ideal was equal justice for all.[76] They failed to realize, though not out of malice, that inherent social inequality largely nullified the concept of equality before the law. Since employers and employees were not equal, working men organized despite the threat of transportation and imprisonment. Because hunger and a sense of social injustice existed in the eighteenth century, men stole, poached, and destroyed property, despite the gallows and the gibbet. The judges' lack of social vision and its consequences for the administration of justice has marred the reputation of the English legal system in the eyes of contemporaries and of posterity. This is regrettable because it undermines the credibility of the law, which as Mr. Thompson has suggested, despite its failings and misuse has acted as a bulwark against arbitrary class rule in England.[77]

---

[75] As quoted in Burn, *Age of Equipoise*, pp. 68-9.

[76] For Blackstone's attitude towards poverty as a justification for theft see William Blackstone, *Commentaries on the Laws of England* IV (Oxford, 1769,) 31-3.

[77] Thompson, *Whigs and Hunters*, pp. 264-9.

5

INCOMES AND INVESTMENTS

The judges of the High Court were among the most affluent professional men in eighteenth- and nineteenth-century England. Since the largest percentage of their wealth was derived from professional practice and office, it seems sensible to begin this inquiry into the economic structure of the bench with an examination of the pre-judicial incomes of the judges. This is followed by a detailed description of the level of judicial remuneration, the pension system for retired judges, and the extent and value of judicial patronage. The next section assesses the social, economic and political implications of the financial reform of the judicial system which was implemented in the nineteenth century. I then consider the investments by members of the judiciary in land and securities. Analysis of these investments should help to explain the financial and socio-professional expectations of the judges, especially as these relate to the development of an industrial society and economy in nineteenth-century England. In the final section, I try to establish the value of the real and personal fortunes accumulated by the judges who served in the eighteenth and nineteenth centuries on the basis of probate records, private papers and accounts, and the *New Domesday Book*.

Incomes at the Bar

The fees which barristers received for their professional services have never been controlled by statute, and, during the eighteenth and nineteenth centuries, advocates could earn anything from 1 guinea to several thousand pounds for an appearance in court. An individual barrister's income could undergo enormous fluctuations from year to year, and even the most successful advocates had to work hard to maintain their incomes at high levels. There were many factors which influenced the size of a barrister's annual income, and it was often difficult to predict whether the acceptance of a particular professional office or rank would affect earning power positively or adversely.

Any attempt to chart the level of the judges' pre-judicial incomes is limited by the scanty amount of available data. I have been able to discover information on the incomes of only a small percentage of the 208 judges included in this study. There is data about the incomes of only 20 judges during the latter stages of their pre-judicial careers, the time when their incomes were approaching their maximum. The

Table 8: Income at the bar 1735-1871

		Annual Income
John Comyns	c.1735	A £3,000[a]
Charles Yorke	1763	E £7,322[b]
Thomas Sewell	c.1764	A £3,000-£4,000 [c]
William De Grey	1770	E £8,037[d]
John Dunning	1771	E £8,535[e]
Lloyd Kenyon	1782	E £11,542[f] (including emoluments as A.G. and Chief Justice of Chester)
John Scott	1796	E £12,140[g]
John Nicholl	1798-1809	E £10,600[h] (average for 11 year period)
Thomas Erskine	c.1800	A £8,000[i] (never reached £10,000)
Charles Abbott	1807	E £8,026[j] (reached £10,000 by end of career in 1816)
Samuel Romilly	1807-1818	A £17,000-£18,000[k]
James Scarlett	1818-1835	A £15,000[l] (never reached £20,000)
Henry Brougham	c.1830	A £8,000-£9,000[m]
Edward B. Sugden	c.1830	A £17,000[n]
Frederick Pollock	1831	A £9,000-£10,000[o]
Thomas Talfourd	c.1845	A £5,000-£6,000[p]
Charles Austin	1847	A £40,000[q] (result of railway mania; retired 1848)
John Jervis	1847-1849	A £10,000[r]
Richard Bethell	c.1856-61	A £24,000[s] (reached almost £30,000)
Alexander Cockburn	1856	A £15,000-£16,000[t]
Fitzroy Kelly	c.1860	A £25,000[u]
John Duke Coleridge	1866	A £19,000[v]
George Jessel	1871	A £29,000[w]

Note: The letter E or A in front of the income of each judge refers to the quality of the income data i.e. whether it is exact (E) or approximate (A). The exact data is derived from the fee books of the judges during their pre-judicial careers, while the approximate data comes either from estimates made by the judges themselves, from well-informed contemporaries or from biographers. *Sources: a History of Parliament, The House of Commons*

1715-54, I, 569; *b* Foss, *Judges of England,* VIII, 223; *c Correspondence of the Earl of Chatham,* II 268-9; *d* Walsingham MSS, XIII/6; *e* Peter Brown, *The Chathamites* (London, 1967), p. 239; *f* Kenyon MSS, fee books; *g* Jeafferson, *A Book about Lawyers* I, 296; *h* Merthyr Mawr Collection, E/116/4; *i* Campbell, *Lives of the Chief Justices,* p. 282; *j ibid.,* and *Annual Biography and Obituary* (London, 1822), p. 383; *k* Patrick Mead, *Romilly: A Life of Samuel Romilly, Lawyer and Reformer* (London, 1968), p. 194; *l* Peter Campbell Scarlett, *A Memoir of the Right Honourable First Lord Abinger* (London, 1877), p. 85 and *Report of the Select Committee on Official Salaries,* p. 174; *m* New, *The Life of Henry Brougham to 1820,* p. 316; *n Report of the Sel. Committee on Official Salaries,* p. 164; *o* Pollock MSS, Box 4; *p* Newdick 'Sir Thomas Talfourd D.C.L.', p. 98; *q DNB* I, 734; *r Report of Sel. Committee on Official Salaries,* p. 183; *s* Nash, *The Life of Richard, Lord Westbury,* I, 132 and *Salaries,* p. 183; *t* Holdsworth, *History of English Law;* XV, 431; *u* DNB, X, 1236, *v* Ernest H. Coleridge, *Life and Correspondence of John Duke Lord Coleridge,* II, 150; *w* Sir Elwyn Jones, 'The Office of Attorney-General', *Cambridge Law Journal* 27 (1969), 45-6.

incomes of the 20 judges (and also those of 3 barristers who were most successful advocates but were never appointed to the bench) are listed in chronological order in Table 8. Fortunately, a high percentage of the barristers for whom income data is available were considered the most successful and most highly paid members of the profession in their day. Consequently the maximum levels of barristers' incomes throughout the eighteenth and nineteenth centuries can be identified, and the rise, stagnation, and decline of income levels can be charted.

I have been able to find only limited data on pre-judicial incomes during the first half of the eighteenth century. The fee books of Charles Yorke, a younger son of Lord Chancellor Hardwicke, provide us with the first year-by-year account of the fees received by a leading member of the eighteenth-century bar. Yorke began his practice in 1746 and 11 years later in 1757, after his father's retirement from the woolsack, was appointed Solicitor-General and earned £3,400. In 1758 his income rose to £5,000 and in 1763, the last year of his first term as Attorney-General, his income reached a career high of £7,322. He was among the most highly paid barristers in the 1760s and his income was considered most impressive.

Less than a decade later, at least two barristers, one a future judge, had surpassed Yorke's income of 1763. The first of these two men was William De Grey, who left complete records of his income for the last nine years of his career at the bar. In 1762, twenty years after his call to the bar, he earned £2,604. By 1766, his first year as Attorney-General, De Grey was earning £6,037, and in 1767 the figure had increased to £6,916. The next two years, 1768 and 1769, were less successful and he earned £5,644 and £6,829 respectively. Then in 1770, his last full year at the bar, he became one of the first barristers to earn more than £8,000 in one year; his income of £8,037 probably made him the most highly paid barrister in England. The other barrister of note in the 1760s and early 1770s was John Dunning who, though a leader of the bar, was prevented from being appointed to the bench by his political associations and early death at the age of 53. Dunning was called to the bar in 1757 and within ten years was earning over £5,000 per year. In 1770, his last year as Solicitor-General, he earned £8,014, placing him just slightly behind De Grey, and in the following year, the last one for which the records of his fees survive, he earned £8,535 without the benefit of holding a government office.

Between 1771 and 1820 the leading barristers in each decade set new income records. In 1782 Lloyd Kenyon surpassed Dunning's 1771 income by £3,000, earning a total of £11,542. Kenyon was serving both as Attorney-General and Chief Justice of the Chester circuit at the time, and these offices added £3,487 to the £7,555 which Kenyon earned from his appearances for private clients. In the 1780s at least two barristers were earning more than £10,000 a year. John Scott, later Lord Eldon, was called to the bar in 1776 and made rapid progress in his profession. By 1789 he had exceeded £9,000 a year and in 1791 he surpassed £10,000 for the first time. He was appointed Attorney-General in 1793 and in that year earned £10,330. His most successful year came in 1796, three years before he was raised to the bench, when he earned £12,140. The other top advocate was John Nicholl, who was one of the leading civilian lawyers and who served as King's Advocate from 1798-1809. Although the civilian lawyers usually earned much less than their common-law counterparts, Nicholl was lucky to have reached the top of the civilian side during the Napoleonic Wars. He was thus able to benefit from the large number of prize cases which were the result of these wars. Those cases, which constituted the most lucrative business available to civilian lawyers, were no doubt the reason why between 1798 and 1809, the year in which he was appointed to the bench, Nicholl's average annual income was £10,600.

The quality of data on pre-judicial incomes deteriorates for those judges who practised law after the first decade of the nineteenth century. The fee books of this post-1810 group have not survived, and the information which does exist consists entirely of estimates either by the judges themselves or by well-informed contemporaries. The most highly paid barrister in the first quarter of the nineteenth century was Samuel Romilly. He was called to the bar in 1783, and at first his progress was slow and his success on the Midland circuit was indifferent. By 1793 he was earning only £2,000. After that his fortunes began to change, and by 1807 he had an income of £17,000-

£18,000 per annum. His income remained at this level for the remainder of his career although despite his success he was never appointed to the bench.

No further increases in barristers' incomes were registered in the 1820s and 1830s but at least two barristers, James Scarlett and Edward B. Sugden, had incomes which approached that of Romilly. Scarlett's earnings averaged £14,000-£15,000 per annum between 1818 and 1834 and in some years he may have earned close to £20,000, although by his own testimony he never reached that plateau. Sugden had a reputation of being one of the most highly paid barristers in the first half of the nineteenth century, and it was reported that before his appointment to the Irish judiciary in 1834, he was earning upwards of £17,000 per annum.

After the middle of the 1830s the incomes of leading members of the bar seemed to drop significantly. Neither John Jervis nor Frederick Pollock, both of whom served as Attorney-General during this period, earned much in excess of £10,000 per annum. The only two contemporary barristers who may have had an income comparable to that of Romilly, Sugden, and Scarlett were Charles Austin and William Follett. The latter practised at the bar for 21 years and at his death in 1845 at the age of 47 he left a fortune of £200,000. Unfortunately his fee books have not survived and there are no estimates of his yearly income, although he was said to be most successful and was considered the *enfant terrible* of the Western Circuit in the early 1830s. Austin was the leader of the Parliamentary Bar in the 1840s and he had an enormous income due to the railway mania of that decade. His fees in 1847 were said to have been in excess of £40,000, which if accurate was a record for the nineteenth-century bar. Austin retired in 1848 from overwork and died in 1875 leaving an estate of £140,000.

Members of the profession were well aware of the decline in incomes which had occurred after 1835. In testimony before the Select Committee on Official Salaries, the witnesses who gave evidence about the incomes of barristers agreed that there had been a decline.[1] While the total amount of fees paid to barristers had increased, the structure of professional remuneration had changed and the leaders were absorbing a smaller proportion of the fees than they had in the first third of the century.

From the testimony presented to the Select Committee on Official Salaries, we can reconstruct the income structure of the profession circa 1850. There were, according to the Attorney-General, John

[1]*Report of the Select Committee on Official Salaries,* pp. 175 and 191.

Jervis, 5 barristers earning above £11,000 per annum, 3 earning between £8,000-£11,000 and 15 or 16 earning between £5,000-£8,000 per year.[2] Behind these 23 or 24 leaders there were the Queen's Counsels, very few of whom were earning more than £3,000 annually — most of them had incomes of £1,500. While the most successful junior barristers earned £2,000 per annum, the average annual income for the junior bar was from £500-£1,200.[3]

Actually by the time Jervis was giving his evidence in 1850, the slump in barristers' incomes had already ended, and the Attorney-General stated that he knew of one barrister who was earning £20,000 annually.[4] He may well have been speaking of Richard Bethell, who while serving as Solicitor-General between 1852 and 1856 was said to have had an income of £24,000 per annum from his private practice and from the emoluments of his office. In 1856 he became Attorney-General and retained that office until his elevation to the bench in 1861, when, according to his biographer, he was earning almost £30,000 annually. None of the judges and in fact no member of the bar who practised during the third quarter of the nineteenth century seems to have surpassed Bethell's income. There were, however, two other men appointed to the judiciary before 1875 who earned more than £20,000. Fitzroy Kelly, who served as Solicitor- and Attorney-General in the 1840s and 1850s and was then appointed Chief Baron of the Exchequer in 1866, is said to have earned £25,000 in a single year. Finally, George Jessel, who was Solicitor-General until 1873, at which time he was appointed Master of the Rolls, had an income in excess of £29,000 per annum.

If we compare the common law and equity sides of the bar after 1800 with reference to incomes, the evidence strongly suggests that the most successful equity men could earn higher incomes than their common law counterparts. Among the six leading post-1800 barristers including Romilly, Scarlett, Sugden, Bethell, Kelly, and Jessel, four practised in the Equity and two in the Common Law Courts.

Throughout most of the eighteenth and nineteenth centuries, the leading barristers in England were paid increasingly higher fees. Their incomes rose steadily from the early 1760s, if not before, until 1815-20. This rise in incomes corresponds to the inflationary period in late eighteenth- and early nineteenth- century Britain, which was especially marked during the war years 1792-1815. After 1820 incomes levelled off and remained stationary until the mid-1830s. After 1835 incomes

[2]*Ibid.*, pp. 173-4.

[3]Thomson, *Choice of a Profession,* pp. 97-8.

[4]*Report of the Select Committee on Official Salaries,* p. 176.

declined; this was undoubtedly connected to the nation-wide depression in the 1830s and 1840s. By 1850 incomes had begun to rise again, and by the second half of the decade they reached new levels which were maintained until 1875. Within a period of 100 years, from 1761 until 1861, the incomes of the most successful barristers increased by more than 300%, while prices rose by only 15-20%.[5] The increase in the incomes of the men at the top of the bar did not benefit the entire profession, and the gap between the leaders and the majority of barristers widened. Not surprisingly the judges, who were often leaders during their pre-judicial careers, benefited most from the rise in incomes.

Judicial Salaries and Patronage

The period 1727 to 1875 also witnessed a revolution in the system of judicial remuneration. During the first half of this period the judges derived their incomes from a complex combination of salaries, fees, and patronage. The system was so complicated and so concealed from public scrutiny, even from that of Parliament, that it is impossible to state with any accuracy the exact or even the approximate size of judicial remuneration in England prior to the first third of the nineteenth century. In order to clarify the situation, I have divided this examination into three sections. First I present the available information on the fees and salaries received by the judges of the High Court in the eighteenth century. Then I discuss the patronage, both legal and clerical, which was controlled by the judges, the way in which patronage was turned into income by the judges, and the characteristics of the pension system as it existed in the second half of the eighteenth century. Finally, I consider the changes which occurred in the nineteenth century to remedy the confusion which reigned in the system of judicial remuneration. An abstract of the changing patterns of judicial remuneration between 1750 and 1850 appears in Table 9.

In 1790 the salary of the Lord Chancellor was £5,000 per annum from which he had to pay taxes of about £350. His salary was augmented by a steady flow of fees to the Lord Chancellor, which fluctuated each year but rarely added less than £5,000 to his income. Thanks to a House of Commons inquiry in 1811, we have complete data on Lord Eldon's income from salaries and fees between 1801 and 1811. The lowest sum in those years was £9,926 in 1801-2

[5] B.R. Mitchell and P. Deane, *Abstract of British Historical Statistics* (Cambridge, 1971), pp. 468-71.

Table 9: Salaries and emoluments of the judges 1750-1832

	1750	1790	1799	1825	1832	Comments
Lord Chancellor	—	£5,000	£5,000	£5,000	£10,000	Lord Eldon's average income p.a. 1801-1809 £16,950.
Master of the Rolls	£2,400-£2,500	—	£4,000	£7,000	£7,000	Information for 1750 includes both salary and fees.
Vice-Chancellor	None	None	None	£6,000	£6,000	In 1841 2 more V.C.s were named with salaries of £5,000.
C.J. King's Bench	£4,000	£4,000	£4,000	£10,000	£8,000	Had vast patronage; actual income before 1825 £14,000-£16,000.
C.J. Common Pleas	£2,000	£3,500	£3,500	£8,000	£8,000	Had vast patronage before 1825. Income greater than salary.
Chief Baron Exchequer	£2,000	£3,500	£4,000	£7,000	£7,000	Prior to 1825 salary is increased by fees.
Puisne Judges and Barons	£1,000	£2,400	£3,000	£5,500	£5,000	Prior to 1825 the salary of these offices was increased by fees. *(continued)*

Table 9 continued

	1750	1790	1799	1825	1832	Comments
Admiralty Judge	—	£1,380	£2,500	£2,500	—	Value of this office rose in war years by £2,500-£5,000. By 1850 salary was £4,000.
Judge of the Prerogative Court of Canterbury	—	—	—	£2,800-£3,000	£3,300	By 1850 the salary of this office was £4,300.

Note: — = unknown. The incomes of the judges in the eighteenth and nineteenth centuries placed them among the highest salaried individuals in England. In the eighteenth century their emoluments were comparable to incomes of the members of the squirearchy (£1,000-£3,000 *per annum*), the greater gentry (£3,000-£5,000 *per annum*), and segments of the aristocracy (an average of £10,000 *per annum*). According to an estimate of the incomes of various occupations in the first decade of the nineteenth century compiled by Patrick Colquhoun, few men outside of the landed classes had annual incomes comparable to those of the judges. For example, bishops were estimated to average £4,000 *per annum*, civil servants from £200-£800 *per annum*, merchants between £800-£2,600 *per annum*, clergymen from £200-£500 *per annum*, shop-keepers and tradesmen £150 *per annum*, and artisans £55 *per annum*. By the middle of the nineteenth century, the system of judicial remuneration had been reorganized, but the judges remained among the most highly paid salaried individuals in Britain. According to the returns for Income Tax Schedule E (which included the incomes of most salaried individuals) just under 3% of those filing returns in 1851 were earning £1,000 or more per annum, while by 1871 the percentage of incomes over £1,000 *per annum* had dropped to slightly less than 2%. During the middle years of the nineteenth century the incomes of the judges were greater than or equal to those of leading cabinet ministers (the Prime Minister, Chancellor of the Exchequer, and Home Secretary all earned £5,000 *per annum*), members of the greater gentry (whose incomes ranged from £3,000-£10,000 *per annum*), and the bishops (they had an average income of £6,000 *per annum*).

Other examples of the incomes received by various occupational categories in the mid-nineteenth century are as follows: government medical officers earned from £200-£2,000 *per annum*, ecclesiastical incumbents earned an average of £285 *per annum*, civil servants £125-£1,000 *per annum*, clerks £70-£600 *per annum*, and skilled workers £100 *per annum*. The preceding data has been taken from the following works: G.E. Mingay, *English Landed Society in the Eighteenth Century* (London, 1963), p. 26, Patrick Colquhoun, *Treatise on Indigence* (London, 1806) as quoted in Dorothy George, *England in Transition* (Baltimore, 1967), pp. 152-5. Banks, *Prosperity and Parenthood*, pp. 107, 111, and 179. *Report of the Select Committee on Official Salaries*, pp. 5, 44, and 132, F.M.L. Thompson, *English Landed Society in the Nineteenth Century* (London, 1963), p. 114, and Geoffrey Best, *Mid-Victorian Britain 1851-1875* (London, 1971).

and the highest figure is £15,532 in 1810-11. In total, Eldon earned
£100,502 between 1801 and 1811, averaging approximately £11,167
per annum.[6]

Apart from his judicial income the Chancellor also received a
regular remuneration for officiating as Speaker of the House of
Lords. Between 1736 and 1755 Lord Hardwicke earned £31,765 as
speaker, or just under £1,100 per year. His lowest income from this
source in any one year was £570 in 1745, while in 1755 he earned
£2,299.[7] Fifty years later, the Chancellor's income as Speaker of the
House of Lords had increased more than fivefold. Between 1801 and
1809 Lord Eldon earned £45,056 as Speaker, which provided him
with an average annual income of £5,767 from that source. Thus
between 1801 and 1809 Lord Eldon's income averaged approximately
£16,950 per annum.[8]

The second judicial office of the Court of Chancery was the
Master of the Rolls. According to an account in the papers of Lord
Hardwicke, the income which accrued to the Master of the Rolls from
fees and from the Hanaper Office ranged between £2,400-£2,500 per
annum in the period 1751-3.[9] This is supplemented by another
account also found in the Hardwicke papers, in which an attempt is
made to estimate the total annual income received by the Master of
the Rolls from all fees, salaries, and rents. According to these
calculations, the total income of this judge was £3,168 per annum.[10]

At the end of the reign of William III, the Chief Justices of the
three common law courts received salaries of £1,000 per annum,
which were raised to £2,000 at the beginning of the reign of George
I.[11] The salary of the Chief Justice of the King's Bench was further
increased to £4,000 in 1734 when Philip Yorke insisted on a rise
before he would accept this office.[12] By 1790 the salary of both the
Chief Justice of Common Pleas and of the Lord Chief Baron had
been increased to £3,500. In 1799 and 1809 the Chief Baron received

---

[6]*House of Commons Commission on the Delay of Suits in the High Court of Chancery,* 1st Report 1811, pp. 33-5.

[7]British Library, Hardwicke MSS., 36, 118, pp. 42-58.

[8]*Commission on the Delay of Suits in the High Court of Chancery, 1811,* p. 5.
According to his biographer, Eldon's income for his entire chancellorship (1801-1827)
was £14, 718 per annum. Twiss, *Life of Lord Eldon,* p. 315.

[9]Hardwicke MSS, 36, 118, p. 101.

[10]*Ibid.,* pp. 89-94.

[11]Foss, *Judges of England* VII, 10.

[12]George Harris, *The Life of Lord Chancellor Hardwicke,* (London, 1847), I, 256-7.

additional rises, bringing his salary to £5,000 per annum. This gave the Chief Baron the highest salary of the Chiefs, although his total emoluments amounted to less than those of his two colleagues.[13]

Unlike the Chiefs, the Chancellor, and the Master of the Rolls, the puisne judges received most of their income from salary, and only a small part from fees. As a result we are able to estimate their total earnings more accurately. During the reign of George I the puisnes received £1,000 per annum.[14] In 1759 that figure was raised to £1,500, in 1779 to £1,900, in 1799 to £3,000, and in 1809 to £4,000.[15] In addition to their salary, the puisnes also received fees from their offices of several hundred pounds a year. Sydney Stafford Smythe has left us an account of his total income from salary and fees for the years 1750-7, at which time the official salary was still £1,000 a year. His lowest income in any single year was £1,426 (1750-1751) and the highest was £1,731 (1754-1755).[16]

Finally, we must consider the incomes of the judges of the Prerogative and Admiralty Courts. Although there are few official statistics, we are able to estimate the incomes of the civil law judges from biographical data and private accounts. The incomes of the Judges of the Court of Admiralty fluctuated tremendously depending on whether there was war or peace. The judge was given a share of the money awarded in prize cases in wartime, and as a result the salary of approximately £2,500 which was unsupplemented in peacetime could rise to £7,000-£8,000 during war.[17] The income of the Judge of the Prerogative Court of Canterbury was, on the other hand, very stable. Sir John Nicholl, of the Prerogative Court, told a parliamentary inquiry in 1827 that the leading ecclesiastical judge in England earned between £2,800-£3,000 per annum, plus an additional £50 from the office of Dean of the Arches.[18] By 1850 the income of both judicial offices had increased, according to testimony presented to a Parliamentary inquiry by Stephen Lushington, the Judge of the Court of Admiralty. He estimated that the Judges of the Court of Admiralty

[13]*Return of the Salaries and Emoluments in 1790 of the Judges of the Several Courts in England, Ireland and Scotland,* PP XXXIII, 1850, pp. 1-2.

[14]Foss, *Judges of England,* VIII, 10.

[15]*Return of Salaries and Emoluments in 1790,* pp. 1-2.

[16]Hardwicke MSS., 36, 223, pp. 292-3.

[17]Article on Christopher Robinson in *Annual Biography and Obituary,* (London, 1834), p. 330.

[18]Merthyr Mawr Collection, L/209. Merthyr Mawr House, Glamorganshire, quoted by permission of Mr. M.A. McLaggan.

earned £4,000 per annum, while the salary of the Judge of the Prerogative Court of Canterbury was £4,300.[19]

For a majority of the judges the income derived from salaries and fees constituted their entire remuneration. However, for three of the judges in particular, the Chancellor, the Chief Justice of King's Bench, and the Chief Justice of Common Pleas, the emoluments of office also included a large amount of legal patronage. In some cases the offices in a judge's gift could be sold, with the proceeds going directly to the judge who controlled each office. In other cases, judges could keep valuable offices for themselves and add the income derived from those offices to their income. Finally, important offices were often given to the sons or close relatives of the judges, while lesser offices were given to more distant relatives and friends. Unfortunately the data on judicial patronage and income is incomplete and it is impossible to assemble a full account of the offices which were in the gift of each of the judges. As a result, there is no way to calculate with accuracy the supplementary income which accrued to members of the judiciary, directly or indirectly, from these offices. We can simply survey distribution and the dimensions of judicial patronage.

By the 1730s the patronage belonging to the Lord Chancellor had already been subject to public criticism. In 1725 Lord Chancellor Macclesfield was impeached and fined £30,000 on account of the embezzlement of court receipts in excess of £100,000 by officials who had purchased their offices from Macclesfield. As a result, the practice of sale of offices began to come under attack, and the sale of the office of the Master in Chancery, (the men guilty of the embezzlement had served in this capacity) was forbidden. Despite this incident, however, the Chancellor continued to control a huge amount of patronage.[20] In 1810 a House of Commons committee report on the value of sinecures in the various courts revealed that the current Lord Chancellor had offices in his gift worth £6,391 per annum, and offices worth another £8,790 per annum were held by relatives of former Chancellors. One of these offices, the Clerk of the Hanaper, was held by the 'sisters and co-heiresses of the Earl of Northington' as a result of a patent issued to the first Earl (a former Chancellor) forty or fifty years earlier.[21].

---

[19]*Report of the Select Committee on Official Salaries,* pp. 208-9.

[20]For a complete list of the offices in the gift of the judges see Appendix XIII in Holdsworth, *History of English Law,* I, 684-6.

[21]Details from the will of the Earl of Northington, Public Record Office, PROB 11/1772/64.

Of course, not all Chancellors benefited equally by the patronage invested in their office. To a large extent the value of patronage to any individual Chancellor depended on which offices became vacant during his term of office. The longer Chancellors, or for that matter Chief Justices, held office, the more likely they were to benefit fully from the patronage attached to their office. In this respect the two Chancellors who were able to take fullest advantage of their patronage were Lord Hardwicke, who held the Great Seal for 19 years, and Lord Eldon, who held it for 25 years. Both men liberally distributed offices among their children and relatives. Hardwicke, for example, gave two of his younger sons the office of Clerk of the Crown in Chancery, which was worth £1,200 per annum,[22] while his eldest son received the office of Chief Clerk of King's Bench by royal patent in 1737 when Hardwicke agreed to be transferred from King's Bench to the woolsack.[23] Lord Eldon granted his eldest son, William, 6 Chancery sinecures, Clerk of Patents, Registrar of Affidavits, Receiver of Fines, and Cursitor — offices which were in Eldon's possession. In addition, William was granted the reversion of the Clerk of the Crown in Chancery and the office for the execution of the Statutes of Bankrupts.[24]

The office of Lord Chancellor was more richly endowed with patronage than any other judicial office. Not only did the Chancellor control the numerous and valuable legal sinecures to which few duties were attached, but he also had the right to appoint court officials, including the judges of the Royal Courts, the judges of the County Courts, and the judges of the Welsh circuits, all of whom continued to perform essential legal functions. Even after the reforms in Chancery offices during the years 1825-35, the Chancellors were still able to provide for relatives in a number of inferior legal offices. A striking example of the post-reform possibilities is found in a letter written in 1859 from the Lord Chancellor Chelmsford to Sir Hugh McCalmont Cairns, the Solicitor-General, concerning criticism of one of Chelmford's legal appointments.

> Apropos to Lunacy I understand that there is a storm brewing about my appointment of Higgins to the Mastership. My answer is that he certainly would not have been appointed if he had not been my son in law, but that being my son in law he would not have been appointed if I hadn't considered him perfectly

[22]Yorke, *Life and Correspondence of Philip Yorke,* II, 143.

[23]Harris, *Life of Lord Chancellor Hardwicke,* I, 362-3.

[24]Twiss, *Life of Lord Eldon,* III, 171. The value of those offices was £3,000 *per annum* according to Eldon's own estimate. *Ibid.,* p. 556.

competent (after a little instruction) to the duties of the office. . .
He is certainly only *formally* qualified being a Barrister of more
than ten years standing, but the present & late Masters were, one
of them, Principal Secretary and the Secretary of Presentations
to Lord Lyndhurst at the time they were made.[25]

In addition to his control of legal patronage, the Chancellor was
also one of the most important patrons of ecclesiastical offices in the
realm. In 1736, according to an account in the papers of Lord
Hardwicke, the Lord Chancellor was patron of 1,276 clerical livings
in England and Wales, which had a nominal value of between £7
and £400 per annum.[26] Although by 1850 the number had declined,
the Lord Chancellor still had some 700 livings in his gift, according to
an estimate given by Lord John Russell.[27]

The Chancellors did not receive direct personal financial benefit
from appointments to post-reform court offices or clerical livings. In
some cases, court offices were bestowed on eligible relatives or
friends, as Chelmsford's letter indicated, but the vast majority of legal
and clerical positions were filled by men who had no connection with
the Chancellor. As might be expected, Chancellors were deluged with
requests for appointment to these situations, and members of the
judiciary were often asked to intercede with them, on behalf of one
applicant or another. In 1774 one correspondent requested that
Lady Apsley, wife of Henry Bathurst, help secure the living of St.
George, Hanover Square, for 'a worthy Clergyman'. He promised
Lady Apsley that if she succeeded he would provide her or any friend
of hers with either a lump sum of £3,000, or £500 per annum for as
long as his friend held the living.[28] Although this request was out of the
ordinary due to the apparent value of the living and the offer to pay for
the appointment, it was only one among thousands that crossed the
desks of every Chancellor. We can imagine that more than one
Chancellor would have agreed with Lord Eldon when he wrote to Sir
Richard Richards, the Lord Chief Baron, with regard to a request for a
living:

> Mr. Moore's venerable father told me on the day, I think, in
> which I first appeared in the House of Lords as Chancellor that
> my Church Patronage would destroy all my Peace — and
> certainly it has done so in a very great Measure — No man could
> think of believing if I were to state how many pending

[25]Cairns MSS. PRO 30/51/9, letter 5. On the Lord Chancellor's use of patronage
after the reforms of the 1830s see Vincent, *Formation of the British Liberal Party,* pp.
78-9 and 82-3.

[26]Hardwicke MSS., 36, 857.

[27]*Report of Select Committee on Official Salaries,* pp. 134-5.

[28]British Library, Bathurst MSS., Loan 57/1-2, letter 88.

applications are before me on behalf of young Clergymen in order that they may marry — how many on behalf of older Clergymen, who have married, and have from ten to fourteen children.[29]

The total patronage belonging to the Chief Justice of King's Bench could not compare with that of the Chancellor. The former could appoint no members of the judiciary and few legal officers outside his own court. Yet the absolute value of the court sinecures which he had in his gift may very possibly have been greater in value than the sinecure offices belonging to the Chancellor. In the first quarter of the nineteenth century the Chief Justice controlled legal patronage which had an annual value of approximately £23,000.[30] Usually a large part of that income accrued to the sons and other close relatives of the Chief Justice. We find that in 1825 almost 75% of these offices (based on their annual value) were either held directly by the sons of the two previous Chief Justices, Lords Kenyon and Ellenborough, or were sub-patronage attached to their offices.[31] The most valuable of these offices, the Chief Clerk, which was worth £7,700 in 1825, was sometimes kept by the Chief Justice.[32]

Not only did the Chief Justice of King's Bench have an enormous amount of patronage which could be used for his own direct financial benefit or for that of his children, but in addition, some of the officials who held sinecures in the Court of King's Bench were required to pay part of their fees to him for his own use. This added another £3,000 to his official salary of £4,000 and was further supplemented by other fees, the sale of offices, and sometimes the direct receipt of income from the sinecures.

Before the reformation of the patronage and sinecure system, Chief Justices rarely hesitated in appointing near relatives to the most lucrative positions. Those who filled the office of Chief Justice after the reorganization of the courts in the 1830s could no longer benefit from patronage to the same extent as did their predecessors. This does not mean, however, that they were unable to find offices for their sons and relatives, although the offices that were available paled by comparison to what had been. Lord Denman, who became Chief Justice in 1832, was able to appoint one of his sons to the office of Marshall and Associate of the Chief Justice, which was reportedly

[29]Merioneth Record Office, Caerynwch MSS., DA/M/1/704, letter 33.

[30]*Report of the House of Commons Select Committee on Sinecure Offices*, 1834, p. 3, and Holdsworth, *History of English Law*, I, 687.

[31]*Report of the Select Committee on Sinecure Offices*, 1834, p. 3.

[32]This was the practice of Lord Ellenborough before he granted the office to his son, according to Copley. *Parliamentary Debates*, XIII, 2nd Series, p. 634.

worth £1,500 per annum.[33] Even offices which were under judicial patronage but which required their holders to have professional qualifications were often filled by the sons of judges. Of the 22 Masters of the Supreme Court, for example, who were serving in 1881 and who received salaries of between £1,000 and £1,500 per annum, seven or just under one third were sons of former judges of the High Court.[34]

The third largest share of judicial patronage belonged to the Chief Justice of Common Pleas. The offices in his gift amounted to approximately £10,000, and the most valuable one was that of the Clerk of Errors in Exchequer Chamber, an office not even in his own court. Most of the offices were worth no more than £300, and a list of office-holders in 1825 indicates that the Chief Justice of Common Pleas was less likely to appoint his immediate relatives to the offices in his gift than were the Chancellor or the Chief Justice of King's Bench.[35] The Chief Justice of Common Pleas also received fees directly from his appointees. The income received from this source, though considerably less than that of the Chief Justice of King's Bench, amounted to £1,100 per annum.

The patronage of the Chief Baron was much smaller than that of the Chancellor or Chief Justices. He was able to appoint 8 officials, but these offices did not even include the most valuable sinecures in the Court of Exchequer. The Master of the Rolls also had some judicial patronage, and although I have not been able to find its value in the nineteenth century, during the first half of the eighteenth century it stood at £6,900 for a total of 13 offices.[36]

The Judges of the Admiralty and the Prerogative Court did not control the offices connected with their courts, although the judge of the Prerogative Court did have the right to appoint an official known as the Registrar of the Arches and Vicar General's Office.[37] One puisne justice of the King's Bench had the right to appoint the Clerk of the Home Circuit, worth £400, while a justice of Common Pleas appointed the Clerk of the Western Circuit.[38] In addition, the senior justice on each circuit had the right to appoint revising barristers, in accordance with the provisions of the 1832 Reform Bill, who helped

[33] *Report of the Select Committee on Official Salaries*, p. 186.
[34] *Patronage of the Lord Chief Justice, etc.,* PP, LXXVI, 1881, pp. 1-2.
[35] *Report of the Select Committee on Sinecure Offices,* 1834, p. 4, and Holdsworth, *History of English Law,* I, 687-8.
[36] Hardwicke MSS., 36, 118, pp. 89-94.
[37] Merthyr Mawr Collection, L/205/1-29.
[38] *Report of the Select Committee on Sinecure Offices,* 1834, p. 45.

prepare and check voting lists. These positions were 'uncommonly sought after — it being unusual to displace anyone once appointed, if he conducts himself well — it becoming a place of £200 a year, the work only in the long vacation interfering with no other call'.[39]

Not only did the Chancellor and the two Chief Justices benefit from their extensive patronage but they were also frequent recipients of royal patents, which guaranteed them pensions after their retirement from office and sometimes provided lucrative government sinecures to their progeny. Such arrangements were almost routine with regard to the Chancellor, because unlike the other judges he did not hold office for life. Since there was no official judicial pension system until 1799, it was considered essential to guarantee former Chancellors the financial requisites which would enable them to live in the style suitable to their rank as peers of the realm. Furthermore, the lucrative sinecures granted to the eldest sons of many Chancellors were probably intended to provide these men, who would some day inherit their fathers' titles, with the ability to support that honour.

In 1766 Lord Northington resigned as Chancellor to become President of the Privy Council. At that time, he received an immediate pension of £2,000 per annum and a promise that he would receive an additional £2,000 per annum when he resigned from the latter post. He was also granted the reversion of the office of Clerk of the Hanaper in Chancery for two lives.[40] In 1770 Lord Camden received a royal patent which provided him with an annuity of £2,300 and the reversion of one of the Tellerships of the Exchequer for his son.[41] This lucrative office, which was worth upwards of £25,000 per annum in the early nineteenth century, was also granted to the eldest sons of Lords Hardwicke and Bathurst and to the nephew and successor of Lord Thurlow.[42]

The other judges were not treated as liberally as were the Chancellors, although some of the Chief Justices were also able to secure pensions and/or offices for their sons. On becoming Lord Chief Justice of Common Pleas, William De Grey insisted that his son receive some sort of royal favour, which was soon forthcoming in the form of the office of the Groom of the Bed Chamber. His predecessor in the office of Chief Justice, John Eardley Wilmot, was provided with a pension of £2,400 per annum, which after taxes and

[39]Coleridge MSS., d. 295, p. 130.

[40]Jeafferson, *A Book About Lawyers,* I, 348.

[41]Camden MSS., U 840 07.

[42]Halevy, *England in 1815,* p. 10.

other deductions was worth £1,800.[43] Thomas Parker, Chief Baron of the Exchequer, who retired the year after Wilmot in 1772, received the identical pension. The frequency with which pensions were granted to the other judges is unknown, though some men who held positions below the Chiefs were sometimes provided with retirement allowances. In 1799 James Marriot retired as Judge of the Admiralty with a pension of £2,000. Also in the 1770s two puisne judges, Edward Clive and George Perrot, were both granted pensions of £1,200 per annum at the time of their retirement.

There were obviously discrepancies between the emoluments and rewards attached to the various judicial offices. In addition, there was a vast amount of unnecessary expense and waste in the judicial establishment which cost the nation many thousands of pounds each year and benefited only the lucky individuals who had been appointed to fill the various sinecures. As we have seen, public discontent with the sinecure system had begun as early as 1725, and this was followed by a parliamentary commission in 1733 which investigated the operation of the Court of Chancery.[44] Although no action was taken to rectify the situation, opposition to sinecure offices erupted periodically, and finally in the early nineteenth century the attack on the entire system of legal patronage and income began in earnest. Between 1810 and 1825 at least five parliamentary reports on the offices and judicial salaries in the various courts were published. As a result, the entire structure of the courts and the method of judicial remuneration were overhauled and rationalized.

With regard to the reform of the salary system, the two most important years were 1825 and 1832. In 1825 the salaries of all the judges except the Chancellor were established in the form which they would retain, with some slight modifications, until the middle of the twentieth century. Not unexpectedly the most heated debate arose over the new salary of the Chief Justice of King's Bench who, as a result of the reforms, was stripped of the better part of his valuable patronage. In that debate John Singleton Copley, the Attorney-General, supported the proposal of fixing the Chief Justice's salary at £10,000 per annum, by noting that previously the emoluments of the office were £9,000, which could be increased by the sale of offices or by direct receipt of income from sinecures. According to Copley, Lord Ellenborough had an income of £16,000 per annum during his tenure as Chief Justice, although neither his predecessor nor his

[43]John Eardley Wilmot, *Memoirs of the Life of the Right Honourable Sir John Eardley Wilmot, Knt.* (London, 1811), pp. 157-8.

[44]Holdsworth, *History of English Law,* I, 252.

successor had as high an income.[45] Later in the same debate James Scarlett, a future Chief Baron, provided additional support for the government's salary proposal when he told the House that 'in the last thirty or forty years the salary and fees of the chief justice amounted to between £14,000 and £15,000 a year, to add only £1,000 to the lowest sum he received during any one of these years'.[46]

Those who had advocated a salary of £10,000 for the Chief Justice were victorious. In addition, the salaries of almost all the other judges were increased, while fees were eliminated, sale of offices prohibited, and most sinecure offices were abolished. According to the new salary schedules the Chief Justice of Common Pleas received £8,000 per annum, the Chief Baron and the Master of the Rolls £7,000, the Vice-Chancellor £6,000, and the puisne justices and barons £5,500.

Not everyone approved of the new salaries — some reformers felt that they were too high. Thomas Denman, who was soon to be Chief Justice, attacked the proposal because of what he saw as its deleterious effects on the life-style of the judiciary. In the debate he was quoted as saying,

> This bonus, as he might term it, to the judges, of £2,000 a year, would, in his mind be injurious to their dignity. It was impossible, by any increase of salary that they could ever be raised to an equality with the great. At present, they might be said to be at the head of people of middling fortune, which was better than being at the foot of the higher order; and, though some aristocrat gentlemen in the House had treated their usual residence with so much contempt, as to profess that they did not know where Russell Square was, he thought they were much more respected in that quarter than they would be were they to intrude themselves amongst the wealthy inhabitants of Grosvenor-Square. . . [47]

Denman was true to his conviction, and upon his appointment he never accepted the full £10,000 due to the Chief Justice, but only £8,000, which became the official salary under his successor, Lord Campbell. The new salary scale may not have been the motivating force, but Denman's 1825 prediction came true, and by the 1850s the judiciary had abandoned Bloomsbury and had moved en masse to the West End.

[45] *Parliamentary Debates,* XIII, 2nd series, p. 634.
[46] *Ibid.,* p. 928.
[47] *Ibid.,* p. 620.

In the early 1830s the financial reforms in the three Common Law Courts were extended to the Court of Chancery and the jurisdiction of the Lord Chancellor. Following a very heated debate, the Chancellor was provided with a permanent salary and was deprived of his fees and much of his legal patronage in 1832. Many of the arguments in Parliament revolved around the income of the Chancellor prior to the reform. Estimates ranged from £12,000 to £20,000 although the most commonly mentioned figure was £14,000. Despite the objection of some reformers that the government's salary proposals were excessive, the official recommendations were accepted. The Chancellor was given a salary of £10,000 per annum in his judicial capacity, and another £4,000 as Speaker of the House of Lords.[48]

The reorganization of the courts was a protracted process. The sale of offices was attacked in 1826, and was to all intents and purposes eliminated by 1833. The 1820s also saw the abolition of the most valuable sinecures in the Court of King's Bench and the opening round of the reformation of the offices in the Court of Chancery. It was not, however, until the 1850s that the reform movement could be said to have approached the realization of the goals that had been set thirty years before.

As part of the reform of the system of judicial remuneration in the 1820s and 1830s, the pensions for retiring judges, which had been first established in 1799, were augmented during the parliamentary session of 1825.[49] Pensions were an essential part of the reform because they helped to eliminate one instrument which the government could use in theory to control the judiciary — the power to provide for retirement. As we have seen, in the eighteenth century every judge who hoped to receive a pension or an office for his son upon retirement had to depend on the generosity of the government. Although this situation did not necessarily make the judiciary susceptible to governmental pressure, it was a possible avenue of ministerial influence which was best removed. The creation of a regular pension system for the members of the judiciary, then, may be seen as another step in the continuing process to free the judges from the possibility of governmental manipulation and control.

[48] *Parliamentary Debates,* XIV, 3rd series, 1834, pp. 1055-1263.

[49] In 1799 the pensions of the judges were set at £4,000 *per annum* for the Chancellor, £3,000 for the Chief Justices and Chief Baron, £2,500 for the Master of the Rolls, £2,000 for all the other judges. In 1825 the Chief Justice of King's Bench had his pension raised to £4,000, the Chief Justice of Common Pleas, Chief Baron of the Exchequer, Master of the Rolls, and Vice-Chancellor to £3,750, and the puisne judges and barons to £3,500.

Furthermore, many people, both in and out of Parliament, felt that the lack of a pension system encouraged old men to remain even after their capacity to function efficiently had disappeared. It was hoped that a permanent pension arrangement would encourage older judges to retire without major financial sacrifice when they felt their powers beginning to wane. The evidence on retirement patterns indicates that in fact the desired results were achieved. In the first two periods 1727-90 only 35% of the judges retired, while the other 65% died in harness. In contrast, during the last three periods (1790-1875) after the introduction of pensions, these figures were reversed with 39% of the judges dying while in office and 61% retiring from their posts.[50]

Of all the late eighteenth- and early nineteenth-century reformers who attacked the traditional methods of remuneration, one voice stands out from the rest — that is the one belonging to Jeremy Bentham. His criticisms of the judicial establishment ran the gamut from legal procedure to the behaviour of particular judges, to the structure of the law itself, to the issue of salaries and fees, patronage, and pensions. Bentham attacked the 'fee-gathering system' as a pernicious influence on the administration of justice 'since it is from this source alone that they [the judges] can generally be considered liable to corruption, and that so much more easily, since they may be subject to its influence without perceiving it'.[51] The abolition of the system of remuneration by fees and its replacement by an all inclusive salary was accordingly an essential first step in any attempt 'to establish identity of interests between the magistrates and the public. . . '.[52]

Bentham was equally hostile to the use and abuse of the patronage system and the sale of legal offices which, he maintained, was merely a means by which the judges could further increase their power, income, or both. The practice of appointing their sons to lucrative legal offices, which as we have seen was almost universal among the pre-reform Chief Justices and Chancellors, was condemned by Bentham in no uncertain terms.

> But, by every fee received by any such subordinate of his, the
> effect produced on the mind of the Judge is in kind the same as if

[50]Since in fact a judge was only given a retirement pension after 15 years of service, Abel-Smith and Stevens questioned its efficacy in encouraging judicial retirement. Abel-Smith and Stevens, *Lawyers and the Courts,* p. 38.

[51]Jeremy Bentham, *The Works of Jeremy Bentham,* John Bowring ed., II, (New York, 1962), 209.

[52]Elie Halevy, *The Growth of Philosophic Radicalism* (Boston, 1966), p. 395.

> received by himself to his own use. . . . In this case [when the
> Judge gives an office to his son] the patronage is worth even more
> than the incumbancy for, in the money-market phrase, the life of
> the son is of course worth more than the life of the father, it may
> be worth several times as much.[53]

Of course when an office was not given to a close relative but rather
sold for profit, the results were even more undesirable. In such an
instance the judges will, according to Bentham, 'of course sell it to any
one who will give the most money for it; and any thought bestowed
upon the fitness of the purchaser will be the mere work of super-
erogation'.[54]

Finally, Bentham also unconditionally attacked the lack of regular
pension systems. Pensions which were bestowed as a result of
government favour were disparaged by Bentham 'as a fund of
peculation and corruption', and the basis upon which pensions were
granted was seen as destructive to the proper functioning of the
judiciary and of the courts. Thus,

> The cases where the pension is granted are, where a lazy judge
> has a minister for a friend, and where the minister has a friend
> whom he wants in the judge's place. The cases where the pension
> is not granted are, when the judge is too incapable to pretend to
> do business, and where he does it so badly that his not pretending
> to do it would be a blessing.[55]

While Bentham probably overstated the evils inherent in the unre-
formed system of judicial remuneration and patronage, he did
expose very real problems and suggested solutions, many of which
were adopted during the course of the nineteenth century.

Investments in Land and Securities

English law does not require inventories of property to be kept by the
state as part of the probate records. Inventories did exist in England
for many individuals who died in the seventeenth century and before;
however, they gradually disappeared in the eighteenth century, and
became non-existent by 1800. As a result the possibility of recon-
structing the investment patterns of the members of any social group
in England is limited. Fortunately I have been able to discover the
wills of 95% of the judges included in this study, and these documents
are a valuable source of information on their investments in land and

[53]Bentham, *Works,* III, 339-40.
[54]*Ibid.*, IV, 375.
[55]*Ibid.*, IV, 361.

securities. Other important sources of data on the personal and real property owned by the judges are account books, bank books, estate papers, and the *New Domesday Book*.

This last source, the only complete survey of English land ownership since the reign of William I, includes a county by county register of the acreage, rental, and details of ownership of all the land in the United Kingdom, with the exception of the English boroughs and London. Compiled by order of Parliament in 1872-3, it allows for an accurate reconstruction of the land belonging to the judges appointed between 1850 and 1875, most of whom were still alive at the time of the survey. For those judges who were raised to the bench between 1820 and 1850 the data is less exact. Some of these men were still alive in 1873, and the land-holdings of many more can be traced through their immediate heirs. Naturally, there are dangers in trying to determine the amount and value of the land owned by judges who died prior to 1873 by extrapolating backwards from the data in the *New Domesday Book*. The difficulties inherent in this procedure are compounded the further we move away from 1873. In order to minimize these problems I have only used the information from the *New Domesday Book* for judges who died after 1830, and I have checked the location of land owned in 1873 against that listed in the judges' wills, so that any major purchases made after their deaths will not be included.

At least 151 of the 208 judges or 73% owned some landed property, although there is no information on the cost, acreage, or rental of land owned for just over half of them. In 68 cases data is available on the annual rental of the estates; in 3 cases we only know the purchase price of the estates; in 1 instance only the acreage is known; 7 other estates were, according to descriptions in the wills, country houses with only small parks surrounding them. These were usually located in the home counties, and the wills refer only to the disposition of the house and sometimes of a home farm, but no mention is made of extensive real estate or the rents that could be expected from such property. The sizes of the remaining 72 estates are unknown.

In Table 10 the estates whose annual rentals are known are divided into the following 6 categories: great landowners with rentals of over £10,000 per annum, greater gentry with rentals of between £3,000-£10,000 per annum, squirearchy with rentals of between £1,000-£3,000 per annum, and then three divisions of smaller landowners — those with rentals of between £300-£1,000 per annum, those whose rentals were worth between £100-£300 per annum, and

Table 10: Annual value of judicial estates 1727-1875

Annual Rental	1727-1875		1850-1875	
	No.	*%*	*No.*	*%*
Over £10,000	2	3	0	0
£3,000-£10,000	17	25	4	12
£1,000-£3,000	22	32	13	41
£300-£1,000	10	15	6	19
£100-£300	9	13	6	19
Under £100	8	12	3	9
Total	68	100	32	100

those with rentals of under £100 per annum.[56] Column 1 indicates the distribution of all 68 of the estates with known rentals, while column 2 includes only the 32 estates owned by judges appointed between 1850 and 1875, the period for which information on the rentals of judicial estates is almost complete.

As is evident from Table 10, the vast majority of judges who invested in land owned property comparable either to members of the landed gentry or to the smaller landowners. Only a tiny minority of the judges owned estates which qualified them as full-fledged members of the landed aristocracy. Even if we lower the qualifications from £10,000 per annum to £5,000 per annum for those judges appointed in the eighteenth century as suggested by Professor Mingay, only 5 judges definitely rank as great landowners.[57] Of these four were men who amassed great wealth while serving as either Lord Chancellor or Chief Justice prior to the reforms of the 1820s and 1830s. They included Lords Hardwicke, Kenyon, Rosslyn, and Eldon.

The majority of the 68 judges whose annual estate rentals are known purchased all their land. However, more than one third of the 68 men had inherited at least part of it. The more land a judge owned, the greater was the probability that he had inherited some of it. Among the judges who owned small estates, worth under £1,000 per annum, 6 (22%) had inherited some. Inheritance was more common among the owners of estates worth between £1,000 and £3,000 per annum; 7 of these judges (32%) inherited some of their land. The percentage of judges who inherited part of their estates was

[56]The categories used in this analysis have been taken from Thompson, *English Landed Society in the Nineteenth Century,* pp. 32, 114, 115, and 117.

[57]In the eighteenth century the minimum qualification for being considered a great landowner was a rental of £5,000 *per annum* according to Mingay, *English Landed Society in the Eighteenth Century,* p. 26.

even greater among those with rentals of £3,000-£10,000 per annum; this accounted for 10 judges (59%). Finally, both the judges who owned estates worth more than £10,000 per annum inherited some of their landed property.

Despite the fact that many judges had land bequeathed to them, in most instances the large judicial landowners acquired the major portion of their estates through purchases and not through inheritance. At this point it may be useful to examine the histories of three of the largest judicial estates for which documentation is available, in order to determine whether any general pattern of growth exists.

The first of the great estates belonged to the Earl of Hardwicke who began his life as Philip Yorke, the attorney's son from Dover. Yorke did not inherit any land from his father. He began buying land in his native Kent in 1722, just seven years after his call to the bar and 2 years after his appointment as Solicitor-General. In that year he bought several farms in Sandwich for an undisclosed sum, and paid £7,500 for 200 acres in Upton and Eastry which were worth £290 per annum.[58] Three years later, in 1725, soon after his appointment as Attorney-General, Yorke purchased the Hardwicke estates in Gloucestershire, which were then worth £1,000 per annum, for £24,000.[59] In 1730 he increased the size of his Gloucestershire property by purchasing additional lands for £6,000.[60] The most important year in the history of the expansion of the Hardwicke estates was 1740. Lord Hardwicke had already been Chancellor for three years and according to his biographer, may have felt that the Gloucestershire estates were too small for a man of his station. Therefore in 1740 he purchased the Wimpole estate in Cambridgeshire from the second Earl of Oxford for £86,740. He also invested another £16,000 in additional purchases and improvements, over half of which was spent on expanding the country house at Wimpole.[61] Hardwicke became one of the leading landowners in Cambridgeshire, and his eldest son Philip was elected a knight of the shire and was also appointed Lord Lieutenant of the county. In that same year Philip married Jemima Campbell, niece and heiress of the Duke of Kent. The old Duke died later in the same year, leaving his large landed possessions to Philip. The final extent of Lord Chancellor Hardwicke's landed holdings can be seen in the rent roll for his estates for

---

[58] Yorke, *Life and Correspondence of Philip Yorke, Earl of Hardwicke,* I, 108.

[59] Harris, *Life of Lord Chancellor Hardwicke,* I, 190.

[60] Yorke, *Life and Correspondence of Philip Yorke, Earl of Hardwicke,* I, 206-7, and Hardwicke MSS., 36, 228.

[61] Yorke, *Life and Correspondence of Philip Yorke, Earl of Hardwicke,* I, 210.

the years 1765-6, the year after his death. According to the list, the family owned property in Cambridgeshire, the Isle of Ely, Bedfordshire, Essex, Suffolk, Kent, Gloucestershire, Leicestershire, and Wiltshire, with rents totalling £6,771 per annum.[62]

The most valuable of the estates acquired by any of the judges in the eighteenth or nineteenth centuries probably belonged to two brothers, John Lord Eldon and William Lord Stowell. Their father bequeathed £24,000-£25,000 in real and personal property to the two brothers.[63] The bequest included the estate of Usworth in Durham, which was given to the elder son, William. The first major purchase was made in 1792 by John the year before he was appointed Attorney-General. He bought the 1,300 acre estate of Eldon, in the southern part of Durham, for £22,000.[64] In 1807 he made his second major purchase, the Encombe estate in Dorset. This 2,000 acre estate cost Lord Eldon, who was by then in his second term as Chancellor, £52,000-£53,000.[65] Eldon's brother, William, did not begin to buy land of any consequence until more than a decade after his appointment as Judge of the Admiralty. In 1811-12 he purchased the Gloucestershire estate of Stowell for £65,000.[66] During the next few years he bought another estate in Gloucestershire which had formerly belonged to the Earl of Chedworth. William paid approximately £300,000 for this second estate, which gave a very low rate of return, averaging only 2% per annum.[67] Stowell, who had been raised to the peerage in 1821, died in 1836. Since he was predeceased by his only son, most of his landed property, which was said to be producing £8,000-£12,000 per annum,[68] was inherited by his brother Lord Eldon. In the course of their legal careers, Eldon and Stowell both made large fortunes from their profession. They invested much of their wealth in landed estates in five counties, which in 1885 included 25,761 acres which were worth £28,457 per annum.

The last of the three estates belonged to Sir John Nicholl. Nicholl was the younger son of a small Glamorgan landowner, John Nicholl of Llanmaes. He acquired his first two tracts of land in the early 1770s while still a boy: in 1770 he inherited a contingent interest in the

[62]Hardwicke MSS., 36, 229.

[63]Twiss, *Life of Lord Eldon,* I, 102.

[64]*Ibid.,* I. 216.

[65]*Ibid.,* II, 39-40.

[66]*Ibid.,* II, 183.

[67]Thompson, *English Landed Society in the Nineteenth Century,* (London, 1963), p. 55.

[68]*Ibid.,* and Jeafferson, *A Book About Lawyers,* I, 342.

property of the Reverend J. Nicholl, his godfather, and in 1771 he came into possession of the Tondue estate valued at £8,000, after the death of Edward Powell.[69] He did not begin purchasing land until 1804, six years after his appointment as King's Advocate and four years before his appointment as Judge of the Prerogative Court of Canterbury and Dean of the Arches. His first purchase, the Merthyr Mawr estate in Glamorganshire, which became his seat, was acquired from the executors of Charles Bowen for £30,000.[70] In 1800 Merthyr Mawr included 1,169 acres which had an annual rental of £925, but which, with the improvements, were estimated to be worth £1,278 per annum.[71] All Nicholl's later purchases were made in Glamorgan, and many were tracts of land adjoining his Merthyr Mawr estate. In 1808 he purchased the Coity estate for £13,000, in 1811 the Wich property for £2,000, in 1812 the Tymaen property for £5,000, in 1812 the Park property for £4,000, in 1812 the Reverend Iltid Nicholl's property (Llanmaes) for £7,000, in 1812 the Castle on the Avon for £2,000, and in 1825 Verville for £4,000.[72] In total, Nicholl's landed estates were worth at least £75,000 at the time when they were purchased or inherited. The largest of the estates, Merthyr Mawr, had grown from the original 1,169 to 2,790 acres worth £3,448 per annum by 1839.[73] In 1885 the Nicholl estates included 4,894 acres which had an annual rental of £6,565.

Lords Hardwicke, Eldon, Stowell, and Sir John Nicholl all had most successful careers as advocates, and furthermore their fortunes had been swollen by their acquisition of high legal office. Lord Hardwicke held the lucrative offices of Chief Justice of King's Bench and Lord Chancellor for an uninterrupted period of 23 years from 1733 until 1756. Similarly Eldon, who was appointed as Chief Justice of Common Pleas in 1799, served in that office and as Lord Chancellor until 1827 with only a short break during the years 1806-7. Eldon's brother Stowell served as Judge of the Court of the Admiralty, an office whose emoluments grew dramatically during the Napoleonic Wars as a result of prize cases, during the years 1798 to 1828. Finally, Nicholl also benefited from the increased fees in the Court of Admiralty during the war years. He had been appointed to the office of King's Advocate General in 1798, an office which he held until 1809, and as a result was the chief representative of the crown in the civil courts of which the Admiralty was one.

[69]Merthyr Mawr Collection, Catalogue and E/116/4.

[70]*Ibid.* E/116/4.

[71]*Ibid.*, E/1.

[72]*Ibid.*, E/116/4.

[73]*Ibid.*, E/133.

Although of these four judges only Lord Stowell had been appointed to the bench prior to his earliest purchases of land, Hardwicke, Eldon, and Nicholl were all well on their way to professional fame and fortune by the time they first bought landed estates. These early purchases were, as we have seen, augmented once Hardwicke, Eldon and Nicholl were provided with the financial security of a judicial office. The earliest purchases of land made by all four men provided them with estates whose rentals exceeded £1,000, enough to support an eldest son as a landed gentleman. This would indicate their early interest in founding a landed family. While the acquisition of peerages by Hardwicke, Eldon, and Stowell may have accentuated this desire to provide landed estates for their progeny, their purchases of land pre-dated their ennoblement.

Other members of the eighteenth- and early nineteenth-century judiciary who invested large sums in land prior to their receipt of peerages include Dudley Ryder (who died before his title as Lord Harrowby could be confirmed), Lord Kenyon, and Lord Walsingham. Prior to the period of reform in the 1820s and 1830s many judges, especially those who held the premier judgeships, were desirous of establishing a landed family, and while a title added to their families' prestige, it was not necessarily the factor which motivated the judges to purchase large landed estates.

As a result of professional duties which required their attendance in court either in London or on the circuit from October to August, judicial landowners could only direct the affairs of their estates *in absentia.* Unlike the majority of aristocratic and gentry landowners, the judges, with the exception of those who owned estates located in their home counties, were able to reside on their estates for only short periods.

Few judges had estates which were large enough to demand the services of a full-time agent, but they did require someone to oversee their estate accounts, to collect rents, to attend to repairs and improvements, to make recommendations on the renewal of leases, and to provide a communications link with the tenants.[74] I have found no correspondence between the judges and their agents. The estate records which do exist are confined to annual or semi-annual accounts in the agent's hand informing the judge of the current rent of his estates, the payments received, the amount of rents in arrears, the

[74] Although many of the judges had small estates, unlike full-time landowners of estates with annual rentals of £1,000 or less, the judges were not able to collect their own rents. For a complete discussion of the services required of estate agents by landowners with small, medium, and large estates see David Spring, *The English Landed Estate in The Nineteenth Century: Its Administration* (Baltimore, 1963), chapter 1.

cost of repairs and improvements, the taxes paid, and the balance for the year which was usually remitted directly to the judge's London bankers.

The accounts for Lord Brougham's, Lord Camden's and Lord Walsingham's estates indicate that these three judges bore the cost of all capital improvements undertaken on their estates, including drainage, fencing of fields, construction of new buildings, and repair of old ones.[75] Their agents' accounts usually include lists of repairs or improvements made on the estates, the cost of the work, and whether it was done by a tradesman or a tenant. The tradesmen were either paid directly by the agent, or the agent would reimburse the tenant if the latter had paid for repairs or improvements undertaken on his farm. If the tenant made the repairs himself, as was often the case, then he was granted a rent reduction which was indicated in the accounts by the agent.

In addition to their financial obligations, the agents acted as a link between the judge and his tenants and also, perhaps, with neighbouring landowners. Professors Chambers and Mingay, for example, in their study of the agricultural revolution in Britain, cite two requests from Gloucestershire farmers to Lord Hardwicke which were addressed to his agent. It may be assumed that the latter then transmitted the messages to Hardwicke, depending upon their importance.[76]

The function of the agent as an intermediary between the judicial landlord and his tenants is well illustrated by a review of Lord Walsingham's Suffolk estates, which was prepared by the agent in 1781 after the death of the first Lord Walsingham. The report indicates that Lord Walsingham was very much concerned with the quality of his tenants and with their welfare. It indicates furthermore

[75] Unfortunately I have been able to discover only a limited amount of data on the organization of landed estates owned by members of the judiciary. Most of the material presented here has been derived from the records of the following estates: Lord Brougham's estates in Westmoreland and Cumberland, which covered 2,244 acres with annual rental of £2,551. Accounts for these estates are available for the years 1828-34 and 1837-8. Lord Brougham's agent was J. Crosby. Brougham Financial MSS. Lord Walsingham's estates in Norfolk and Suffolk covered 4,100 acres, worth £2,364 *per annum.* Records for these estates are available for the years 1769-81. They were kept by Lord Walsingham's agent W. Black. Walsingham MSS., XXV/5 and XXV/10. Lord Camden's estates were located in London, Westminster, Middlesex, Gloucester, and Suffolk. The exact acreage of these estates is not known but they had an annual value of £1,400. The accounts which exist for the years 1782-93 were drawn up by Lord Camden's agent, Augustine Greenland, who was paid 5% of the gross annual rental, approximately £70 *per annum.* Camden MSS., U840 AL9.

[76] J.D. Chambers and G.E. Mingay, *The Agricultural Revolution 1750-1880* (London, 1966), pp. 41 and 90. One letter dealt with non-payment of rent and the other with the advisability of exchanging lands in order to facilitate enclosure.

that his agent was attentive to these concerns. An indication of this concern is the agent's description of one farm in which he notes that the former tenant 'Wm. Marven having by indiscretion lately fail'd, the Farm was by the late Ld. Walsingham's permission assign'd to a person who appears to be an industrious good Tenant'.[77] In another instance he wrote that one farm which had been previously divided in two and shared by two men, Thomas Mays and Edward Tussell, was now to be united and rented to Mays alone. This, he explained, was because 'Tussell's Buildings being unnecessary on the Estate and himself a single drunken man, it has some years been propos'd that these two farms should be laid together to save buildings — Mays who is a very industrious man has undertaken the whole from Mich[aelm]-as last. . . '.[78] Those tenants who were industrious and responsible could look forward to consideration by their landlord. One such tenant, George Marven, was granted a rent reduction, and although his farm was worth £200 per annum, he only paid £180. The agent remarked that the reduction was granted to Marven 'in consideration of his being an Old Tenant much esteem'd by his late lordship and all the family. . . '.[79]

While there is little evidence available on the management of the estates of the judges, at least one member of the judiciary was, according to the testimony of Arthur Young, an enthusiastic improving landlord. In his *Annals of Agriculture,* Young reports on his visit to the estate of Sir Francis Buller at Princetown in Dartmoor. He described Buller as 'that active, spirited, and enlightened improver', who 'in the midst of this dreary desert [Dartmoor] . . . has built a very comfortable house, with everything necessary to live in plenty, from a farm which was lately a black moor'.[80] Buller owned 600 acres of land in Dartmoor and he had invested much time and money in enclosing and draining, in experimenting with burning, with the use of lime and of granite gravel in order to bring peat wastes under cultivation, and finally with the use of a variety of rotations of turnips, oats, and red and white clover.[81] Young was obviously most impressed with Buller's work when he wrote: 'To see a person of ample private fortune, high in rank, and filling an office that requires an almost incessant employment and anxious labour of mind, to discharge those important duties on which the lives and properties of his fellow

[77]Walsingham MSS., XXV/10.

[78]*Ibid.*

[79]*Ibid.*

[80]Arthur Young, *Annals of Agriculture,* XXIX (London, 1797), 569.

[81]*Ibid.*, pp. 570-6.

subjects depend upon — to see such a person filling his leisure moments with agricultural experiments, in the walk of all others the most useful to the state, is a spectacle so uncommon, and so highly meritorious, that too much cannot be said in his praise.'[82]

While most of the judges' estates were devoted exclusively to agriculture, several judges found other ways to exploit their land. William Alexander, who retired as Chief Baron of the Exchequer in 1831, discovered iron on his estate in Airdrie, Scotland, at about the time when he resigned from the judiciary.[83] Lord Eldon's exploitation of the mineral rights on his estates as is attested to by the inclusion of a particular clause in his will, which made provision for mining on his Durham estates by granting his heirs the 'authority to sink, bore, dig, drive, search for, win, work, get & raise the said mines, layers, veins, seams, beds, & strata of ironstone, coal, copper, copper ore, load, loadore, marl, sand, limestone, and other stones, minerals, metals, and substances'.[84] Finally, Thomas Lord Erskine, who was most unlucky in business affairs throughout his life, invested more than £40,000 in land in Sussex with the hope of becoming a major supplier of birch timber to London. His plan failed and in order to recoup his losses he tried to establish a factory which was to make brooms from the timber, but this scheme also ended in failure.[85]

The non-landed investment opportunities which were available to the members of the eighteenth-century judiciary were limited in variety. Capital not used to buy land was usually invested in a variety of government securities. These were seen as a very secure investment, and as a result were often chosen by the judges as the most appropriate means of providing annuities to support their wives and younger children. In addition, they often instructed their executors to purchase these securities with their residuary personal estates. Some examples of judges in the eighteenth and early nineteenth centuries who invested large sums in government securities were Edward Clive (£10,000), Lord Eldon (£96,000), Lord Ellenborough (£148,000), and Lord Kenyon (£31,358).[86]

---

[82]*Ibid.*, pp. 577-8.

[83]Foss, *Judges of England,* IX, 74.

[84]Public Record Office, PROB 11/1838/58.

[85]Lloyd P. Stryker, *For the Defense, Thomas Erskine* (Garden City, 1947), pp. 493-5.

[86]The value of Clive's and Eldon's government securities is derived from those specifically mentioned as bequests in their wills and in fact the total value of the government securities which they owned may be significantly higher. Public Record Office, PROB 11/1771/200 and PROB 11/1838/58. The data for Lord Ellenborough

Some of the more prosperous members of the eighteenth-century judiciary invested money in personal loans. In 1767 William De Grey had £15,500 on loan to private individuals, but from this sum he received an extremely low rate of interest — only 1.5%[87] Lord Kenyon's accounts from the end of the eighteenth century show that from 1794 to 1802 he had between £17,324 and £26,141 on loan, and that the interest on these loans ranged from just over 1% in 1794 to 5.6% in 1797.[88] Some of Kenyon's loans went to enterprising landowners who had borrowed capital in order to exploit the resources of their estates. In 1779 he loaned £1,000 at 5% to the Duke of Bridgewater, whose mining and canal ventures were so successful, and two years later he loaned £1,500 at the same rate to the Duke of Chandos, almost all of whose ambitious projects ended in failure.[89]

While government funds and private loans and mortgages may have accounted for most of the non-landed investments of the eighteenth-century judges, they were certainly not the only investment opportunities available. At least three judges invested in the annuities of the South Sea Company — Thomas Reeve (£5,000), George Lee (£5,000), and John Willes (£3,000).[90] Two other mid-eighteenth-century judges were owners of stocks in government charter companies — Thomas Clarke (£4,310) and Dudley Ryder (£24,800).[91] Ryder also subscribed £10,000 to the Government Loan of 1748, while Lord Hardwicke had participated in the land tax loans of 1743 and 1744 in which he had invested £21,000 and £11,000 respectively.[92] Lord Camden invested small sums in a colliery (an initial investment of £500) and in a 1/16 part of a ship carrying goods to the East Indies (which cost him £1,176).[93] Lord Kenyon, who according to the

is derived from an inventory which appears in his private papers. Public Record Office VIIB 30/12/17/5. The data for Lord Kenyon is found in an entry in the diary of George, second Lord Kenyon, from 1802, Kenyon MSS., Gredington, Shropshire. Quoted by permission of the Rt. Hon. Lord Kenyon, DL.

[87]Walsingham MSS., XIV/17. There is no list of who the recipients of these low interest loans were.

[88]In 1802, the year of his death, Lord Kenyon had £21,941 out on private loan. Kenyon MSS., from a list entitled 'cash out on interest'.

[89]Kenyon MSS., Account Book 1779-1802, and G.E. Mingay, *English Landed Society in the Eighteenth Century,* pp. 190-1.

[90]Public Record Office, PROB 11/1761/454 and PROB 11/1737/13. Lee Papers D/LE/15/41, Buckingham Record Office.

[91]P.G.M. Dickson, *The Financial Revolution in England* (London, 1967), pp. 292-7.

[92]*Ibid.,* pp. 290, 424.

[93]Camden MSS. U840 addn. T295 and C173/74.

available evidence was the first judge to have directly invested in a canal, lent £1,000 to the Chester Canal Company in 1776.[94]

At the very end of the century and continuing into the early years of the nineteenth century, Lord Erskine invested large sums in speculative securities which were no more successful than were his real estate ventures. He purchased American securities, fearing, according to one source, that the French Wars would adversely affect the value of English shares.[95] Erskine's assessment was incorrect and as a result of the War of 1812, which severely disrupted American foreign trade, he lost most of his money.[96]

Despite the fact that the interest on consols, and presumably on the other public funds, decreased after the end of the Napoleonic Wars, these shares remained one of the most popular forms of investment for the judges in the nineteenth century.[97] Although some investors may have been discouraged by the fall in the interest rate, they were by and large compensated by a concurrent rise in the market value of the public funds.[98] Some judges were not content merely to collect interest on their investments, but tried to profit from the fluctuations in the value of the funds by speculating in government securities.[99] The wills and account books of the judges indicate that, after the 1850s, there was a decline in the level of their investments in public funds. The movement away from government securities at that time cannot be explained satisfactorily by reference to the changes in the interest rate, since the decline in those rates which had begun in

---

[94]Kenyon MSS., Diary, 17 August 1776.

[95]Polson, *Law and Lawyers,* I, 272.

[96]Stryker, *For the Defense, Thomas Erskine,* pp. 493-5.

[97]Among the largest judicial investors in public funds during the nineteenth century were Joseph Littledale who owned £100,000 worth of annuities, Public Record Office PROB 11/1842/483, and George Bankes who owned £150,000 worth of consols. Public Record Office PROB 11/1856/609.

[98]The rise in the value of public fund shares after the end of the war is exemplified by a note in the accounts of Sir John Nicholl which reports that the rise in the value of his property from £150,000 in 1810 to £185,000 in 1828 was primarily due to the value of the funds. From Nicholl's bank books we find that consols were valued at £64 1/8 in 1808, while by 1838 they were worth £93 5/8. Merthyr Mawr Collection, E/116/4, F/8/3, F/152. The rise of the value of the funds after the end of the French wars can also be traced in the bank books of Sir John Dodson. In 1823 consols were selling at £75 per share, while twenty years later they were selling at £96 7/8. Bodleian Library, Monk-Bretton MSS., 33. Quoted by permission of the Rt. Hon. Lord Monk Bretton.

[99]Although the values of public fund shares were rising in the long-term, there were short-term fluctuations which allowed for speculation, for example see Monk-Bretton MSS., 33. Sir John Nicholl, on the other hand, bought government funds for long-term investments, but regularly bought and sold Exchequer Bills as speculative investments. Merthyr Mawr Collection, F/8/1-5.

1817 had already ended by the 1830s; the new rate, which was stabilized at a new level of 3.0% to 3.4%, remained there until the late 1880s.[100] A more convincing explanation for the decline in judicial investments in public funds was the emergence of new financial opportunities during the course of the nineteenth century, namely in public works — insurance, railways, canals, and foreign securities.

Some of the judges invested in the new business ventures, apparently believing that the higher interest rates which these securities offered justified the greater risk. Based on the evidence provided by the judges' wills and personal papers, the new enterprises in which members of the nineteenth-century judiciary most frequently invested were canals and insurance companies (at least 8 judges owned shares in each of these),[101] railway shares (owned by at least 5 judges), and turnpike bonds, East India shares, bridge bonds, and foreign securities (each of which was owned by at least 3 judges). Naturally, there were great variations in the size of the investments made by the judges. John Nicholl, for example, owned shares in turnpike, railways, and a bridge, yet the total value of his shares was only £890 with annual dividends of just £40 6s; this investment was negligible next to the £91,000 worth of consols which he possessed.[102] On the other hand, Colin Blackburn, who died in 1896, owned stock in 6 railways which were worth more than £95,000 and also canal shares which were worth an additional £21,000.[103]

The data which has been presented on the investments of the judges must be treated cautiously, since information is available for only a small minority of the 208 men. Not only is the data incomplete in many cases, but in addition, the judges for whom data exists do not constitute a random sample of the eighteenth- or nineteenth-century judiciary. Having cautioned the reader as to the limitations of the data, I will nevertheless present some tentative observations about the structure of judicial investments in real estate and securities.

---

[100]Mitchell and Deane, *Abstract of British Historical Statistics,* p. 455.

[101]In at least one instance a judicial decision was appealed on the grounds that the presiding judge, Lord Chancellor Cottenham, was involved in a conflict of interests. He was at the time a shareholder in the Grand Junction Canal 'to the amount of several thousand pounds'. As a result the House of Lords set aside his order against a Mr. Dimes who was involved in litigation against the Grand Junction Canal Company. 1852 III H.L.C. 759 and Holdsworth, *History of English Law,* XVI, 28-9.

[102]Merthyr Mawr Collection, F/152.

[103]Somerset House, The Testament of the Right Honourable Colin Baron Blackburn, issued in Scotland on January 24, 1896.

We find that most of the judges who were elevated to the bench after 1820 did not invest in large landed estates. Of the 103 judges who were appointed after that date, only 30 (29%) owned landed estates which had gross annual rentals of over £1,000. This may well represent a significant decline in judicial investment in real estate by those men appointed after 1820; however, the lack of comparable data for the judges appointed prior to 1820 prevents us from testing this hypothesis. Nevertheless, the evidence indicates a noteworthy decline in land investment by judicial peers appointed after 1820. Twenty-seven judicial peers were appointed after this date, yet only eight of them possessed landed estates worth more than £1,000 per annum. By contrast, of the 18 judicial peers appointed prior to 1820, nine definitely had landed estates worth more than £1,000 per annum, and according to Professor F.M.L. Thompson there were four others who should certainly be included in this category.[104] If these four judicial peers (Lords Alvanley, Bathurst, Mansfield, and Rosslyn) are counted, then 13 of the pre-1820 judicial peers (72%) owned landed estates with gross annual rentals of more than £1,000, as compared with only eight post-1820 judicial peers (30%).

The evidence indicates that among the nineteenth-century judges there was a marked preference for investing in securities rather than in land. Of the 112 judges, (all of whom died after 1802) for whom data on real and personal wealth is available, only 25 (21%) had invested as much as 40% of their fortune in landed property. Unfortunately it is impossible to discover the ratio between the real and the personal property owned by the eighteenth-century judges, since prior to 1802 no records were kept of the exact size of those personal estates valued at more than £10,000.

The most popular of all the non-landed investments among the judiciary during our entire period were the public funds. Even in the nineteenth century, at a time when there were many opportunities to purchase stocks and bonds issued by private enterprise, most judges seemed to prefer investing the majority of their personal property in the funds. Only a tiny minority of judges invested the major part of their savings in canals, railways, insurance companies, mortgages, or other speculative ventures, although there were more than a few judges willing to risk several thousand or even tens of thousands of pounds in these enterprises.

We can now begin to consider the dimensions of the judges' personal and real fortunes. The most important sources for the study

---

[104]Thompson, *English Landed Society in the Nineteenth Century,* pp. 57-8.

of personal wealth in England are the valuations of estates which were made when a will was probated and which were recorded in a document known as the Probate Act. For the purposes of this study the Probate Act only becomes useful in 1802, for in that year the value of all estates worth up to £100,000 began to be recorded. As a result, none of the judges who were appointed between 1730 and 1760 is included in this analysis, since they all died prior to 1802. In Table 11, the distribution of the personal estates of the judges in the periods 1760-90, 1790-1820, 1820-50, and 1850-75 is indicated by means of percentiles. In each of these four periods the value of the lowest decile, the lower quartile, the median, the upper quartile, and the highest decile have been calculated from the valuations of the judges' personal estates.

The data in Table 11 demonstrates that between the years 1760 and 1875 there was an overall increase in the size of the personal estates of the judges, but that this rise was not steady. Thus from 1760/90 to 1790/1820 there was a rise in the value of judicial estates, from 1790-1820 there was a decline, and finally from 1820/1850 to 1850/1875 there was once again a rise. The decline in the value of the estates left by those judges appointed between 1820 and 1850 can

Table 11: Size and distribution of the judges' personal estates — 1760-1875

	1760-1790	1790-1820	1820-1850	1850-1875
Total no. of judges in group	38	29	44	59
No. of judges for whom data is available	14	25	41	59
Range of estate valuation	£5,000-£180,000	£1,000-£700,000	£2,000-£250,000	£3,000-£300,000
Lowest decile of estate valuation	£7,500	£5,000	£10,000	£12,000
Lower quartile of estate valuation	£12,000	£25,000	£18,000	£25,000
Median of estate valuation	£25,000	£70,000	£35,000	£60,000
Upper quartile of estate valuation	£40,000	£120,000	£80,000	£84,101
Highest decile of estate valuation	£100,000	£250,000	£120,000	£148,168

be explained by the coincidence of two factors. Firstly, the reforms in the system of judicial remuneration in the 1820s and 1830s reduced the salaries of the top judges. Secondly, there was, as we have seen, a decline in the income of leading barristers during the period 1835-50. Both of these changes had adverse effects upon the wealth of the judges appointed between 1820 and 1850.

The most skewed distribution of wealth in any one period occurred between 1790 and 1820: the judges included in the first decile were poorer than the judges in any other period, while the judges in the last decile were far wealthier. On average, the men appointed between 1790 and 1820 were the wealthiest of the judges, and this may be explained in several ways. First, the men in this group who served as Chief Justice or Lord Chancellor were not affected by the reforms in the method of judicial remuneration and the abolition of court sinecures, which adversely affected the incomes of judges appointed from the 1830s. Secondly, some of the judges in this group were still in office in the mid-1820s, and therefore benefited from the rise in judicial salaries which was instituted at that time. Lastly, the income of the Admiralty judge was greatly augmented during these years as a result of the French Wars, and the man who held that post for most of the period, Lord Stowell, was the wealthiest of all the civil law judges.

The data on the personal estates of the judges which was presented in Table 11 is supplemented by Table 12, in which the judges appointed in the periods 1790-1820 and 1850-1875 are divided into 6 categories according to the size of their total fortunes, that is the combined value of their personal and real property.[105]

The data in Table 12 indicates that the size of judicial fortunes underwent a twofold change between 1790 and 1875. First, an increasing number of fortunes fell into a middle category of £50,000 to £200,000. In 1790-1820 only 24% of the judges' fortunes were within this range. The percentage rose in the period 1820-50 to 29%; while between 1850 and 1875, over half the judges (59%) had estates worth between £50,000 and £200,000. Second, we find that at the same time the percentage of very wealthy judges (with fortunes of over £200,000) was decreasing. Earlier evidence which indicated that there was a higher percentage of very wealthy judges in the period

---

[105]The data in Table 11 is based on the total wealth of the judges, both real and personal. The value of their personal estates is derived from the figures listed in the Probate Acts, while the value of their real estate is derived from a calculation of thirty years' purchase, based on the gross annual valuation listed in the *New Domesday Book,* or from the purchase price of the land in those cases in which this information is available.

1790-1820 than at any other time is confirmed. In that period, 17% of the judges had estates worth more than £200,000. The percentage declined slightly to 14% in the period 1820-50, and dropped to 9% in the last period.

The data in Table 12 provides additional support for two conclusions which were reached earlier. In the first place, the rise in the incomes of the leading barristers and the increase in the salaries of the judges ranking below the Chief Justices or the Chancellor, tended to increase the number of barristers who left medium-sized fortunes of between £50,000 and £200,000. In the second place, the reforms which gave the Chiefs and the Chancellor a fixed salary while eliminating their fees and court sinecures were instrumental in reducing the percentage of judges who left fortunes in excess of £200,000. Nevertheless at least seventeen men included in this study who died after 1802 had estates of that magnitude (cf. Table 13).[106.]

Table 12: Real and personal wealth of the judges 1790-1875

Values of the estates	1790-1820 No.	%	1820-50 No.	%	1850-75 No.	%	Total No.	%
£10,000 and under	1	3	1	2	4	6	6	5
£10,000-£50,000	4	14	12	27	16	27	32	24
£50,000-£100,000	4	14	11	25	17	29	32	24
£100,000-£200,000	3	10	3	7	17	29	23	17
£200,000-£300.000	3	10	5	11	4	7	12	9
over £300,000	2	7	1	2	1	2	4	3
Unknown	12	41	11	25	0	0	23	17
Total	29	99	44	99	59	100	132	99

The data listed in Table 13 adds credence to the contention that there was a progressive decline in the purchase of land by members of the judiciary during the course of the nineteenth century. Five of the judges listed in Table 13 were appointed to the bench between 1850-75, and four of these men owned land worth less than £30,000 (that is, with a gross annual rental of less than £1,000). Seven of the judges

[106]The data in Table 11 is derived from the same sources used in Table 12. See above p. 141, n. 105.

were appointed in the period 1820-50 and of these men, two had estates worth less than £30,000. Finally, of the five judges appointed prior to 1820 who are listed in the table, none owned landed property worth less than £30,000 — the smallest estate being John Nicholl's which was worth £75,000. Since the purchase of land is so closely connected with the subject matter of this chapter, it will be useful before concluding this examination of the investment patterns and wealth of the judges, to analyse the decline in their purchase of real property in the nineteenth century.

The changing pattern of judicial landed investment can usefully be explained in two ways. First, the reforms in the system of judicial remuneration before 1832 acted to decrease the wealth of the Chief Justices and Chancellor (the judges most frequently raised to the peerage). As a result, few of the judicial peers appointed after 1820 had fortunes equal to those of Lords Eldon, Stowell, or Kenyon.

Table 13: The fortunes of English judges in the nineteenth century

	Personal Estate	Land	Total Fortune
Lord Eldon (d.1838)	£700,000	£600,000	£1,300,000
George Bankes (d.1856)	£200,000	£450,000	£650,000
Lord Stowell (d.1836)	£250,000	£350,000	£600,000
Lord Westbury (d.1873)	£300,000	£4,000	£304,000
George Jessel (d.1883)	£260,529	–	£260,529
Lord Kenyon (d.1802)	£60,000	£200,000	£260,000
H. Jenner-Fust (d.1852)	£25,000	£228,000	£253,000
Lord Manners (d.1842)	£250,000	£540	£250,540
Lord Cottenham (d.1851)	£80,000	£170,000	£250,000
Joseph Littledale (d.1842)	£250,000	–	£250,000
John Byles (d.1884)	£201,446	£39,000	£240,446
Montague Smith (d.1891)	£238,000	–	£238,000
William Grove (d.1896)	£216,734	£21,000	£237,734
Lord Campbell (d.1861)	£120,000	£100,000	£220,000
John Nicholl (d.1838)	£140,000	£75,000	£215,000
Thomas Coltman (d.1849)	£35,000	£166,000	£201,000
Lord Ellenborough (d.1818)	£200,000	amt. unkn.	£200,000[+]

Therefore post-1820 judicial peers could not endow their peerages with large landed estates in the style of their eighteenth- and early nineteenth-century counterparts.

Second, the judges appointed after 1820 who had sizeable fortunes of £100,000 or £150,000, deliberately decided not to invest in large landed estates because of what they believed were sound financial, social, or familial reasons. For example, there was a total of 20 judicial peers who owned land worth less than £500 per annum, of whom all but 3 were appointed between 1820 and 1875. Of these 20 men, 5 were life peers and 15 were hereditary peers, 9 of whom had male heirs. Nine of the 20 judicial peers had fortunes in excess of £80,000 and 7 of them had more than £100,000. Furthermore, of the 9 hereditary peers with male heirs, 6 had fortunes which were greater than £80,000 and 2 of them, Lord Manners and Lord Westbury, had more than £250,000. Finally, there were 9 other judges who were not peers, and who owned little or no land, but possessed personal estates greater than £80,000. All these judges, peers and commoners alike, had the financial capability to purchase large amounts of real estate, but decided for a variety of reasons to avoid major investments in land.

6

AT HOME AND IN SOCIETY

A social analysis of any professional group must remain incomplete if it restricts itself to occupational concerns alone. Not only does an examination of extra-professional evidence provide a more balanced view of the members of an occupation, but it better enables the historian to place the particular group in a larger socio-economic context. As important as the law was to the judges, it constituted only one aspect of their lives. The extra-professional social history of the judiciary can be read in a variety of institutions and activities including residential patterns in town and country, non-legal avocations and pursuits, style of life, and most importantly, the family. Without doubt it is this last institution which stands at the centre of the judges' lives outside the confines of their chambers and courtrooms. It was the repository of the social, economic, and cultural values and expectations of the profession. Fortunately, the domestic evidence which is available for the judges, including marriage patterns, occupational choices of the sons, dynasticism in the law, and the inter-generational transmission of wealth, provides an excellent foundation for an examination of the relationship between the judicial family, the legal profession, and English society.

Residences in Town and Country.

As a result of their professional duties, most judges spent the greater part of the year in London. In order to trace the changing residential patterns of the judges in the metropolis, I have divided London into 14 districts, and the judicial population of each one is displayed in Table 14. Unfortunately little information is available on the London addresses of the 44 judges appointed between 1727 and 1760, but of the 164 judges in the other four periods, 1760-1875, I have been able to discover the addresses of 137.

If any district in eighteenth- or early nineteenth-century London could have been designated the legal quarter, it would have been the one which extended from Lincoln's Inn Fields in Holborn, close to the Inns of Court, northwards to Bloomsbury. The older of the two districts was Lincoln's Inn Fields, which had begun to develop as a living quarter at the end of the reign of Charles I, and was for the most part completed by the middle of the eighteenth century.[1] The earliest buildings in Bloomsbury were erected soon after the Restoration, with

[1] John Summerson, *Georgian London* (Harmondsworth, 1969), pp. 32-4.

the establishment of Bloomsbury Square. Some further development took place at Bedford Square in the last quarter of the eighteenth century, and the district was completed by extensive building during the first third of the nineteenth century.[2] As we can see in Table 14, the importance of Lincoln's Inn Fields as a place of judicial residence was declining during the periods 1760-90 and 1790-1820, while at the same time the judges were converging on Bloomsbury.[3] The prominence of these two districts as residential areas for the judges between 1760 and 1820 is apparent: the homes of at least 47% of the judges appointed between 1760 and 1790 and 86% appointed between 1790 and 1820 were situated within these two districts.

The domination of Lincoln's Inn Fields and Bloomsbury prior to 1820, was followed by their rapid decline as legal quarters between 1820 and 1875. Before 1820 there were a few judges who took up

Table 14: Judges' London residences 1760-1875

	1760-1790		1790-1820		1820-1850		1850-1875		Total	
	No.	%	No.	%	No.	%	No.	%	No.	%
Soho	1	3	1	0	0	0	0	0	2	1
City	1	3	1	3	0	0	0	0	2	1
Lincoln's Inn Fields	6	19	2	7	1	2	0	0	9	6
Bloomsbury	9	28	17	59	9	20	0	0	35	21
St. James/ Westminster	4	12	3	10	2	4	2	3	11	7
Mayfair	1	3	3	10	8	18	4	7	16	10
St. Marylebone	0	0	0	0	5	11	9	15	14	9
Hyde Park	0	0	0	0	4	9	9	15	13	8
Belgravia	0	0	0	0	3	7	10	17	13	8
Knightsbridge/ Kensington	0	0	0	0	1	2	8	14	9	5
Regent's Park	0	0	0	0	1	2	1	2	2	1
Bayswater/ Notting Hill	0	0	0	0	0	0	8	14	8	5
South of River	0	0	0	0	0	0	3	5	3	2
Temple	0	0	0	0	0	0	1	2	1	1
Unknown	10	31	2	10	10	23	4	7	26	15

[2]*Ibid.*, pp. 164-73.

[3]Lincoln's Inn Fields was past its heyday as a residence for the leading members of the legal profession by the time this study opens. It became a favourite residential district for the judges after the Restoration and between 1696 and 1711. Newcastle House which was situated in Lincoln's Inn Fields served as the official residence for 6 Lord Chancellors. John C. Jeafferson, *A Book About Lawyers,* American edn. (New York, 1868), pp. 26-33.

residence outside these districts, but such instances were rare. Lord Bathurst, who was raised to the woolsack with the title of Lord Apsley in 1771, built his town house, Apsley House (later the home of the Duke of Wellington) at Hyde Park corner at about the time of his elevation. In the later 1750s Lord Hardwicke, who had been a long-time resident of Bloomsbury (he lived at Powis House on Great Ormond Street), moved to a house at No. 29 Grosvenor Square, which he had purchased from Lord Exeter for £6,300.[4] Additionally, four judges (12%) in the period 1760-90 lived in the more southerly St. James and Westminster district, near Westminster Hall and the Royal Courts.

After 1820 the movement away from Bloomsbury and Lincoln's Inn Fields to the south and to the west began in earnest. In the period 1820-50 less than a quarter of the judges lived in the old legal districts, and almost as many inhabited St. Marylebone and Mayfair. In the last period, the judges completely abandoned Bloomsbury and Lincoln's Inn Fields and they continued the movement westwards and south-wards. Mayfair, which had been very popular among the judges appointed between 1820 and 1850, accounting for almost 20% of the judiciary, attracted but a small percentage of the judges after 1850 — only 7%. After that date no one district could be proclaimed the residential quarter of the judiciary. There were five districts in which the judges' homes were concentrated: Belgravia (17%), St. Maryle-bone and Hyde Park (16% each), and Knightsbridge/Kensington and Bayswater/Notting Hill (14% each). As fashionable London society moved to districts in the west and southwest in the late eighteenth and nineteenth centuries, the judges abandoned their old living quarters and joined this migration.

As we have already noted in the last chapter, many judges had homes in the country as well as in London. Some of the judges built large new country houses on their estates, while others rebuilt or renovated existing structures. Some judges who were not interested in purchasing large estates did buy small tracts of land upon which to build a country house, while several judges rented country houses rather than building their own. Since the judges spent much less time on their estates than did full-time landowners, their houses were often not as large or as costly as their status and wealth would have allowed. There were of course exceptions, one of the most striking of which was Wimpole Hall in Cambridgeshire, which was purchased by Lord Hardwicke in the 1740s. This house, first built in the mid-seventeenth century, was one of the largest in the county, as befitted Hardwicke,

---

[4]Yorke, *Life and Correspondence of Philip Yorke,* II, 556.

who was one of the great landowners there. After purchasing Wimpole, which had previously belonged to the Earl of Oxford and the Duke of Newcastle, Hardwicke commissioned the architect Henry Flitcroft to redesign part of the house; these alterations were executed during the years 1743-45 at a cost of £8,241.[5]

In terms of the history of architecture in England, Kenwood House, which was built for Lord Mansfield on his Hampstead estate by the famous Georgian architect Robert Adam, is the most important of the country houses owned by any of the judges. Mansfield, who bought the house from Lord Bute in 1754, commissioned Adam to rebuild the existing house in the mid-1760s. The work continued under Adam's direction for many years, although most of the details of the construction are unknown, since a fire set by the Gordon rioters in 1780 at Mansfield's town house destroyed his accounts and papers. The house designed by Adam was surrounded by a great park which included a lake. The interior was decorated with furniture and ornaments designed by the Adam brothers, by Thomas Chippendale, as well as by several other artists and craftsmen.

Kenwood and Wimpole stood out among the country houses of the eighteenth- and nineteenth-century judiciary because of their grandeur and elegance. Most of the judges built large comfortable homes which were probably similar to those of the landed gentry. The judges' country residences were probably designed by local architects and executed by local craftsmen, and while they were perfectly suitable for the needs of judges who owned upwards of several thousand acres, they lacked the stateliness of a house like Kenwood. Between 1804 and 1805 Sir John Nicholl built a house on his newly acquired Glamorganshire estate of Merthyr Mawr for £10,600, including the cost of constructing a farm house.[6] Just over 50 years later in 1857, Lord Campbell 'rebuilt and refurnished the house and reformed the pleasure gardens' on his estate at Hartigge in Roxburghshire for a cost of almost £10,000.[7] Finally, in the 1870s, several years after the death of the former Lord Chancellor Brougham, his family home, Brougham Hall, was valued for insurance purposes at £9,500.[8] These three country houses provide an indication of the

---

[5]Hardwicke MSS., 36,228.

[6]Merthyr Mawr Collection, E/11/1 and E/11/17.

[7]Campbell, *Life,* II, 214-15.

[8]It should be noted that this valuation for Brougham Hall is based on its insurable value and not on the cost of erecting the building. Brougham Financial Papers, Box 2.

level of expenditures which were made on housing by some of the larger judicial landowners.[9]

The judges did not confine their purchase of estates and building of country houses to Britain. At least two of the judges owned estates and houses on the continent — one in France, the other in Italy. Soon after his departure from the woolsack, Lord Brougham bought an estate on the Riviera in Cannes. He had a chateau built on this land between 1836 and 1840 at a cost of 58,849.48 francs (approximately £2,300).[10] He was, according to one of his biographers, 'the first distinguished Englishman to take up his residence in the Riviera and it was mainly due to the force of his example that Cannes became a popular winter resort for the wealthy and leisured class of his country'.[11] Similarly, Lord Westbury, who retired as Chancellor in 1865, acquired soon afterwards an estate in Pistoja near Florence. In fact he spent very little time in Italy and only resided at the estate on three visits there between 1865 and his death in 1873.[12]

Non-Professional Activities

The men who sat on the bench during our period were by and large not merely professional men who had a single-minded devotion to the law to the exclusion of all other pursuits and interests. They were remarkably successful students, as has been observed, and their abilities outside their profession were not abandoned when they began their careers. Some judges were prolific authors: sixty-seven (one third of the total) published works which are listed in the British Library's catalogue of printed books, and six others either edited or translated books written by other authors. While the majority of these judicial authors wrote about legal subjects, their interests ranged far beyond the precincts of their profession. Of the 67 authors, 31 wrote solely on legal subjects, 10 wrote on other topics as well as the law, and 26 wrote on subjects other than the law. These subjects included science and mathematics, prose and poetry, biography and history,

[9]The expenditures made on these houses by the judges were very small compared to the cost of building a country house suitable for one of the great landed aristocrats. Two such houses, Wentworth Woodhouse and Audley End cost £83,000 and £100,000 respectively. Most landed aristocrats and some wealthier gentry spent many tens of thousands of pounds on their houses and the expenses of building sometimes exceeded £100,000. It was not necessary for an aristocrat to spend such high sums to build his house. For example, Lord Sidmouth built a house on his Devon estate of Up Ottery in 1845 for £6,440. Mingay, *English Landed Society in the Eighteenth Century,* p. 160, and Thompson, *English Landed Society in the Nineteenth Century,* pp. 87-93.

[10]Brougham Financial Papers, Box 4.

[11]Aspinall, *Lord Brougham and the Whig Party,* p. 220.

[12]Nash, *Life of Richard Lord Westbury,* II, 146.

religion, politics, literary criticism, economics, and education. In order of popularity we find 14 works about politics, 10 on religion, 9 works each of prose and poetry, and history and biography, 4 of literary criticism, 3 on mathematics and science, and 1 each on economics and education.

Nine of the judges wrote and published literary works, including novels, poetry and plays. The most noted of these judicial authors was Thomas Talfourd, who is best known for his dramatic tragedies. Talfourd wrote a number of plays which were produced on the London stage with varying degrees of success. His works included *Ion* (1836), *The Athenian Captive* (1838), and *Glencoe* (1840). The most successful of these three works was *Ion,* a Greek style tragedy which established Talfourd's reputation as a playwright. Talfourd was also an accepted member of London's literary fraternity, and he was intimately associated with many important nineteenth-century authors and writers. He was a close friend of Charles and Mary Lamb, and was, as a result of this connection, named Charles's literary executor; he was the author of the first edition of the Lambs' letters. He also befriended the young Charles Dickens who, as a tribute, dedicated *Pickwick Papers* to him.

On the other hand, a number of judges made reputations for themselves in mathematics and science. More than a few of the members of the eighteenth- and nineteenth-century judiciary could claim the distinction of being members of the Royal Society. One of these scientist-judges, William Robert Grove, was the inventor of a voltaic battery in 1840 which bears his name. In addition, a series of lectures on physics which he wrote was published in 1846 under the title 'The Correlation of Forces'. This volume went through six editions and was translated into French. Grove retired from the bench in 1887 in order to pursue his interest in science. During the course of his career he held a number of posts connected with his scientific research, and was the recipient of several science awards. He was Vice-President of the Royal Institution, a royal medalist, professor of experimental philosophy at the Royal Institution, member of the Chemical Society, member of the Accademia dei Lincei of Rome, and a knight of the Brazilian Order of the Rose.

Some judges were successful in a number of fields outside their profession. For example, there was Francis Maseres, who was elected a fellow of the Royal Society as a result of his mathematical treatises. He was also a classical scholar, and was chosen as the Chancellor's Medalist in classics at the end of his undergraduate career at Cambridge in 1752. Furthermore, Maseres wrote on a wide range of political and social subjects, including the political conditions in Canada (where he served as Attorney-General of Quebec from 1766-9) and aid to the poor, thereby contributing to the debate on the Old Poor Law which was raging in the late eighteenth and early nineteenth century.[13]

Many judges wrote for periodicals and newspapers in the early years of their legal careers, as was noted in chapter 3, but two of the judges, Henry Brougham and John Taylor Coleridge, were not only frequent contributors to many English journals, but they were involved in the management of two of the most important nineteenth-century political and literary reviews, the *Edinburgh Review* and the *Quarterly Review* respectively. Henry Brougham, prior to coming to London to try his luck at the English bar, became acquainted with Francis Horner, Francis Jeffrey, and Sydney Smith. In 1802 these four men founded the *Edinburgh Review,* which became one of the major organs of Whig thought in nineteenth-century Britain.[14] This connection was very useful for Brougham, since he was able to support himself during his early years in London by writing for the journal. The major Conservative periodical, the *Quarterly Review,* was edited by John Taylor Coleridge for eleven months — from December 1824 until November 1825. Coleridge, who had written articles for the review early in his legal career, became associated with that periodical through his uncle Samuel Taylor Coleridge and his uncle's literary friends. As a result of this connection, John Coleridge was eventually appointed editor of the review, but served for only a short period, since he feared that his editorial duties would interfere with his legal career.[15]

The careers of a number of judges were connected with the promotion of both professional and general education in Britain. Sir William Blackstone, who served as a judge in both the King's Bench and the Common Pleas, is best known as a legal scholar, author, and lecturer. Blackstone's career as an educator began in 1753 when he started giving private lectures in jurisprudence at Oxford. He continued in this capacity for 5 years until 1758 at which time he was elected Oxford University's first Vinerian Professor of English Law. As we have seen, Blackstone favoured the teaching of law in the universities, and his professorship, which he held until 1766, served as a platform from which he could express his views. The year before he retired from this office, he published the first volume of his

[13]J. R. Poynter, *Society and Pauperism: English Ideas on Poor Relief 1795-1834* (London, 1969), pp. 35-6.

[14]New, *The Life of Henry Brougham,* pp. 13-4.

[15]Lord Coleridge, *Story of a Devonshire House,* p. 285.

Commentaries on the Laws of England. This work, which was one of the great landmarks in English jurisprudence, was completed in 1769 and went through eight editions during Blackstone's lifetime (he died in 1780). It is estimated that Blackstone earned between £14,000-£16,000 from the *Commentaries.*[16]

Although Blackstone's contribution to legal education was unique among the eighteenth- and nineteenth-century judiciary, other judges helped to carry on the fight for educational reform. One of the most active reformers was Richard Bethell, a most successful barrister who later served as Lord Chancellor with the title of Baron Westbury. During the late 1840s and early 1850s Bethell agitated in both the Inns of Court and in Parliament for the reform of the system of legal education. In addition, he was one of the founders in the 1850s of the Juridical Society, whose object was the promotion of the science of jurisprudence, and he served as the Society's first president.

The educational interests and activities of some judges extended beyond the boundaries of their profession. Several judges retained close contact with their universities, and at least two served as masters of their college (Sir James Marriot and Sir William Wynne, both of Trinity Hall, Cambridge). There was one member of the judiciary whose efforts in support of general education were outstanding: that man was Henry Brougham. He was one of the founders of the Society for the Diffusion of Useful Knowledge in 1825 and he also collaborated with Dr. George Birkbeck in the development of the Mechanics' Institutes. Both of these institutions, which were designed to foster continuing working-class education, were less than completely successful, but nevertheless they did have an impact on the development of popular adult education. The audience, which was in fact attracted by Brougham's educational programmes, was composed not of mechanics or skilled workers but rather of members of the middle classes.

Brougham also participated in the campaign to improve primary education for the working classes. He served as the chairman of the 1816 Charity Commission. During the two succeeding decades the Commission continued his work by investigating, reforming, and rationalizing endowed charities in England, including many educational facilities for the poor. He was also instrumental in securing the appointment of the Select Committee on the Education of the Poor in the Metropolis, which became a Royal Commission in 1818.[17]

[16]*DNB,* XII, p.1083.

[17]David Owen, *English Philanthropy 1660-1960,* (Cambridge, Mass. 1964), pp. 183-91.

However, the most famous of Brougham's educational projects was the creation of a non-sectarian university in London. In order to realize this aim Brougham, along with other radicals and dissenters, most notably Jeremy Bentham, founded University College in 1828, thus laying the foundation for what would later become the nucleus of the University of London.

The possible extent of involvement of some judges in extra-professional activities may be gauged from a list compiled by Sir John Nicholl of the organizations and societies of which he was a founder, member or financial supporter, including the following: the National Society for Church Enlargement, the Foundling Hospital, St. Bartholomew's Hospital, Deptford School, St. George's School, Christ's Hospital, the Clergy Orphan Asylum, St. George's Dispensary, the Royal Society, the Antiquarian Society, the British Institution, the Geographical Society, the Horticultural Society, the British Society, Bridgend School, Bridgend Savings Bank, the District Commission, the Clergy Charity, and the Agricultural Society (Glamorganshire).[18]

Not only were the judges leaders of their profession and often of political affairs, but they were also pillars of society. On both the national and local levels, in education, the liberal arts, science, religion, and charitable causes, the judges of England were organizers and supporters of voluntary associations and productive members of the nation's intellectual community. They were active in public affairs and utilized their prestige and wealth, which were the result of professional success, as a platform from which to influence public opinion.

Judicial Life Styles

In 1867 a book on the legal profession in Britain described the plight of junior barristers who, having been recently called to the bar, were put under excessive social and economic pressures to conform with the demands of an extremely elevated life style. According to the author of this work,

> Society will not let him live after the fashion of 'juniors' of eighty or a hundred years since. He must maintain two establishments — his chambers for business, and his house in the west-end of town for his wife. Moreover, the lady must have a brougham and liberal pin money, or four or five domestic servants and a drawing-room well furnished with works of art and costly decorations. They must give state dinners and three or four

[18]Merthyr Mawr Collection, F/2/4.

routs every season; and in all other matters their mode of life
must be, or seem to be, that of the upper ten thousand.[19]

The author estimated further that a barrister who hoped to live in this
way had to allow for an annual expenditure of £1,500 per annum.

Unlike the junior barristers, most of the judges had no financial
difficulty in fulfilling the social demands which were made upon them.
Several of them had the reputation of being parsimonious, most
notably Lord Kenyon and Lord Eldon,[20] but as a group the judges
lived in accordance with their financial resources, which were in most
cases considerable.

Not unexpectedly, in the early years of their careers many of the
judges had to spend more than they were earning from their
profession.[21] One judge, Sir John Nicholl, has left a very valuable set
of personal and household accounts which begin in the early years of
his career as an advocate and continue intermittently until 1835, three
years before his death. Because this is the most complete set of accounts
that exists for any of the judges, it may be useful to begin this
examination of the patterns of expenditure in judicial households with
Nicholl's records. Nicholl, who was admitted to Doctors' Commons
in 1785, did not earn over £2,000 per annum until 1793, which was
also the first year in which his professional income had exceeded his
expenditures. In that year he earned £2,143 from his profession while
his total expenses were £1,919.[22] Between 1789 and 1793 Nicholl's
expenses had outstripped his earnings by approximately £500 per
year. After 1793 his expenditures continued to rise, but his income
both from his profession and from his investments rose even faster,
and his fortune began to increase.

Nicholl's annual expenses exceeded £4,000 per annum for the
first time in 1800, and from that date until his appointment to the
bench in 1809 they fluctuated between £4,290 and £5,800 per
annum. In 1810, his first full year on the bench, his expenditures rose
to £8,690 and then declined to £7,500 in 1811 and £6,190 in 1812.[23]
It seems probable that at least part of the additional outlay in the years
immediately following his appointment to the bench was the result of

[19] Jeafferson, *A Book About Lawyers,* American edn, p. 91.

[20] *Ibid.,* p. 408.

[21] For additional information on the inability of barristers to survive on their
professional earnings and the need for non-professional incomes or financial aid from
relatives or friends, see Chapters 3 and 5.

[22] Merthyr Mawr Collection, L/1/2 and E/116/4.

[23] Merthyr Mawr Collection, E/116/4.

the social requirements of judicial office. This may have been compounded by the general inflation during the Napoleonic Wars.

Two years during the period of Nicholl's tenure on the bench, 1813 and 1820, have been chosen to illustrate the patterns of expenditure in his household. A number of the more outstanding changes between 1813 and 1820 can be explained as the effects of the continental wars raging in the earlier year. Taxes were naturally higher during the war years, especially as a result of the income tax of 1799 to 1816. The price inflation in basic commodities may also help to explain the large proportion of annual income devoted to household expenses, to coals, beer, and wine, and to repairs and improvements in 1813. In 1813 these four categories of expenses accounted for £5,167 or three-quarters of Nicholl's total expenditures for the year; in 1820 they equalled £3,525 or just under one half of the year's total. Clearly the decline in such basic expenses allowed for an increase in more luxurious expenditures, namely clothes and books, and travelling and sundries. These were valued at £1,066 (16%) in 1813 and £2,882 (40%) in 1820.[24]

Table 15: The personal and professional expenses of Sir John Nicholl in the years 1813 and 1820

| | 1813 | | 1820 | |
	£	%	£	%
Rent and Taxes	682	10	301	4
Housekeeping and Wages	232	3	296	4
Carriages and Horses	385	6	461	6
Travelling and Sundries	432	6	1524	21
Clothes and Books	634	9	1358	19
Coals, Beer, and Wine	557	8	315	4
Merthyr Mawr (repairs and improvements)	2198	32	1659	23
Lady Nicholl (includes Household expenses)	1730	25	1250	18
Total	6850	99	7164	99

[24]Merthyr Mawr Collection, F/9/9. Nicholl's expenses in 1813 and 1820 can be compared with a model budget for a middle class family with an income of from £1,000-£5,000 in 1823.
1. Household expenses including provisions, coal, candles, entertainment and medicine.

Another useful set of records is that of Lord Mansfield, which begin in July 1785 and continue until the Chief Justice's death in March 1793. During these years Mansfield lived primarily at Kenwood, but he also kept a town house in Lincoln's Inn Fields. Although he was already 80 when these records begin, he was still active in the profession and he did not retire from the bench until 1788. Mansfield was a widower (his wife died in 1784) and he lived at Kenwood with two nieces and a large staff of servants. During the seven years for which complete accounts are available (1786-1792) Mansfield's expenditures totalled £39,331 or £5,619 per annum. His largest annual expenditure was in 1786 (£6,909) while his lowest was in 1792 (£5,310).[25]

A comparison of Mansfield's accounts in 1786 (Table 16) and Nicholl's in 1820 (Table 15) shows striking similarities.[26] For example, Mansfield spent 30% of his income on household expenses and servants, while Nicholl spent 26% on housekeeping and wages, coals, beer and wine, and Lady Nicholl's expenses, a large proportion of which were apparently devoted to household needs. Carriages and horses accounted for 8% of Mansfield's outlay and 6% of Nicholl's. There is also an almost exact correspondence between the 22% in Mansfield's account devoted to books, travel, professional and miscellaneous expenditures, and the 21% listed by Nicholl for travel and sundries; this figure would be increased somewhat if the precise amount spent by him on books were known. Of course the absence of a detailed itemization of the two sets of accounts may conceal basic differences in the patterns of expenditure, despite superficial similarities.

36%; 2. Servants and Equipage. 22%; 3. Clothes. 12%; 4. Rent, Taxes, and Repairs. 12%; 5. Extra Expenses including Education, Pocket Money, and Private Expenses. 8%; 6. Reserve or Savings. 10%.
Not surprisingly Nicholl as a large landowner spent more on taxes, rent, repairs, and improvements than would any middle-class family. On the other hand, the percentage of his outlay which Nicholl spent on household expenses, even if the entire amount which is labelled Lady Nicholl is included, falls short of the percentage suggested above. This is also true of the amount spent by Nicholl on servants and equipage. Finally, in 1813 the percentage spent on clothes and extra expenses by Nicholl conforms generally with the estimates above, but the percentage he spent in these categories in 1820 is far above the estimate. Banks, *Prosperity and Parenthood,* p. 55.

[25]Lord Mansfield's Account Book, Kenwood House, by courtesy of the Iveagh Bequest.

[26]Nicholl's 1820 account has been chosen for this comparison rather than the 1813 account because by 1820 the inflation of the Napoleonic period had subsided and prices declined almost to their pre-war levels, such as existed in 1786. See Deane and Cole, *British Economic Growth,* long-term trend in British prices (chart at the end of the study).

Table 16: Lord Mansfield's expenses — 1786

1.	Household	£1,831	25%
	a. Housekeeping	£840	11%
	b. Food	£345	5%
	c. Beer and Wine	£359	5%
	d. Coal	£140	2%
	e. Doctor and Medicine	£147	2%
2.	Servants and Equipage	£968	13%
	a. Servants	£390	5%
	b. Carriages, carts, horses	£578	8%
3.	Rentals, Taxes, Repairs	£2,082	28%
	a. Tradesmens' bills, repairs, farm work	£435	6%
	b. Gardens and Woods	£366	5%
	c. Taxes	£949	13%
	d. Rents	£332	4%
4.	Clothes	£289	4%
5.	Extra Expenses	£1,638	22%
	a. Professional Expenses	£200	3%
	b. Travel, holiday	£406	5%
	c. Books	£40	1%
	d. Miscellaneous	£992	13%
6.	Savings	£504	7%
7.	Total	£7,312	100%

Source: Lord Mansfield's Account Book, Kenwood House. Compare with model budget above pp.155-6 n. 24.

One category in the accounts that was devoted to the upkeep of the Kenwood and Merthyr Mawr estates, provides some suggestive clues about the profitability of judicial estates.[27] Mansfield spent £801 on repairs, improvements, farm work, and gardening — 11% of his total outgoings. The income from his Hampstead estate was derived from a number of sources. Mansfield's ledger lists annual remittances from a single tenant, Mr. Way. In 1786 two separate payments were received from Mr. Way at approximately the same time, one for £433 10s and the other for £404 6s 8d. The first amount is clearly recorded as rent 'for land about Kenwood'; however, no explanation is provided for the second sum — whether for land, the rent of buildings, or for services rendered. In addition, Mansfield maintained a productive home farm which in 1786 provided him with an income of £666 14s 7d. The combined value of Mr. Way's payments and the sale of farm produce was £1,504 11s 3d. After the deduction of expenses for repairs and upkeep, Kenwood produced a net income of just in excess of £700.

Nicholl's home estate of Merthyr Mawr was much larger than Kenwood. For the period 1813-20, it contained just under 2,800 acres which produced an annual rental of £3,000. In 1820 Nicholl spent £1,659, or 23% of his total expenditure, on repairs and improvements to Merthyr Mawr, while during the war year 1813 these costs amounted to £2,198 or 32%. For the period 1810 to 1835 seven yearly summaries of expenses survive for Merthyr Mawr; these give an average annual expenditure of £1,750 on repairs and improvements, thus providing Nicholl with a net income of £1,200 per annum before taxes.

Unfortunately a more detailed analysis of Nicholl's expenditure on repairs and improvements is impossible because of the lack of explanatory data in the accounts. As a result, there is no way of knowing what percentage of the total was spent on capital improvement such as enclosures or building as compared with repairs or aesthetic improvement to Merthyr Mawr House and its park. In the case of Kenwood, which had more explicit accounts, annual expenses were by and large evenly divided between farm work and repairs to the big house and its immediate environs.

Large homes in town and country meant that for most members of the judiciary, a retinue of servants formed a basic component of their

[27]Both Mansfield and Nicholl spent a lower percentage of their income on household expenses and a higher percentage on rents, taxes, repairs, and improvements than appears in the model budget.

households. Few judges have left complete lists of the names, functions, and salaries of their servants; nevertheless it is possible to sketch an average judicial domestic establishment from the information contained in accounts and wills.

The wills rarely include the names of all the servants of a judge. In many instances, principal servants or those who had served in the household for many years, were noticed individually by name or by title. From this source, it is possible to estimate the minimum size of the domestic staffs employed by the judges. According to the available evidence, members of the eighteenth- and nineteenth-century judiciary supported, on average, between four and seven servants at any one time. These usually included a butler, a cook, a housekeeper, a coachman, a gardener, and one or more housemaids. Of course judges with very high incomes, with large households, or with great landed estates required more domestic help, and they may have employed as many as 10 or 20 servants.[28] In these large establishments, the more basic staff were often supplemented by a bailiff, a groom, a postillion, a second coachman, a second gardener, a kitchen maid, and a number of miscellaneous servants and maids. The largest of all the judges' domestic establishments seems to have been that of Lord Mansfield. In 1788 he employed 11 male and 11 female servants whose wages totalled £320 per annum, in addition to the cost of their board and lodging.[29]

The judges who served in the eighteenth and early nineteenth centuries, especially the Chancellors and the Chief Justices, were to be found in the best circles of London society. They had their portraits painted by the great artists of the day — Reynolds, Gainsborough, Copley, Romney, Lawrence, and Dance. They were great hosts, and their dinner parties included not only their colleagues but also members of the cabinet, important literary figures, and members of the aristocracy. In this regard, Lord Lyndhurst's biographer wrote of the Lord Chancellor that

> A man so distinguished for his social qualities, and so con-
> spicuous in his profession, was sure to be courted in the best
> London society. That his wife was handsome, 'lived well, loved
> company,' and was admired by many leading men in the political
> world, was another reason for his finding his way into the
> intimacy of the highest circles . . . The truth was that Copley
> brought around him in his home the men most eminent in

[28]For example, see the wills of Sir John Nicholl and William Lord Walsingham in the Public Record Office and the will of William Ventris Lord Field in Somerset House.

[29]Lord Mansfield's Account Book for 1788.

literature, art, and science, as well as in political life: and it was inevitable that names of great distinction for social rank should become from time to time mingled with theirs in the pages of his wife's visiting book.[30]

Many of the judges for their part received invitations to the parties given by the leading figures of London society. Thomas Talfourd, who entertained his literary friends such as Charles Dickens at his Russell Square home, was a frequent guest at the parties of such notables as Lord John Russell, Lord Lansdowne, and Lord Melbourne.[31]

Another indication of the judges' standing in London society was their affiliation with the leading London political and social clubs. Of the 59 judges who were appointed between 1850 and 1875, forty-four (75%) were members of one or more London clubs. Thirty judges were members of the most prestigious of the literary and artistic clubs, the Athenaeum. Eleven belonged to the leading Conservative club, the Carlton, eight to the leading Liberal club, the Reform, and six to the Whiggish Brooks's. The other clubs which could claim judges as members were the Oxford and Cambridge (6), the Windham (2), the University (2), the Garrick (1), the Marlborough (1), the National (1), the Turf (1), and the Portland (1).

The judges' closest friendships were generally with their colleagues. They traditionally referred to one another as 'brother', and their relationships were often closer than professional bonds necessitated. In the later eighteenth century John Dunning, a leading barrister though never a judge, held weekly gatherings of members of the legal profession, some of whom were already judges and many others who would soon be elevated to the bench, including Wedderburn, Ashurst, Hotham, Mansfield, Grose, Ley, Jack Lee, Impey, Mitford, Skynner, Rooke, Day, Pepper Arden, and Scott.[32] The judges also took an interest in the well-being of their colleagues and their families, as is illustrated in the following letter written in 1831 by the Chief Justice of King's Bench, Lord Tenterden, and the Chief Justice of Common Pleas, Nicholas C. Tindal, to the Chancellor, Lord Brougham.

> We take the liberty to trouble your Lordship with this communication on behalf of the widow and only daughter of our late friend Sir Geo. Holroyd. The daughter is, as you probably will recollect, unmarried. They are both left with very slender means,

---

[30]Sir Theodore Martin, *A Life of Lord Lyndhurst* (London, 1883), pp. 200-1.

[31]Robert S. Newdick, 'Sir Thomas Talfourd D.C.L.', p. 142.

[32]Kenyon, *Life of Lloyd, First Lord Kenyon*, p. 48.

& neither of the sons is in a condition to offer much assistance. A pension was granted to the widow of Sir Wm. Blackstone, & another to the widow of Sir Giles Rooke. They are precedents & we trust that by your kindness and zeal, you may be able, even in these days of Economy, to obtain some pension from his majesty for these ladies.[33]

Husbands and Fathers

The road to success at the bar was long and unsure, as we have noted, and the young barrister had to face many years of professional and economic uncertainty. As a consequence of these professional facts of life, the barrister often had to postpone any thoughts of marriage until he had made his reputation at the bar and had secured his livelihood. For example, in 1814, eight years after his call to the bar, John Campbell wrote the following to his brother concerning a career at the bar and marriage.

My receipts still go on increasing [he had been earning between £1000-£1500 per annum for several years already], but I am forced to enslave and devote myself in a manner which I very much dislike. I am cut off from all society except what I meet in the courts of justice. Nor do I know how I could act otherwise. I cannot say, I will go into company three days in the week and give up half my business. Were I to make the experiment, I should soon be left without any. This is a very great drawback upon the profession of the law in England. Marriage seems to be out of the question for me. I have not conversed for many months with any women I would marry.[34]

The conditions of professional life faced by the budding barrister, such as those described by Campbell, had important implications for the demographic patterns of the judiciary.

Although 87% of judges, including Campbell, did marry eventually, their mean age of marriage was extremely high, even exceeding that of the British peerage. In his exhaustive demographic study of that social élite, T.H. Hollingsworth found that the mean age of marriage for male cohorts born between 1675 and 1824 ranged from 30 years 10 months to 33 years 11 months, a somewhat higher average than that of the general population.[35] By comparison, the mean age of

[33]Brougham MSS., 25,636.

[34]Campbell *Life,* I, 311.

[35]T.H. Hollingsworth, 'The Demography of the British Peerage', Supplement to *Population Studies* 18 (1964), 27.

marriage for the members of the judiciary appointed between 1727 and 1875 (most of whom were born between 1680 and 1820) ranged from 32 years to 35 years. The reasons for the late marriages within the judiciary are clear. Most of these men were not in a position to begin earning a living in their chosen profession until they were already in their late twenties. Even then they almost invariably had to wait for a number of years to pass before they made their reputation and began to build up a solid and permanent practice upon which it would be possible to support a family. By this time the barrister was already in his early or mid thirties. These circumstances may have been aggravated by the pace of professional life, which according to Campbell, prevented the young barrister from developing relationships with suitable women. An examination of Campbell's own career provides an indication of the difficulty which faced the young barrister. He was called to the bar at the age of 27, but not until 1814 when he was already 35, did Campbell have the financial resources, if not the social contacts, to enable him to contemplate marriage.

In all, 13% of the judges never married as compared with 19.5% of male members of the peerage born between 1675 and 1824.[36] Of those judges who did marry, 18% had no children (16% of the total judicial population), while among the married male members of the peerage and of their sons born between 1675 and 1824, 19.7% were childless.[37] Although the percentage of judges in each of these two categories is somewhat lower than for the peerage, it is much higher than for the English population at large. Combining the data on never-married judges with that on childless judicial marriages, we find that 29% of the judges had no offspring.

This data emphasizes the significance of the evidence concerning the lateness of judicial marriages. Professional and consequently financial factors seemingly contributed to the high percentage of childless judges by producing conditions which were not conducive to marriage, or by delaying marriage until an age which adversely affected the childbearing potential of judicial couples.

The 181 married judges had a total of 218 spouses; of these it has been possible to trace the social origins of 124 (57%). This data provides some clues about the social milieu inhabited by the judges during the early years of their legal careers; however, the high percentage of wives with unknown origins makes it necessary to treat any conclusions with caution.

[36]*Ibid.*, p. 20.
[37]*Ibid.*, p. 46.

Table 17: Social origins of judges' wives

Father's occupation	1727-60 No.	%	1760-90 No.	%	1790-1820 No.	%	1820-50 No.	%	1850-75 No.	%	Total No.	%
Landed	8	15	6	21	4	16	6	13	11	17	35	16
Professional	13	25	10	35	6	24	21	44	23	36	73	33
Merchant/business	1	2	1	3	3	12	4	8	4	6	13	6
Other	0	0	1	3	1	4	1	2	0	0	3	1
Unknown	30	57	11	38	11	44	16	33	26	41	94	43
Total	52	99	29	100	25	100	48	100	64	100	218	99

Clearly, the missing data could alter considerably this profile of judicial marriage partners. For example, the unknown groups may very well conceal a number of lesser gentry or yeoman farmers which could swell the landed group, although there seems little chance that large landowners have been omitted. Similarly additional clergymen, military and naval officers, and government office holders as well as merchants and businessmen would undoubtedly be found among the unknown fathers-in-law. Nevertheless it is possible to draw some tentative conclusions. There seems to be no evidence that the members of the judiciary used marriage as a means of upward social mobility, while few wives with known origins were from the lower social strata. A few judges did marry the daughters of titled aristocrats, and some others married women whose fathers could variously be described as small merchants or large retailers; one even allied himself with the daughter of a clerk, but these were the exceptions. Most of the judges found their wives among the daughters of men belonging to the upper professions and the middling and lesser gentry. Based on the age at which the judges married and their marriage patterns, as well as the social origins of their wives, there seems to be little evidence that the judges selected their partners with an eye to improving their professional chances by choosing the right father-in-law. The fact that only 4 men married the daughters of solicitors gives the lie to the amusing parody of a judicial marriage in Gilbert and Sullivan's 'Trial by Jury';

> In Westminster Hall I danced such a dance,
>   Like a semi-despondent fury;
> For I thought I should never hit on a chance
>   Of addressing a British jury —
> But I soon got tired of third class journeys,
>   And of dinners of bread and water;
> So I fell in love with a rich attorney's
>   Elderly ugly daughter.
> The rich attorney he jumped for joy,
>   And replied to my fond professions:
> You'll reap the reward of your pluck, my boy
>   At the Bailey and Middlesex Sessions.[38]

On the contrary, the judges seem to have married women who inhabited those social circles in which one would expect to find up and coming barristers, who had already achieved a moderate degree of professional success and whose social life reflected their professional advancement.

---

[38] W. S. Gilbert and Arthur Sullivan, 'Trial By Jury', in *The Complete Plays of Gilbert and Sullivan*, (New York edn, 1941), p. 41.

The 148 judges who had children produced a total of 370 sons. An examination of the occupational choices of these men should help us gain a clearer understanding of the values and social outlook of their families. Such a connection would be natural, since the choices of the sons would probably be influenced by their social milieu and perhaps more directly by the social and professional attitudes of their families. Any significant changes in the career choices of the judges' sons could be indicative of a change either in the status or in the attitudes of the judges and their families. However, since evidence on judicial incomes, origins, and life styles did not suggest any major transformation in regard to social or occupational status of the judiciary in the period 1727-1875, modifications in attitudes and values will probably serve as a more satisfactory explanation.

In Table 18 the sons of the judges are listed according to their principal sources of income. A special category has been included for those sons who died before they had entered a particular profession, that is before age twenty-five. The revolution which occurred in the occupational choices of the sons of the judges is at once evident. In the first period, just under one quarter of the sons were landowners, 22% followed their fathers' profession, and 22% entered one of the other higher professions — the armed services, the church, or government service. In the second period, apart from an almost five-fold increase in the percentage of sons entering the military, the pattern was much the same. During these two periods, a majority of sons were either landowners or members of one of the upper professions, and they seemed to favour their fathers' profession only to a limited extent. This pattern began to change in the period 1790-1820 at which time the percentage of sons who became landowners declined to just over 5%, while almost one third of all the sons were barristers. The attraction of the law became even greater during the next two periods, so that by the period 1850-75, 44% of the sons of the judges were earning their living at the bar.

Even after 1790 the sons of the judges were still reluctant to enter the lower professions or business. A small number became solicitors, doctors, artists, school teachers, businessmen, and merchants, but the bar, military, and church remained far and away the most attractive professions.[39]

[39]The decline in the importance of government office as an occupation among the sons of the judges appointed after 1820 may be explained by the elimination of lucrative sinecures in the courts and by the establishment of a permanent pension system. This resulted in the elimination of *ad hoc* retirement awards which sometimes included permanent appointments to government offices for sons of the judges (see Chapter 5). An additional factor may have been the professionalization of the civil service in the second half of the nineteenth century, which culminated in the introduction of an examination system in 1870.

Table 18: Occupations of judges' sons

	1727-60		1760-90		1790-1820		1820-50		1850-75		Total	
	No.	%	No.	%	No.	%	No.	%	No.	%	No.	%
Landed	12	24	8	19	3	5	6	6	7	6	36	10
Bar	11	22	8	19	18	33	39	37	50	44	126	34
Clergymen	5	10	6	14	13	24	25	23	10	9	59	16
Military	2	4	8	19	6	11	13	12	14	12	43	12
Civil Service/Gov't Office	4	8	3	7	5	9	6	6	3	3	21	6
Doctors	0	0	0	0	0	0	1	1	1	1	2	1
Solicitors	0	0	0	0	0	0	1	1	2	2	3	1
Teachers	0	0	1	2	0	0	1	1	1	1	3	1
Misc. Professionals	1	2	0	0	0	0	0	0	2	2	3	1
Businessmen	0	0	0	0	0	0	0	0	3	3	3	1
Large Merchants	0	0	0	0	0	0	1	1	1	1	2	1
Misc. Merchants	0	0	0	0	0	0	0	0	1	1	1	0
Died before age 25	5	11	7	16	4	7	14	13	7	6	37	10
Unknown	10	20	2	5	6	11	1	1	12	11	31	8
Total	50	100	43	101	55	100	108	102	114	101	370	102

In explaining the career choices of the sons of the judges appointed between 1727 and 1790, it must be remembered that the eighteenth-century judges lived in a society in which the landed classes still held an unchallenged position of political, social, and economic leadership. The ideal in that society was to acquire the accoutrements of gentility, and if possible to provide for one's progeny by founding a landed family. From this point of view, appointment to the judiciary conferred gentility upon the judge and his family, and provided them with the credentials which enabled them to enter the world of the landed gentry and aristocracy. As a result, we find that the occupational choices of the sons of the eighteenth-century judges are the same ones that we might expect of the sons of the landed classes. Those who were provided with estates became landed gentlemen, while the others entered the most gentlemanly professions, scrupulously avoiding the lower professions and business. Except for the slight preference for the bar, the profession in which they had the best connections, there is no special emphasis in the career choices of the judges' sons from which it is possible to discern that their fathers were leading members of the legal profession. For the sons of the eighteenth-century judges, the real importance of their fathers' professional success was the gentility it conferred upon them.

The occupational choices of the sons of the judges appointed after 1790 indicate the gulf which lay between their social attitudes and those of their eighteenth-century counterparts. During the three periods 1790-1820, 1820-50, and 1850-75, the professional nature of the judiciary became successively more evident in the career choices of the sons. The change from eighteenth-century choices, which stressed gentility, to the more professional choices of the nineteenth century are most notably represented by the decline in the percentage of landowners and the expansion in the percentage of sons who entered the law.

The increasing professionalization of attitudes, as represented by the occupational choices, did not, however, signify a decline in social consciousness. As we have seen, the sons of the judges continued to avoid the lower professions and business in the nineteenth century. What seems to have occurred is not a change in the sons' concern with status, but rather a redefinition of the nature of status. The sons of the nineteenth-century judges no longer needed the concept of landed gentility to buttress their social standing. They were the sons of men who had reached the pinnacle of success in their profession and who were able to mingle comfortably with ministers and peers. In addition, by the mid-nineteenth century the ideal of the gentleman, which had been strongly connected with the position of the landed classes in eighteenth-century England, no longer held a pre-eminent position, Lionel Trilling has written that 'in nineteenth-century England the ideal of the professional commitment inherits a large part of the moral prestige of the ideal of the gentleman'.[40] This change in the attitudes of society is reflected in the occupational choices of the sons of the nineteenth-century judges. These choices also indicate the special position of the legal profession in their consciousness as the occupation which provided the judges and their families with superior social status.

At least since the Middle Ages there had been a tendency within the ranks of the legal profession towards the formation of professional dynasties.[41] There were, however, periodic fluctuations in the percentage of barristers' sons who followed their fathers' profession. As a result, legal dynasties flourished in one period and practically disappeared in another. As is apparent in Table 18, such a decline occurred among the sons of the judges who were appointed in the period 1760-90. The percentage of sons who entered their fathers' profession was smaller than in either the preceding or succeeding periods, and in addition not one of the judges appointed between 1760 and 1790 had a son who also sat on the bench. The sons' waning interest in the law during this period is mirrored in the findings of Professor Paul Lucas, who has noted in a recent article that among barristers called by Lincoln's Inn between 1765 and 1804, a much lower percentage came from legal backgrounds than in the period 1695-1764.[42]

In the first decades of the nineteenth century, the trend began to reverse, and more and more judges' sons began to follow their fathers' profession. Yet, only one of the judges appointed in the period 1790-1820 had a son who also sat on the bench. The rise in dynasticism continued in the periods 1820-50 and 1850-75. In fact the earlier of these two periods saw the creation of two judicial dynasties which were to last for three generations: the Coleridges and the Pollocks.

[40]Lionel Trilling, *The Opposing Self* (New York, 1955), p. 215.

[41]As Dr. E.W. Ives had noted: 'The combination of a tendency for the son to follow the father in the law and for a lawyer and his children to marry within the profession, might be expected to produce a very closely knit group in society, and this in fact, was the case at the end of the medieval period'. Ives, 'Some Aspects of the Legal Profession in the Fifteenth and Sixteenth Centuries', p. 182.

[42]Lucas, 'A Collective Biography of Students and Barristers of Lincoln's Inn, 1680-1804', pp. 232, 241, and 255.

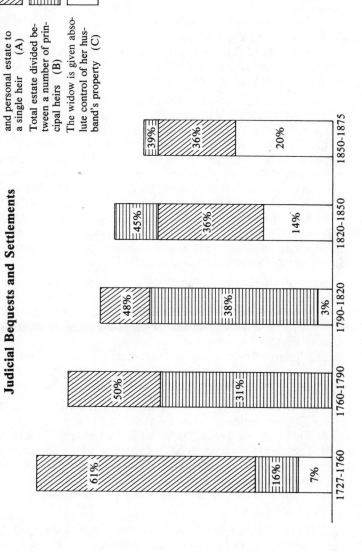

169

Figure 1

Judicial Bequests and Settlements

KEY

75% of the real or real and personal estate to a single heir (A)

Total estate divided between a number of principal heirs (B)

The widow is given absolute control of her husband's property (C)

	1727-1760	1760-1790	1790-1820	1820-1850	1850-1875
A	61%	50%	48%	45%	39%
B	16%	31%	38%	36%	36%
C	7%		3%	14%	20%

The first judge in the Coleridge family was John Taylor Coleridge, who was appointed a judge of the King's Bench in 1834. John Taylor's eldest son was John Duke Coleridge, who was appointed Lord Chief Justice of Common Pleas in 1873, created Lord Coleridge in 1874, and elevated to the office of Lord Chief Justice of England in 1880. Similarly John Duke's eldest son, Bernard John Seymour, was appointed to the judiciary in 1907 and held the same office, judge of the King's Bench, as had his grandfather.

The Pollock family was no less distinguished in the law than were the Coleridges. David Pollock, saddler to King George III, had two sons who were both judges: David, Chief Justice of Bombay, and Frederick, Lord Chief Baron of the Exchequer. Frederick's fourth son, Charles Edward, followed his father into the Court of Exchequer as a puisne baron, while two of his brothers served as Masters in Chancery. The younger of those two brothers, George F. Pollock, had a son, Ernest Murray Pollock, who was appointed Master of the Rolls in 1923, and was raised to the peerage as Viscount Hanworth in 1926. The older brother, William F. Pollock, who succeeded his father as baronet, also had a son who was well known in the legal profession — Sir Frederick Pollock, the famous legal historian.

Not surprisingly, the influx of the sons of the judges, including many first sons, into their fathers' profession in the nineteenth century, coincided with the decline in the tendency of members of the judiciary to found landed families. Fewer and fewer of the judges' sons became country gentlemen, since the vast majority of nineteenth-century judges were reluctant to invest their capital in landed estates which were sufficiently large to support a man even as a member of the squirearchy (that is, with a rental of £1,000 per annum or more).

The decline in the importance of the landed ideal among members of the English judiciary is reflected not only in the occupational profiles of their sons, but also in the settlement patterns found in their wills. The choice of a system of succession in which the eldest sons received most of the patrimony would suggest a desire to follow in the footsteps of the aristocracy, while any alteration in favour of a more equal distribution of wealth would indicate a reassessment of social attitudes and values.

The settlement patterns followed by the judges in their wills have been classified into three categories according to the extent to which they deviate from absolutely favouring the eldest son or nearest male heir: A. a single heir, usually the eldest son, receives 75% or more of the real or of the real and personal estate; B. the estate is divided into roughly equal shares which are distributed among a number of heirs, most often the children of the testator; C. the wife is named sole heiress and is usually given absolute control of the entire estate. The percentage of the wills which conform to each of these patterns during the five periods is traced in Figure 1.[43]

A majority of judges in the first three periods adopted the settlement pattern which is most frequently associated with the landed classes, namely the favouring of one heir. This individual, most often an eldest son or nephew, inherited most if not all of the familial land, and often the greater part of the personal estate as well. In addition these wills usually contain provisions for the strict settlement of landed estates, as a means of protecting the integrity of the property and preventing sub-division and alienation by future generations. However, even during the years 1760-1820, at which time almost half of the judges named a single heir, the pattern was clearly in decline.

In the years after 1820, a new more egalitarian spirit came to dominate the settlement patterns of the judges. Division of property supplanted the older tradition as the leading pattern. The break with the past was even more evident in regard to the third pattern, the bequeathing of all property, real and personal, to the judges' wives. In these cases, the women were appointed as the sole executrices with absolute control of their husbands' estates. This pattern is of particular interest because of the light it sheds on the position of some women in nineteenth-century society. Of course a more general examination of the wills of the middle class and especially of professional men, would be necessary to evaluate fully the significance of these findings. However, at the very least the evidence indicates that at a time when the right of married women to control their own property was far from settled, more than a few judges were concerned with giving their wives complete control of the family property, and not merely an allowance or jointure for their maintenance. Perhaps these men had begun to see their wives as full-fledged partners rather than as dependent subordinates.

Although comparable data on settlement patterns of members of other social groups is limited, there are two studies of English wealth-holders in the late nineteenth and early twentieth centuries which can provide some basis for comparison. In an analysis of the wills of millionaires and half millionaires between 1858 and 1899, Dr. William Rubinstein found that 32% left 50% or more of their estates

---

[43] Seven of the 208 judges (3%) bequeathed their estates to non-relatives or to institutions. The settlement patterns of another 15 (7%) are unknown. By period the unknown category is divided as follows: 1727-60, 4, (9%); 1760-90, 3 (10%); 1790-1820, 2 (7%); 1820-50, 2 (4%); 1850-75, 4, (7%).

to a single heir, 53% divided their property between heirs of the second generation, and 14% bequeathed their property to an heir of their own generation, most frequently their wives.[44] In their outlines, these results are similar to those of the judges appointed between 1850 and 1875, in which 39% favoured one heir, 36% divided their property equally, and 20% left the bulk of the estate to their wives. Another study of wealthholders in the mid-1920s found that there was a predominance of primogeniture among men worth over £200,000, while equal division was the rule among those with estates of between £10,000-£200,000,[45] the group into which a large majority of judges would have fallen.

The changes in settlement patterns, in the occupations followed by the judges' sons, and in the level of judicial investment in land, which first became apparent for those judges appointed during the years 1790-1820, indicates the depth of the social and professional transformation of the judiciary in the nineteenth century. Their behaviour had begun to diverge from that of the landed classes to whom they had formerly been closely allied. No longer was a professional career seen primarily as a means of realizing the social ideal of life as a country gentleman. On the contrary, the behaviour of the nineteenth-century judges and their families indicates that they had little interest in the founding of a great landed family. By rejecting strict settlement and by dividing their property among their heirs, these men consciously prevented the accumulation of real and personal property in the hands of one individual. In this way the nineteenth-century judges demonstrated that as a group they had little desire to join the ranks of the landed classes, and that they were well satisfied with their status as leading members of Britain's professional classes, a position which they had achieved through their success in the law.

[44]W.D. Rubinstein, 'Men of Property: some aspects of occupation, inheritance and power among top British wealthholders', in Philip Stanworth and Anthony Giddens *Elites and Power in British Society* (Cambridge, 1974), pp. 154-5.

[45]Josiah Wedgwood, *The Economics of Inheritance* (Harmondsworth edn, 1939), chapter IV.

7

PROFESSIONALIZATION AND THE LAW

With the advent of the social and administrative revolutions of the nineteenth century, the members of the English judiciary and bar found themselves in an ambiguous position. On the one hand, the status and traditions of their profession were firmly anchored in ancient and gentlemanly foundations: on the other, the law was an intensely competitive and laborious occupation. The resulting lack of consensus within the bar and bench over the question of professional reform reflected in miniature the outlines of a struggle also being waged in English society. While the specific version of professionalism arrived at by the judges and barristers was unique, the transformation of attitudes and institutions which it entailed provides an excellent illustration of the professionalization process in the eighteenth and nineteenth centuries.

Returning to an earlier description of that process, it will be recalled that three distinct elements were detailed: first, internal reforms which were largely concerned with training and examining new members; second, administrative professionalization, which regulated and reformed the structure of the profession and related institutions; and third, changes in the social composition and attitudes of professional men. While the primary emphasis will be placed on the last of the three elements, I preface that social analysis with a short summary of the progress of internal and administrative professionalization of the judiciary and the law between 1727 and 1875.[1]

During the nineteenth century, internal professionalization was accomplished by means of both voluntary and statutory reform. The institutional spokesmen of the bar, the Inns of Court, were disinclined to establish a system of lectures and examinations for prospective barristers despite the clamour for these in the profession and Parliament. Legal education was the subject of two parliamentary inquiries in 1846 and 1854, both of which pressed for far reaching reforms. Leading members of the profession including three future or sitting Lord Chancellors — Richard Bethell, Lord Hatherley, and Roundell Palmer — and one future Lord Chief Justice, John Duke Coleridge, actively supported proposals in Parliament to reform the educational functions of the Inns. A few tentative steps were taken in

---

[1] The following discussion of administrative and internal professionalization is taken largely from Holdsworth, *History of English Law*, XIII, XV, XVI; Abel-Smith and Stevens, *Lawyers and Courts*; Robert Stevens, 'The Final Appeal: Reform of the House of Lords and Privy Council 1867-1876', pp. 343-69.

the direction of reform in 1846 and 1852, but it was not until 1872, under the threat of parliamentary intervention, that obligatory lectures and examinations were introduced into the curriculum at the Inns of Court. By surrendering to the most moderate of the suggested reforms, the Inns staved off attempts by radical reformers within the profession to strip them of their role as the qualifying association of the bar, and to establish in their stead a comprehensive Legal University in London.

The bar was the last of the professions to introduce a mandatory examination system for candidates, trailing two years behind the home civil service and the army. The extreme reluctance of the bar to implement educational reform, while perhaps out of character in an age of professional reform, can be traced to the hierarchical organization of the profession, its high status, small size, political importance, and the antiquity of the Inns of Court themselves. These factors provided the profession with a unique ability to withstand demands for institutional rationalization. Of all the professional corporations and societies which pre-dated the rise of the new professionalism, only the Inns were able to retain their ancient constitutions and identities virtually intact.

The progress of the administrative professionalization of the judiciary, aspects of which have been described earlier, was much smoother than internal reform. The major achievements were the elimination of fees and sinecure offices, the establishment of all-inclusive salaries for judges as well as a pension system, and rationalization of the judicial machinery both on the national and local levels. Organized obstruction to reform ended in 1827 with Lord Eldon's retirement from the woolsack. In the following year Henry Brougham made his mammoth speech on law reform which initiated a series of parliamentary inquiries into the state of the judicial machinery in England. Supported by men who could best be described as 'second degree Benthamites' and led by Brougham, who in 1830 became Lord Chancellor, the reform movement eradicated instances of judicial amateurism and inefficiency throughout the British legal system.

Despite the success of these early reformers, a second generation of reformist lawyers had by the 1860s embarked on a campaign thoroughly to restructure and consolidate 'all Superior Courts of Law and Equity, together with the courts of Probate, Divorce, and Admiralty, into one Court, to be called 'Her Majesty's Supreme Court', in which Court shall be vested all the jurisdictions which are now exercisable by each and all the Courts so consolidated'.[2]

[2]Judicature Commission, 1st Report, PP. XXV, 1868-9, p. 17.

Standing at the head of this movement were Lords Cairns and Hatherley, John Duke Coleridge, Roundell Palmer, and Richard P. Collier. Almost all their stated objectives were achieved in the Judicature Acts of 1873 and 1875, which unified the previously divided jurisdictions, and established the Supreme Court consisting of a High Court and a Court of Appeal. However, administrative professionalization was prevented from reaching its logical conclusion, complete judicial centralization, when in 1875-6 a concerted effort by Conservative backbenchers in alliance with members of the bar defeated proposals to eliminate the House of Lords as a court of final appeal.

This episode marked the only successful attempt by members of the profession to block institutional reform. If administrative professionalization was not greeted with the active support of the legal rank and file, it does seem to have gained at least their acquiescence. This was true not only of the reform of the courts and judicial machinery but of financial reforms as well, which as had been clearly demonstrated, adversely affected the purses of leading members of the bar and bench.

In one sense, at least, the professionalization of judicial social structure and attitudes is the most difficult of the three elements to assess. There are no legislative initiatives, no administrative changes, and no speeches or tracts directed to the need and value of reform.

Since such traditional means of tracing the progress of institutional transformations are inapplicable, it would seem essential to construct a more impressionistic framework within which to interpret the data. For decades historians and sociologists have attempted to do just this, and there is no shortage of descriptions and definitions of the professions both as historical and modern entities. Despite the enormous quantity of literature on the professions, none of the existing definitions has been able to explain successfully the reformulation of the professional ideal and of the concept of professionalism which occurred between the middle of the eighteenth century and the 1870s. As a result, the existing descriptions can hardly serve as an explanatory framework for an analysis of the social and attitudinal professionalization of the judiciary.

In order to remedy this situation, I have endeavoured to define the professionalization process within an historical context and to distinguish between the ideology of the professions and their actual structure. The categories incorporated into this description have been derived from historical, literary, and sociological sources.[3] Perhaps

[3] A.M. Carr-Saunders, P.A. Wilson, *The Professions* (London, 1933), *passim;* Reader, *Professional Men, passim;* N.D. Jewson, 'Medical Knowledge and the

the best known of this literature are the sociological 'trait' definitions of the professions[4] which have recently come under severe criticism for 'accepting the professionals' own definitions of themselves. There are many similarities between the "core elements" as perceived by the sociologists and the preambles to and contents of professional codes'.[5] Clearly the value of the 'trait' definitions is limited as objective descriptions of the professions. However, if the 'traits' do in fact represent 'the professionals' own definitions of themselves', then they can provide us with an insider's view of the values, beliefs, and occupational and social attitudes of leading members of the professional community.[6] The analysis of the actual structure of the professions, which will I hope act as a counter-balance to the ideological descriptions, has been derived from both historical and sociological studies.

An attempt has been made in Table 19 to provide a balanced description of the progress of professionalization in the eighteenth and nineteenth centuries. The fourteen selected characteristics represent no more than a composite picture of the pace of professionalization between 1750 and 1870. No single profession conforms exactly to the descriptions, each one having developed at its own speed and in its own direction. Despite certain structural and historical similarities in

Patronage System in Eighteenth Century England', *Sociology* 8 (1974), 369-85; C.B. Otley, 'The Social Origins of British Army Officers', *Sociological Review* 18 (1970), 213-38; Michael Lewis, *A Social History of the Navy 1713-1815* (London, 1960), *passim;* Michael Lewis, *The Navy in Transition* (London, 1965), *passim;* W.H.G. Armytage, *A Social History of Engineering* (London, 1966), *passim;* R. Robson, *The Attorney in Eighteenth Century England, passim;* C.E. Newman, *The Evolution of Medical Education in the Nineteenth Century* (London, 1957), *passim;* George Clark and A.M. Cooke, *A History of the Royal College of Physicians,* 3 vols., Oxford,1964-72), *passim;* Geoffrey Millerson, *The Qualifying Associations: A Study of Professionalization* (London, 1964), *passim;* William Goode, 'Community within a Community: The Professions', *American Sociological Review* 22 (1957), 194-200; Philip Elliott *The Sociology of Professions* (London, 1972), *passim;* D.J. Hickson and M.W. Thomas, 'Professionalization in Britain: A Preliminary Measurement', *Sociology* 3 (1969), 37-53; T.H. Marshall, 'The Recent History of Professionalism in Relation to Social Structure and social Policy', *Canadian journal of Economics and Political Science* 5 (1939), 325-40; J. and N. Parry, *The Rise of the Medical Profession,* (London, 1976), *passim.*

[4]Among the most important formulations of the 'trait' definitions of the professions are E. Greenwood, 'Attributes of Profession', *Social Work* 2 (1957), 44-55; Morris L. Cogan, 'Toward a Definition of Profession', *Harvard Educational Review* 23 (1953), 33-50. William Goode, *Explorations in Social Theory* (New York, 1973), pp. 354-55.

[5]Terence J. Johnson, *Professions and Power* (London, 1972), p. 25. See also Julius A. Roth, 'Professionalism — The Sociologist's Decoy', *Sociology of Work and Occupations* 1 (1974), 17.

[6]For a detailed discussion of the nineteenth-century professional ideology see Daniel Duman, 'The Creation and Diffusion of the Professional Ideology in Nineteenth Century England', *Sociological Review* 27 (1979), 113-38.

those occupations known as professions, each one was unique, and their multifarious natures must not be overlooked in an attempt to discover common characteristics and patterns of development. With these limitations in mind, we can now turn to a comparison between the restructuring of the judiciary between 1727 and 1875 and the general progress of professionalization in the eighteenth and nineteenth centuries.

The English bar has long inhabited an intermediate position between the high status gentlemanly professions and the lower status competitive ones. It was characterized, as we have seen repeatedly, by both high status and severe competition. With the rapid increase in the number of prospective barristers beginning in the late eighteenth century, the social composition of the profession began to change. This process was precipitated by the limited value of social and political patronage in advancing a man at the bar. Clients naturally eschewed barristers who were not of proven ability, regardless of their social origins or connections. This emphasis on skill was probably accentuated by the convention that attorneys employed barristers on behalf of their clients. Not only were the attorneys better acquainted with the reputations of the members of the bar than were laymen, but the success or failure of an advocate reflected on the attorney who selected him.

As a consequence of these special conditions, the bar was atypical of the eighteenth-century gentlemanly professions. Early in its development the bar had adopted a client-professional system. This uniqueness was also reflected in the social composition of the bar and bench, which was apparent even in the last quarter of the eighteenth century. In the *Wealth of Nations,* Adam Smith asked rhetorically: 'In England, success in the profession of the law leads to some very great objects of ambition; yet how many men, born to easy fortunes, have ever in this country been eminent in that profession?'[7] While it is not within the scope of this study to answer Smith, an analysis of the social origins of the judiciary offers indirect confirmation of his impressions. Few judges, even those appointed as early as the period 1727 to 1760, could claim direct descent from the territorial nobility. While a few were younger sons of wealthy members of the gentry, the typical judge of landed origins descended from a middling or small gentry family, with at most one or two thousand acres. Towards the end of the eighteenth century, even these limited connections with the landed classes began to disappear as the social origins of the judges became increasingly dominated by the urban middle classes, especially by professional men.

[7]Adam Smith, *The Wealth of Nations,* p. 717.

**Table 19: Professional ideology and structure
in eighteenth- and nineteenth-century England**

		Eighteenth Century	Nineteenth Century
		IDEOLOGY	
1.	Occupational ideal	Gentlemanly life.	Service to society.
2.	Self image	Gentleman who earns his living from an honourable occupation.	Skilled practitioner with high moral and social status.
3.	Attitude toward the professions	Occupations from which practitioners derive superior status, maximum leisure.	Strenuous occupations of superior moral orientation, which ensure ethical behaviour of members and provide them with respectable incomes.
4.	Educational ideal	Classical 'gentlemanly' education.	Intensive training and examinations in professional knowledge and principles after general education.
5.	Criteria for membership	Restricted to gentlemen.	Open to talent regardless of social origins.
6.	Basis for advancement	Professional and social suitability.	Professional success determined through open competition.
7.	Discipline of members	By professional institutions only.	By professional institutions only.

Table 19 (continued)

8.	Ultimate goal	Acceptance by or entry into landed society.	To rise to the head of one's profession and the receipt of professional honours and offices.

STRUCTURE

1.	Basis of professional relationships	Patron-Professional.	Professional-Client.
2.	Character of professional knowledge	Traditional, non-innovative.	Increasingly receptive to new advances, discoveries, and theories.
3.	Educational structure	General education; formal or informal apprenticeship.	General education, professional education and examinations; apprenticeship.
4.	Social origins	Land, professions — socially exclusive.	Professions, business, land — socially exclusive.
5.	Determinants of success	Connections, favour, wealth, ability.	Professional achievement (dominant), connections, wealth.
6.	Control of professional discipline	Closed and established professional hierarchy.	Professional associations, and governmental boards and agencies.

The slow severing of social and occupational connections with the landed classes, which was due, at least in part, to the rise of industrial society, finds a corresponding expression in the changes in the attitudes and ideals of the judges. While they continued to see themselves as gentlemen, based on evidence of life style and family structure, the members of the judiciary no longer associated that status with a need to assimilate the style and values of the landed gentry. While even in the mid-nineteenth century a few judges in each generation established landed and even titled families, the ideal of life as a country gentleman seems to have lost its glamour and prestige in their eyes increasingly after 1820.

In 1835 Tocqueville wrote that English barristers

> constitute, as it were, the younger branch of the English aristocracy; and they are attached to their elder brothers, although they do not enjoy all their privileges. The English lawyers consequently mingle the aristocratic tastes and ideas of the circles in which they move with the aristocratic interests of their profession.[8]

While this may have been an accurate description of the bar and bench in the eighteenth century, the evidence on judicial investment patterns, property settlements, and the occupational choices of the judges' sons indicate that it was far off the mark by the time de Tocqueville wrote these words.

Thus far the progress of the social and ideological professionalization of the judiciary has been sketched in very broad lines. However, it is possible, by utilizing some of the data presented earlier, to refine our description through the introduction of a more precise dating of some of the more important indicators of professionalization. For this purpose four sets of data have been chosen, namely those on the social origins of the judges, the length of their pre-judicial careers and their ages at the time of appointment to the bench, the occupational choices of their sons, and the settlement patterns found in their wills.

The first of the indicators, the social origins of the judges, began to show a significant shift from the landed to the professional classes among the members of the cohort appointed to the bench between 1760 and 1790. The vast majority of the men in this group registered their desire to become barristers by enrolling in one of the Inns of Court during the years 1735 to 1760. Since the industrial revolution had hardly begun by then, even according to the earliest chronologies, it does not seem likely that the initial decline in the landed contingent

---

[8]Tocqueville, *Democracy in America,* I, 287-8.

on the bench can be interpreted as a direct consequence of industrialization or related economic or social developments. The process
probably began as a response to competitive pressures in the
profession which discouraged very well connected men from pursuing
a career as a practising barrister. However, once the movement of the
landed classes away from the law had begun, it may well have been
intensified during the late eighteenth and early nineteenth centuries by
social, economic, and professional changes which followed in the
wake of industrialization.

The lengthening of pre-judicial careers and the consequent rise in
the age of judicial appointment first becomes evident among the
cohorts appointed between 1790 and 1820. This generation was
called to the bar between 1760 and 1790. By and large their careers
coincided with the opening years of the industrial revolution, the
French wars, and a period of expansion in the number of professional
offices and honours open to members of the bar. The increase in legal
business during this period, as a result of industrialization and the
intensification of competition for the lucrative places at the bar, which
undoubtedly occurred during these years, were primary factors
which encouraged the extension of pre-judicial careers. In addition,
the general rise in incomes at the bar at this time may have meant that
men who worked for years building lucrative practices were unwilling
to abandon the bar during the height of their powers and earning
capacity, for financially secure, but poorly remunerated junior
judicial posts.

Professionalization of the occupational choices of the judges' sons
also begins with those judges appointed in the years 1790 to 1820.
The sons were probably choosing their careers at about the same
time as their fathers were assuming their judicial responsibilities. The
sons were members of the first generation of Englishmen who had
lived their entire lives in an industrializing society. Their emphatic
choice of the professions and especially the law as occupational
objectives and the dramatic fall in the number who entered the world of
the country gentleman, compared to the previous generation, is ample
evidence of a momentous social and economic transformation. More
than anything else it may have represented a change in attitudes
among the judges and their families. As suggested earlier, there
seems to be evidence that during the first third of the nineteenth
century a new self-confidence appeared among the judiciary and
perhaps in the professional community at large. This is reflected in the
nineteenth-century professional ideology which stressed service over
status and which rejected the primary eighteenth-century goal of
establishing a landed family.

Without doubt a parallel development can be seen in the investment patterns of the judges after 1820. These men consciously turned away from landed investments, thereby diminishing the likelihood that their eldest sons would be landed gentlemen. This profound alteration in social values and expectations is also expressed in the settlement patterns found in the judges' wills. The abjuration of allegiance to the standards of landed society becomes complete with the rejection of primogeniture. While this change is difficult to date with any precision, it had become significant by the years 1820-50. With the weakening of the connection between the bar and bench and the landed classes, the judges began to discard those behaviour patterns which they had derived from their landed associations. The development of an independent course by the members of the judiciary was not unique to the legal profession. This was a movement in which the judges were pioneers but others were soon to follow. The professionalization of social origins and perhaps of ideology as well appeared first in the law, of all the gentlemanly professions, because it was also the most competitive. By the 1870s, even the staunchest professional bastions of the old values had fallen, and a new professional ideology served as an occupational declaration of independence.

The pace of reform and modernization in the years between 1727 and 1875 was erratic, and there was by no means a total commitment by the legal profession to its ultimate success. The leadership role of the judiciary and the bar in both social and ideological professionalization was in sharp contrast to mere acquiescence in administrative rationalization and their downright hostility to internal and educational reform. The reform process was not complete, and critics to this day continue to castigate the profession for its resistance to radical change. Nevertheless, the members of the eighteenth- and nineteenth-century judiciary played a leading role in the professionalization of the law and its institutions according to the new definitions and requirements of the first industrial society.

APPENDIX

The Judges of England 1727-1875

ABBREVIATIONS

Adm.	=	High Court of Admiralty
B.	=	Baron of the Exchequer
C.J. (C.B.)	=	Chief Justice (Baron)
C.P.	=	Court of Common Pleas
Div. and Mat.	=	Court for Divorce and Matrimonial Cases
D. Arches	=	Dean of the Arches
J.	=	Puisne Judge
K.B. (Q.B.)	=	Court of King's (Queen's) Bench
L.A.	=	Lord of Appeal
L.C.	=	Lord Chancellor
L.J.	=	Lord Justice of Appeal
M.R.	=	Master of the Rolls
P.C.C.	=	Prerogative Court of Canterbury
Prob.	=	Court of Probate
P.D.A.	=	Probate, Divorce and Admiralty Division
V.C.	=	Vice-Chancellor

The following list contains the names of all 208 judges included in this study. In several cases, initial appointments to the bench pre-dated 1727 but these judges were translated to another judicial position after the accession of George II; these instances are indicated with (   ). Those judges who were re-appointed to previously held posts at the accession of George II are not included. Two judges (Lords Campbell and St. Leonards), who served as Lord Chancellor of Ireland before their appointments to the English bench, were grouped according to their earlier (Irish) appointment.

James Baron Abinger (Scarlett), C.B. 1834-44.
Thomas Abney, B. 1740-43, J.C.P. 1743-50
Richard Adams, B. 1753-75
Edward Hall Alderson, J.C.P. 1830-34, B. 1834-57

William Alexander, C.B. 1824-1830

Richard Baron Alvanley (Arden), M.R. 1788-1801, C.J.C.P. 1801-04

Richard Paul Amphlett, B. 1874-76, L.J. 1876-77

Thomas Dickson Archibald, J.Q.B. 1872-75, J.C.P. 1875-76

William Henry Ashurst, J.K.B. 1770-99

Richard Aston, C.J.C.P. (Ireland) 1761-65, J.K.B. 1765-78

John Tracy Atkyns, Cursitor B. 1755-73

James Bacon, V.C. 1870-86

George Bankes, Cursitor B. 1824-56

Edward Barker, Cursitor B. 1744-55

Henry Earl Bathurst, J.C.P. 1754-71, L.C. 1771-78

John Bayley, J.K.B. 1808-30, B. 1830-34

John Birch, Cursitor B. 1729-35

Colin Baron Blackburn, J.K.B. 1859-76, L.A. 1876-86

William Blackstone, J.C.P. 1770 J.K.B. 1770 J.C.P. 1770-80

William Bolland, B. 1829-39

John B. Bosanquet, J.C.P. 1830-42

William Bovill, C.J.C.P. 1866-73

George William Baron Bramwell, B. 1856-76, L.J. 1876-81

Henry Baron Brougham and Vaux, L .C. 1830-34

Francis Buller, J.K.B. 1778-94, J.C.P. 1794-1800

John Burland, B. 1774-76

Thomas Burnet, J.C.P. 1741-53

James Burrough, J.C.P. 1816-29

John Bernard Byles, J.C.P. 1858-73

Hugh McCalmont Earl Cairns, L.J. 1866-68, L.C. 1868, 1874-80

Peter Calvert, D. Arches and J.P.C.C. 1778-88

Charles Earl Camden (Pratt), C.J.C.P. 1761-66, L.C. 1766-70

John Baron Campbell, L.C. (Ireland) 1841, C.J.Q.B. 1850-59, L.C. 1859-61

Alan Chambre, B. 1799-1800, J.C.P. 1800-15

William Fry Channel, B. 1857-73

William Chappel, J.K.B. 1737-45

Frederich Baron Chelmsford (Thesiger), L.C. 1858-59, 1866-68

Charles Clarke, B. 1743-50

Thomas Clarke, M.R. 1754-64

Anthony Cleasby, B. 1868-78

Edward Clive, B. 1745-53, J.C.P. 1753-70

George Clive, Cursitor B. 1735-39

Alexander James Edward Cockburn, C.J.C.P. 1856-59, C.J.Q.B. 1859-80

John Duke Baron Coleridge, C.J.C.P. 1873-80, C.J.Q.B. 1880-94

John Taylor Coleridge, J.K.B. 1835-58

Thomas Coltman, J.C.P. 1837-49

John Comyns, (B. 1726-36), J.C.P. 1736-38, C.B. 1738-40

Charles C. Baron Cottenham (Pepys), M.R. 1834-36, L.C. 1836-41, 1846-50

Spencer Cowper, J.C.P. 1727-28

Robert Monsey Baron Cranworth (Rolfe), B. 1839-50, V.C. 1850-51, L.J. 1851-52, L.C. 1852-58, 1865-66

Cresswell Cresswell, J.C.P. 1842-58, J.C. Prob. and J. Div. and Mat. 1858-63.

Charles John Crompton, J.Q.B. 1852-65

Richard Budden Crowder, J.C.P. 1854-59

Robert Dallas, J.C.P. 1813-18, C.J.C.P. 1818-23

Henry Dampier, J.K.B. 1813-16

Thomas Denison, J.K.P. 1741-65

George Denman, J.C.P. 1872-81, J.Q.B. 1881-92

Thomas Baron Denman, C.J.K.B. 1832-50

John Dodson, D. Arches and J.P.C.C. 1852-57

John Earl of Eldon (Scott), C.J.C.P. 1799-1801, L.C. 1801-06, 1807-27

Edward Baron Ellenborough (Law), C.J.K.B. 1802-18

William Erle, J.C.P. 1844-46, J.Q.B. 1846-59, C.J.C.P. 1859-66

Thomas Baron Erskine, L.C. 1806-07

Thomas Erskine Jr., J.C.P. 1839-44

William Baliol Viscount Esher (Brett), J.C.P. 1868-76, L.J. 1876-83, M.R. 1883-97

James Eyre, B. 1772-87, C.B. 1787-93, C.J.C.P. 1793-99

William Ventris Baron Field, J.Q.B. 1875-90

John Baron Fortescue (Aland), (B. 1717-18, J.K.B. 1718-27), J.C.P. 1729-47

William Fortescue, B. 1736-38, J.C.P. 1738-41, M.R. 1741-49

Michael Foster, J.K.B. 1745-63

William Garrow, B. 1817-32

Stephen Gaselee, J.C.P. 1824-37

Vicary Gibbs, J.C.P. 1812-13, C.B. 1813-14, C.J.C.P. 1814-18

George Markham Giffard, V.C. 1868-69, L.J. 1869-70

Robert Baron Gifford, C.J.C.P. 1824, M.R. 1824-26

Henry Gould, B. 1761-63, J.C.P. 1763-94

Robert Graham, B. 1800-1827

William Grant, M.R. 1801-17

Nash Grose, J.K.B. 1787-1813

William Robert Grove, J.C.P. 1871-80, J.Q.B. 1880-87

Nathaniel Gundry, J.C.P. 1750-54

John Gurney, B. 1832-45

Charles Hall, V.C. 1873-83

James Baron Hannen, J.Q.B. 1868-72, J. Div. and Mat. and J. Prob. 1872-75, President P.D.A. 1875-91, L.A. 1891-94

Philip Earl of Hardwicke (Yorke), C.J.K.B. 1733-37, L.C. 1837-56

Anthony Hart, V.C. 1827, L.C. (Ireland) 1827-30

William Page Baron Hatherley (Wood), V.C. 1852-68, L.J. 1868, L.C. 1868-72

George Hay, D. Arches and J.P.C.C. 1764-78

George Hayes, J.Q.B. 1868-69

John Heath, J.C.P. 1780-1816

Hugh Hill, J.Q.B. 1858-61

George S. Holroyd, J.K.B. 1816-28

George Essex Honyman, J.C.P. 1873-75

Beaumont Baron Hotham, B. 1775-1805

John W. Huddleston, J.C.P. 1875, B. 1875-81, J.Q.B. 1881-90

John Hullock, B. 1823-29

William Milbourne James, V.C. 1869-70, L.J. 1870-81

Herbert Jenner-Fust, D. Arches and J.P.C.C. 1834-52

John Jervis, C.J.C.P. 1850-56

George Jessel, M.R. 1873-83

Henry Singer Keating, J.C.P. 1859-75

Fitzroy Kelly, C.B. 1866-80

Lloyd Baron Kenyon, M.R. 1784-88, C.J.K.B. 1788-1802

Richard Torn Kindersley, V.C. 1851-66

James Lewis Knight-Bruce, V.C. 1841-51, L.J. 1851-66

Henry Baron Langdale (Bickersteth), M.R. 1836-51

Soulden Lawrence, J.C.P. 1794, J.K.B. 1794-1808, J.C.P. 1808-12

John Leach, V.C. 1818-27, M.R. 1827-34

Simon Le Blanc, J.K.B. 1799-1816

George Lee, D. Arches and J.P.C.C. 1751-58

William Lee, J.K.B. 1720-37, C.J.K.B. 1737-54

Heneage Legge, B. 1747-59

James Viscount Lifford (Hewitt), J.K.B. 1766-68, L.C. (Ireland) 1768-89

Nathaniel Baron Lindley, J.C.P. 1875-81, L.J. 1881-97, M.R. 1897-1900, L.A. 1900-05

Joseph Littledale, J.K.B. 1824-41

Richard Lloyd, B. 1759-61

Robert Lush, J.Q.B. 1865-80, L.J. 1880-81

Stephen Lushington, J. Adm. 1838-67, D. Arches 1858-67

John Baron Lyndhurst (Copley), M.R. 1826-27, L.C. 1827-30, 1834-35, C.B. 1830-34

Archibald MacDonald, C.B. 1793-1813

Richard Malins, V.C. 1866-1881

Thomas Baron Manners (Manners-Sutton), B. 1805-07, L.C. (Ireland) 1807-27

James Mansfield, C.J.C.P. 1804-1814

William Earl of Mansfield (Murray), C.J.K.B. 1754-98

James Marriott, J.C. of Adm. 1778-88

Samuel Martin, B. 1850-74

Francis Maseres, Cursitor B. 1773-1824

William Henry Maule, B. 1839, J.C.P. 1839-55

George Mellish, L.J. 1870-77

John Mellor, J.Q.B. 1861-79

Robert Baron Monkswell (Collier), J.C.P. 1871, Paid Member Judicial Committee of the Privy Council 1871-86

George Nares, J.C.P. 1771-86

John Nicholl, D. Arches and J.P.C.C. 1809-34, J. Adm. 1833-38

William Noel, J.C.P. 1757-62

Robert Earl of Northington (Henley), Lord Keeper 1757-61, L.C. 1761-66

Francis Page, (B. 1718-26, J.C.P. 1726-27), J.K.B. 1727-41

James Alan Park, J.C.P. 1816-38

James Parker, V.C. 1851-52

Thomas Parker, B. 1738-40, J.C.P. 1740-42, C.B. 1742-72

John Patteson, J.K.B. 1830-52

James Plaisted Baron Penzance (Wilde), B. 1860-63, J. Div. and Mat. and J. Prob. 1863-72

George Perrot, B. 1763-75

Richard Perryn, B. 1776-99

Robert Joseph Phillimore, D. Arches and J. Adm. 1867-75, J.P.D.A. 1875-83

Gillery Pigott, B. 1863-75

Thomas Joshua Platt, B. 1845-56

Thomas Plumer, V.C. 1813-18, M.R. 1818-24

Charles Edward Pollock, B. 1873-81, J.Q.B. 1881-97

(Jonathan) Frederick Pollock, C.B. 1844-66

Edmund Probyn, (J.K.B. 1724-40), C.B. 1740-42

John Richard Quain, J.Q.B. 1871-76

Thomas Reeve, J.C.P. 1733-36, C.J.C.P. 1736-37

James Reynolds, (J.K.B. 1725-30), C.B. 1730-38

James Reynolds, C.J.C.P. (Ireland) 1727-40, B. 1740-47

Richard Richards, B. 1814-17, C.B. 1817-24

John Richardson, J.C.P. 1818-24
Christopher Robinson, J. Adm. 1828-33
John Rolt, L.J. 1867-68
John Baron Romilly, M.R. 1851-73
Giles Rook, J.C.P. 1793-1808
Alexander Earl of Rosslyn (Wedderburn), C.J.C.P. 1780-93, L.C.
    1793-1801
Dudley Ryder, C.J.K.B. 1754-56
Edward Baron St. Leonards (Sugden), L.C. (Ireland), 1834-5,
    1841-46, L.C. 1852
Thomas Salusbury, J. Adm. 1751-73
Roundell Earl of Selbourne (Palmer), L.C. 1872-74, 1880-86
Charles Jasper Selwyn, L.J. 1868-69
Thomas Sewell, M.R. 1764-84
Lancelot Shadwell, V.C. 1827-50
William Shee, J.Q.B. 1863-68
Edward Simpson, D. Arches and J.P.C.C. 1758-64
John Skynner, C.B. 1777-1787
Montague Edward Smith, J.C.P. 1865-71
Sydney Stafford Smyth, B. 1750-72; C.B. 1772-77
William Baron Stowell (Scott), J. Adm. 1798-1828
John Strange, M.R. 1750-54
John Stuart, V.C. 1852-71
Charles Baron Talbot, L.C. 1733-37
Thomas Talfourd, J.C.P. 1849-54
William E. Taunton, J.K.B. 1830-35
Charles Baron Tenterden (Abbott), J.C.P. 1816, J.K.B.
    1816-18, C.J.K.B. 1818-32
Alexander Thomson, B. 1787-1814, C.B. 1814-17
William Thom(p)son, (Cursitor B. 1726-29), B. 1729-39
Edward Baron Thurlow, L.C. 1778-83, 1783-92
Nicholas C. Tindal, C.J.C.P. 1829-46
Thomas Baron Truro (Wilde), C.J.C.P. 1846-50, L.C. 1850-52
George James Turner, V.C. 1851-53, L.J. 1853-67
John Vaughan, B. 1827-34, J.C.P. 1834-39
John Verney, M.R. 1738-41
William Baron Walsingham (De Grey), C.J.C.P. 1771-80
William Henry Watson, B. 1856-60
James Baron Wensleydale (Parke), J.K.B. 1828-34, B. 1834-55
Richard Baron Westbury (Bethell), L.C. 1861-65
John Wickens, V.C. 1871-73
William Wightman, J.Q.B. 1841-63
James Wigram, V.C. 1841-50
Edward Willes, J.K.B. 1768-87

James Shaw Willes, J.C.P. 1855-72
John Willes, C.J.C.P. 1737-61
Edward Vaughan Williams, J.C.P. 1846-65
John Williams, B. 1834, J.K.B. 1834-46
John Eardley Wilmot, J.K.B. 1755-66, C.J.C.P. 1766-71
John Wilson, J.C.P. 1786-93
George Wood, B. 1807-23
Martin Wright, B. 1739-40, J.K.B. 1740-55
William Baron Wynford (Best), J.K.B. 1818-24, C.J.C.P. 1824-
  29
William Wynne, D. Arches and J.P.C.C. 1788-1809
Joseph Yates, J.K.B. 1764-70, J.C.P. 1770
Charles Yorke, L.C. 1770

BIBLIOGRAPHY

I. Manuscripts

Bathurst MSS, British Library, Loan 57

Ridley (Blagdon) MSS, Northumberland County Record Office, papers relating to James Parke, Lord Wensleydale. By courtesy of the Rt. Hon. Viscount Ridley TD DL.

Brougham MSS, D.M.S. Watson Library, University College, University of London

Caerynwch MSS, Merioneth County Record Office, papers of Sir Richard Richards

Cairns MSS, Public Record Office, PRO 30/51

Camden MSS, Kent County Record Office, U 840

Clarke MSS, Public Record Office, PRO 30/26

Coleridge MSS, Bodleian Library, Oxford University

Ellenborough MSS, Public Record Office, PRO 30/12

Erle MSS Letters, Bodleian Library, Oxford University

Hardwicke MSS, British Library, Additional MSS 35,349-36,278

Kenyon MSS, Gredington, Shrophire. By courtesy of the Rt. Hon. Lord Kenyon DL.

Lee MSS, Buckingham Record Office

Lyndhurst MSS, Trinity College Library, Cambridge University

Mansfield Account Book, Kenwood House, London, by courtesy of the Iveagh Bequest

Monk Bretton MSS, Bodleian Library, Oxford University. By courtesy of the Rt. Hon. Lord Monk Bretton

Merthyr Mawr Collection, Merthyr Mawr House, Glamorganshire, the papers of Sir John Nicholl, by courtesy of Mr. and Mrs. M.A. McLaggan

Pollock Family MSS, Cambridge University Library

Talfourd Diaries, Berkshire County Library

Walsingham MSS, Norfolk County Record Office

Wills and Probate Acts, Public Record Office, PROB 11 and PROB 8

Wills and Registers, Somerset House

II. Printed Primary Sources

Aspinall, Arthur, *The Formation of the Canning Ministry, February-August 1827,* Camden Society 3rd series, LIX, London: 1937
The Letters of King George IV, 1812-1830. 3 vols. Cambridge: 1938

Bagehot, Walter, 'Good Lawyers and Bad', *The Life and Works of Walter Bagehot.* ed. Mrs. Walter Barrington, London: 1915

Blackstone, William, *Commentaries on the Laws of England.* 4 vols. Oxford: 1765-9
A Discourse on the Study of the Law, Being an Introductory Lecture Read in the Public Schools, October 25, 1758. Oxford: 1758

Brougham, Henry, Lord, *The Life and Times of Henry Lord Brougham.* 3 vols. London: 1871

Campbell, John, Lord, *Life of John, Lord Campbell.* 2 vols. ed. Hon. Mrs. Hardcastle, London: 1881

Coleridge, Bernard, Lord, *This for Remembrance* (extracts from the Diary of Sir John Taylor Coleridge). London: 1925

Correspondence of William Pitt, Earl of Chatham. 4 vols. London: 1840

Correspondence of George III. 6 vols. ed. Sir John Fortescue, London: 1927-8

Croker, John Wilson. *Correspondence and Diaries.* 3 vols. ed. Louis J. Jennings, London: 1884

Dickens, Charles, *Bleak House.* Harmondsworth edn: 1972.
The Posthumous Papers of the Pickwick Club. Harmondsworth edn: 1972.

Forsyth, William, *Hortensius: or, The Advocate.* London: 1849

Gilbert, W.S. and Sullivan, Arthur, *The Complete Plays of Gilbert and Sullivan.* Garden City: 1941

Hortensius, *Deinology or, the Union of Reason and Elegance being instructions to a Young Barrister.* London: 1801

The Memoirs of the Right Honourable Sir John Rolt 1804-1871. London: 1939

Palmer, Roundell, Earl of Selbourne, *Memorials Family and Personal 1766-1865,* and *Memorials Personal and Political 1865-1895.* London: 1896-8

Smith, Adam, *An Inquiry into the Nature and Causes of the Wealth of Nations.* New York: 1937

Smollett, Tobias, *The Expedition of Humphry Clinker.* Harmondsworth edn: 1971

Stephen, Fitzjames, 'The Morality of Advocacy', *Cornhill Magazine* 3 (April 1861). 447-59

Talfourd, Thomas N., 'On the Profession of the Bar', *London Magazine and Review* n.s. I (March 1825), 323-38

Thackeray, William, *The History of Pendennis.* Harmondsworth edn: 1972

Tocqueville, Alexis de, *Democracy in America,* New York edn: 2 vols. 1954

Wilmot, John Eardley, *Memoirs of the Life of the Right Honourable Sir John Eardley Wilmot Knt.* London: 1811

The Works of Jeremy Bentham, ed. J. Bowring, 11 vols. Edinburgh: 1838-42.

Young, Arthur. *Annals of Agriculture*, XXIX. London: 1797

III. Academic, Professional, and Political Directories

Bateman, John, *The Great Landowners of Great Britain and Ireland.* Leicester: 1971

Foss, Edward, *Biographia Juridica.* London: 1870
  The Judges of England. 10 vols. London: 1864

Foster, Joseph, *Alumni Oxonienses 1500-1714.* 4 vols. Oxford: 1891-2
  Alumni Oxonienses 1714-1886. 4 vols. Oxford: 1887
  Men-at-the-Bar. London: 1885
  Register of Admissions to Gray's Inn, 1521-1889. London: 1889

History of Parliament, The House of Commons 1715-1754. 2 vols. London: 1970

History of Parliament, The House of Commons 1754-1790. 3 vols. London: 1964

Ingpen, A.R., *The Middle Temple Bench Book.* London: 1912

Inner Temple, *Masters of the Bench of the Honourable Society of the Inner Temple, 1450-1883 and Masters of the Temple 1540-1883.* London: 1883
  Supplement to Masters of the Bench 1883-1900 to which is appended a List of Treasurers, 1505-1901. London: 1901

Judd, Gerrit P., *Members of Parliament 1734-1832.* New Haven: 1955

Lincoln's Inn, *The Records of the Honourable Society of Lincoln's Inn, Admissions Register 1420-1893.* 2 vols. London: 1896

Sturgess, H.A.C., *Register of Admissions to the Honourable Society of the Middle Temple.* 3 vols. London: 1949

Venn, J.A. and John, *Alumni Cantabrigenses.* 10 vols. Cambridge: 1922-27

Whishaw, James, *A Synopsis of the Members of the English bar.* London: 1835

IV. Parliamentary Papers

Commission on Delay of Suits in the High Court of Chancery, First Report, (1811)

Patronage of the Lord Chief Justice & c, LXXVI (1881)

Return of the Owners of Land 1872-1873, Parts I-IV (England, Wales, Scotland, and Ireland), LXXII (1874), and LXXX (1876)

Return of the Salaries and Emoluments in 1790 of the Judges of the Several Courts in England, Ireland, and Scotland, XXXIII (1850)

Report of the Select Committee on Legal Education, X (1846)

Report of the Select Committee on Official Salaries, XV (1850)

Report of the Select Committee on Sinecure Offices, X (1810)

Report of the Select Committee on Sinecure Offices, VI (1834)

Report on Judges' Salaries, XXXIII (1850)

V. Unpublished Secondary Sources

Berlanstein, Lenard, 'The Advocates of Toulouse in the Eighteenth Century, 1750-1799'. Unpublished Ph.D. dissertation, Johns Hopkins University, 1973

Ives, Eric William, 'Some Aspects of the Legal Profession in the Fifteenth and Sixteenth Centuries'. Unpublished Ph.D. thesis, University of London, 1955

Newdick, Robert S., 'Sir Thomas Talfourd D.C.L.'. Unpublished manuscript deposited in the Reading (England) Public Library

Peterson, Mildred Jeanne, 'Kinship, Status, and Social Mobility in the Mid-Victorian Medical Profession'. Unpublished Ph.D. dissertation, University of California, Berkeley, 1972

VI. Secondary Sources – General and Biography

Abel-Smith, Brian and Stevens, Robert, *Lawyers and the Courts: A Sociological Study of the English Legal System 1750-1965.* London: 1970

Archer, Peter, *The Queen's Courts.* Harmondsworth: 1963

Armytage, W.G.H, *A Social History of Engineering.* London: 1966

Arnould, J., *A Memoir of Thomas, First Lord Denman.* 2 vols. London: 1873

Aspinall, Arthur, *Lord Brougham and the Whig Party.* Manchester: 1927

Atlay, J.B., *The Victorian Chancellors.* 2 vols. London: 1906

Bamford, T.W., *Rise of the Public Schools.* London: 1967

Baker, J.H., 'Counsellors and Barristers — An Historical Study', *Cambridge Law Journal* 28 (1969), 205-29

Banks, J.A., *Prosperity and Parenthood.* London: 1954

Best, Geoffrey, *Mid-Victorian Britain 1851-1875.* St. Albans: 1973

Bolton, W.W., *Conduct and Etiquette at the Bar.* 5th edn. London: 1971

Brooke, John, *The House of Commons 1754-1790: Introductory Survey*. Oxford: 1968

Briggs, Asa, *The Making of Modern England, 1783-1867*. New York: 1965

Brown, Peter, *The Chathamites, A Study in the Relationship between Personalities and Ideas in the Second Half of the Eighteenth Century*. New York: 1967

Bryson, W.H., *The Equity Side of Exchequer*. Cambridge: 1975

Campbell, John, *Lives of the Lord Chancellors and Keepers of the Great Seal of England*. 10 vols., 5th edn. London: 1868
Lives of the Lord Chief Justices. London: 1857

Carr-Saunders, A.M. and Wilson, P.A., *The Professions*. Oxford: 1933

Cecil, Henry, *The English Judge*. London: 1972

Chambers, J.D. and Mingay G.E., *The Agricultural Revolution 1750-1880*. London: 1966

Clark, George and Cooke, A.M., *A History of the Royal College of Physicians*. 3 vols. Oxford: 1964-72

Cock, Raymond, 'The Bar at the Assizes', *Kingston Law Review*, 6, (Spring, 1976), pp. 36-52

Cogan, Morris L. 'Toward a Definition of Profession', *Harvard Educational Review*, 23, (Winter, 1953), pp. 33-50

Coleridge, Bernard J.S., *The Story of a Devonshire House*. London: 1905

Coleridge, Ernest H., *Life and Correspondence of John Duke Lord Coleridge, Lord Chief Justice of England*. London: 1904

Coote, Charles, *Sketches of the Lives and Characters of Eminent English Civilians*. London: 1804

Cottu, M., *On the Administration of Criminal Justice in England and the Spirit of English Government*. London: 1822

Deane, Phyllis and Cole, W.A., *British Economic Growth 1688-1959*. 2nd edition. Cambridge: 1969

Dewey, C.J., 'The Education of a Ruling Caste: The Indian Civil Service in the Era of Competition', *English Historical Review*, 88 (April, 1973), pp. 262-85

Dodson, Michael, *The Life of Sir Michael Foster Knt*. London: 1811

Duncan, G.I.O., *The High Court of Delegates*. Cambridge: 1971

Edgeworth, Richard L., *Essays on Professional Education*. London: 1809

Elliott, Philip, *The Sociology of Professions*. London: 1972

Fifoot, C.H.S., *Judge and Jurist in the Reign of Victoria*. London: 1959

Forsyth, William, *Hortensius: or, The Advocate*. London: 1849

George, Dorothy, *England in Transition*. Baltimore: 1967

Gneist, Rudolf, *Das heutige Englische Verfassungsund Verwaltungsrecht,* 2 vols. Berlin: 1857

Goode, William, 'Community within a Community: The Professions', *American Sociological Review,* 22 (1957), 194-200
Explorations in Social Theory. New York: 1973

Green, V.H.H., *The Universities.* Harmondsworth: 1969

Greenwood, E., 'Attributes of Profession', *Social Work* 2 (1957), 44-55

Guttsman, W.L., *The British Political Elite.* London: 1968

Halevy, Elie, *England in 1815.* London: 1961
The Growth of Philosophic Radicalism. Boston: 1966

Harding, Alan, *A Social History of English Law.* Harmondsworth: 1966

Hardy, Thomas Duffus, *Memoirs of the Right Honourable Henry Lord Langdale.* London: 1852

Harris, George, *The Life of Lord Chancellor Hardwicke.* 3 vols. London: 1847

Hawes, Frances, *Henry Brougham.* London: 1957

Hay, D., Linebaugh P., *et al., Albion's Fatal Tree.* London: 1977

Heuston. R.F.V.,*Lives of the Lord Chancellors 1885-1940.* Oxford: 1964

Hickson, D.J. and Thomas M.W., 'Professionalization in Britain: A Preliminary Measurement', *Sociology* 3 (1969), 37-53

Hobsbawm, E.J., *Industry and Empire.* Baltimore: 1969

Holdsworth, Sir William, *A History of English Law.* Vols. I, XII, XIII, XV, XVI, London: 1938-1969
'The Rise of the Order of King's Counsel', *Law Quarterly Review* 26 (1920), 212-21

Holliday, John, *The Life of William Late Earl of Mansfield.* London: 1797

Hollingsworth, T.H., 'The Demography of the British Peerage', Supplement to *Population Studies* 18 (1964)

Ives, E.W., 'The Common Lawyer in Pre-Reformation England', *Transactions of the Royal Historical Society,* 5th series 18 (1968), 145-73

Jeafferson, John C., *A Book About Lawyers.* London: 1867

Jewson, N.D., 'Medical Knowledge and the Patronage System in Eighteenth Century England', *Sociology* 8 (1974), 369-85

Johnson, Terence J., *Professions and Power.* London: 1972

Jones, Sir Elwyn, 'The Offices of the Attorney-General', *Cambridge Law Journal* 27 (1969), 43-53

Jones, Ray, *The Nineteenth Century Foreign Office, an Administrative History.* London: 1971

196

Jones, W.J., *Politics and the Bench.* London: 1971

Keeton, G.W., 'The Judiciary and the Constitutional Struggle 1660-88', *Journal of the Society of the Public Teachers of Law* 7 (1962), 56-68

Kenyon, Hon. George T., *The Life of Lloyd, First Lord Kenyon, Lord Chief Justice of England.* London: 1873

Laski, Harold, 'The Techniques of Judicial Appointment', in *Studies in Law and Politics.* New York: 1968

Levack, Brian P., *The Civil Lawyers in England 1603-1641, A Political Study.* Oxford: 1973

Lewis, Michael, *A Social History of the Navy 1713-1815.* London: 1960

The Navy in Transition. London: 1965

Lucas, Paul, 'A Collective Biography of the Students and Barristers of Lincoln's Inn 1680-1804: A Study in the 'Aristocratic Resurgence' of the Eighteenth Century', *Journal of Modern History* 46 (June, 1974), 227-61

'Blackstone and the Reform of the Legal Profession', *English Historical Review* 77 (1962), 456-87

Lyon, Bryce, *A Constitutional and Legal History of Medieval England.* New York: 1960

Maine, Henry Sumner, *Ancient Law.* London: 1930

Marshall, T.H., 'The Recent History of Professionalism in Relation to Social Structure and Social Policy', *Canadian Journal of Economics and Political Science* 5 (1939), 325-40

Martin, Theodore, *A Life of Lord Chancellor Lyndhurst.* London: 1883

Mead, Patrick, *Romilly, A Life of Sir Samuel Romilly Lawyer and Reformer.* London: 1968

Millerson, Geoffrey. *The Qualifying Associations: A Study of Professionalization.* London:1964

Mingay, G.E., *English Landed Society in the Eighteenth Century.* London: 1963

Mitchell, B.R. and Deane, Phyllis, *Abstract of British Historical Statistics.* Cambridge: 1971

Morgan, D.H.J., 'The Social and Educational Background of Anglican Bishops — Continuity and Change', *British Journal of Sociology* 20 (1969), 295-310

Musgrove, Frank, 'Middle-Class Education and Employment in the Nineteenth Century', *Economic History Review* 12 (August, 1959), 99-111

Namier, Lewis, *The Structure of Politics at the Accession of George III.* London: 1957

Nash, Thomas A., *The Life of Richard Lord Westbury.* London: 1888

New, Chester W., *The Life of Henry Brougham to 1830*. Oxford: 1961

Newman, C.E., *The Evolution of Medical Education in the Nineteenth Century*. London: 1957

Norton-Kyshe, James W., *The Law and Privileges Relating to the Attorney-General and Solicitor-General of England*. London: 1897

Otley, C.B., 'The Social Origins of British Army Officers', *Sociological Review* 18 (1973), 213-38

Owen, David, *English Philanthropy 1660-1960*. Cambridge, Massachusetts: 1964

Pares, Richard, *King George III and the Politicians*. Oxford: 1967

Parry, J. and N., *The Rise of the Medical Profession*. London: 1976

Pelling, Henry, *Popular Politics and Society in Late Victorian Britain*. London: 1968

Perkin, Harold, *The Origins of Modern English Society 1780-1880*. London: 1969

Peterson, M. Jeanne, *The Medical Profession in Mid-Victorian London*. Berkeley: 1978

Plucknett, Theodore F.T., *A Concise History of Common Law*. 5th edn. London: 1956

Polson, A., *Law and Lawyers: or sketches and illustrations of legal history and biography*. 2 vols. London: 1840

Poynter, J.R., *Society and Pauperism: English Ideas on Poor Relief 1795-1834*. London: 1969

Prest, Wilfrid R., *The Inns of Court under Elizabeth I and the Early Stuarts 1590-1640*. London: 1972

Radzinowicz, L., *A History of English Criminal Law and Its Administration from 1750*. I. New York: 1948

Razzell, P.E., 'Social Origins of British Army Officers in the Indian and British Home Army, 1758-1962', *British Journal of Sociology* 14 (1963), 248-60

Reader, William J., *Professional Men, the Rise of the Professional Classes in Nineteenth Century England*. London: 1966

Robson, Robert, *The Attorney in Eighteenth Century England*. Cambridge: 1959

Roth, Julius A., 'Professionalism — The Sociologist's Decoy', *Sociology of Work and Occupations* 1 (1974), 17

Rothblatt, Sheldon, *The Revolution of the Dons*. New York: 1968

Rubinstein, W.D., 'Men of property: some aspects of occupation, inheritance, and power among top British wealthholders', in Stanworth P., and Giddens, A., *Elites and Power in British Society*. Cambridge: 1974

Ruggles, T., *The Barrister or Strictures or the Proper Education for the Bar*. 2 vols. London: 1792

Sampson, Anthony, *Anatomy of Britain Today*. New York: 1965

Scarlett, Peter Campbell, *A Memoir of the Right Honourable James, First Lord Abinger*. London: 1877

Spring, David, *The English Landed Estate in the Nineteenth Century: Its Administration*. Baltimore: 1963

Stankey, Rt. Hon. Viscount, 'Lord Stowell', *Law Quarterly Review* 52 (1936), 327-44

Stephens, W.R.W., *A Memoir of the Right Hon. William Page Wood, Baron Hatherley*. 2 vols. London: 1883

Stevens, Robert, 'The Final Appeal: Reform of the House of Lords and the Privy Council 1867-76', *Law Quarterly Review* 80 (1964), 343-69

Strahan, J.A., *The Bench and Bar of England*. Edinburgh: 1919

Stanley, Arthur P., *Life of Thomas Arnold D.D.* London: 1910

Stone, Lawrence, *The University in Society*, I. Princeton: 1974

Stryker, Lloyd Paul, *For the Defence, Thomas Erskine the Most Enlightened Liberal of his Times, 1750-1823*. Garden City: 1947

Summerson, John, *Georgian England*. Harmondsworth: 1969

Surtees, William E., *A Sketch of the Lives of Lords Stowell and Eldon*. London: 1846

Swinfen, D.B., 'Henry Brougham and the Judicial Committee of the Privy Council', *Law Quarterly Review* 90 (1974), 396-411

Thompson, E.P., *Whigs and Hunters*. London: 1975

Thompson, F.M.L. *English Landed Society in the Nineteenth Century*. London: 1963

Thomson, H. Byerley, *The Choice of a Profession, A Concise and Comparative Review of the English Professions*. London: 1857

Trilling, Lionel, *The Opposing Self*. New York: 1955

Twiss, Horace, *The Public and Private Life of Lord Chancellor Eldon*. 3 vols. London: 1844

Vincent, John, *The Formation of the British Liberal Party 1857-68*. Harmondsworth: 1972

Warren, Samuel, *Introduction to Law Studies*. 2 vols. London: 1845

Wedgewood, Josiah, *The Economics of Inheritance*. Harmondsworth: 1939

Willock, I.D., 'Scottish Judges Scrutinized, *Juridical Review* ns. 14 (1969), 193-205

Winder, W.H.D., 'Courts of Requests', *Law Quarterly Review* 52 (1936), 369-98

Wiswall, F.L., *The Development of Admiralty Jurisdiction and Practice Since 1800*. Cambridge: 1970

Wynne, Edward, *Eunomus or Dialogues Concerning the Law and Constitution of England.* 4 vols. London: 1785

Yorke, Philip C., *The Life and Correspondence of Philip Yorke Earl of Hardwicke Lord High Chancellor of Great Britain.* 3 vols. Cambridge: 1913

INDEX

Note: Peers are indexed under family name. Where the peerage title differs from the family name, the latter is given in parentheses. Individuals who appear only in the appendix are not indexed.

Abbott, Charles (Lord Tenterden), 60, 160
Adam, Robert, 148
Addington, Henry (Lord Sidmouth), 97-8
Advocates: civil law, 8-10, 13-14, 94, 108; French, 53; Scots, 62, 89-90
Alexander, Sir William, 86, 135
Appointments, judicial: age at, 72; by Archbishop of Canterbury, 78; connections and, 81-2, 86, 94, 96; criteria for, 79-81; by Lord Chancellor, 78, 81, 85, 117; politics and, 80, 84, 87-96; by Prime Minister, 78, 85; refusal of, 83-5, 91; rewards, 27-30, 70-1; 'translation', 91-2
Arden, Richard Pepper (Lord Alvanley), 85, 139
Arnold, Dr. Thomas, 26, 39
Assizes, 22-4
Attorney-General, 13, 75, 93; appointment to bench, 82-91
Attorneys and solicitors, 8, 10-11, 25, 179; practice, 62; status, 36; study with 36-7
Austin, Charles, 106, 109
Authors, judicial, 149-51

Bagehot, Walter, 64
Bankes, George, 87, 137, 143
Bar: and clients, 178-9; depoliticization, 99; dimensions, 8-9, 179; esprit de corps, 11; etiquette, 10, 26-7, 56; hierarchy, 11; prospects at, 30-2, 57-9; resistance to reform, 179; social quality, 35, 44, 54-5, 179-81; specialization, 12; status, 170
Bar, call to, 15-16, 59
Bar mess, 24-5
Bathurst, Henry, Earl, 81, 121, 139, 147
Barristers, 10; attributes of, 32; briefless, 31-2, 57-8; nominal, 8-9; provincial, 7-8, practising 9, 54; reputation and status of, 25-8; revising, 120-1
Bentham, Jeremy, 22, 125-6, 153
Bentinck, William Henry Cavendish (Duke of Portland), 81
Bethell, Richard (Lord Westbury), 149; income and wealth, 58-9, 106, 110, 143-4; as legal reformer, 16, 21, 152, 173

Bickersteth, Henry (Lord Langdale), 48, 58, 83-4
Blackburn, Colin, Lord, 81, 138
Blackstone, Sir William, 8, 104, 151-2; views on education, 34-6
Bosanquet, Sir John Bernard, 103-4
Bramwell, George W.W., Lord, 104
Brett, William Baliol (Viscount Esher), 83, 92
Brougham, Henry, Lord, 19, 21, 74, 84, 86, 106, 151-3; estates, 133, 148-9; legal and political career, 77, 90-1; speech of 1828, 174
Buller, Sir Francis, 134-5
Byles, Sir John Bernard, 143

Cairns, Hugh McCalmont, Earl, 80, 82-3, 117, 175
Campbell, John, Lord, 27, 81, 83-4, 123, 143, 148; early career, 48, 55, 57-8, 161
Cambridge, University of, 13, 16, 42-52
Canning, George, 85-6
Career, choice of, 28; parliamentary, 13, 75, 77-8, 87-8, 95
Careers at the bar, 24, 47-9, 58-63; connection, 62-71; length of, 72-3, 75, 181; patterns, 73-8
Caroline, Queen, 74, 90
Cases: *King v. the Benchers of Gray's Inn,* 14-15; *O'Connell* 18, 21
Chief Barons of the Exchequer, 2, 18, 78-9; salaries, 22n, 112, 114-15; selection of, 84-7, 95
Chief Justices (Barons), sinecures, 119-20, 123, 125; *see* Sinecures and patronage
Chief Justices of the Common Pleas, 2, 13, 17, 21, 78-9; salaries, 22n, 112, 114; selection of, 87-95
Chief Justices of the King's Bench, 2, 17, 21, 78-9, 97; salaries and income, 22n, 112, 114, 122-3; selection of, 87-95
Circuits, 7, 12, 22-5, 68-9, 100
Cleasby, Sir Anthony, 80
Clive, Sir Edward, 122, 135
Clubs, London, 160
Cockburn, Sir Alexander, 106
Coke, Thomas (Earl of Leicester), 64
Coleridge family, 160
Coleridge, John Duke, Lord, 106, 173
Coleridge, Sir John Taylor, 26, 32, 48, 57, 60, 69, 151
College of Advocates, England, 13
Collier, Robert, P. (Lord Monkswell), 175
Coltman, Sir Thomas, 143
Competition, 29; at the bar, 29-31, 54, 64, 181
Comyns, Sir John, 106
Connections, 29-30, 54, 62-6; local, 63, 65-9

Copley, John Singleton, Jr. (Lord Lyndhurst), 86, 122, 159
Council on Legal Education, 16
Country houses, 147-9; costs, 149n; Kenwood house, 100-1, 148, 156-8; Merthyr Mawr house, 131, 148, 155-6, 158; Wimpole hall, 129, 147-8; see Judges, purchase of landed estates
Courts, 7, 18, 20; of Appeals, 18; assize, 24, 99-100; civil law, 2, 7-8, 46, 79, 94; common law, 3, 7-8, 17, 46; Crown Cases Reserved, 18; of Delegates, 19; Divorce and Matrimonial Cases, 18; ecclesiastical, 17, 46; Exchequer, 20, Exchequer Chamber, 18; High, 18; Judicial Committee of the Privy Council, 18-19; Quarter Sessions, 7; Probate, 18; Prerogative Court of Canterbury, 18; reform of, 17-19; 21-2; 173-5; Requests, 7, 19; Supreme Court of Judicature, 18
Criminal law, 99, 101, 104

Dampier, Sir Henry, 83n
De Grey, William (Lord Walsingham), 64-5, 93, 106-8, 121, 136, 159; as landowner, 132-4
Denman, Thomas, Lord, 74, 90, 119-20, 123
Dickens, Charles, 31, 103, 150
Doctors' Commons, 7, 13, 68, 94
Dodson, Sir John, 137
Dublin University, 16, 41
Dunning, John (Lord Ashburton), 58, 106, 108, 160
Dynasties, legal, 168-70; see Judges, sons of

Education, legal, 47-8; courses of study, 17, 36-8; at the Inns of Court, 15-17, 173-4; see also Blackstone, Sir William, views on education
Education, university, 8, 34-6, 41-5, 59; see also individual universities
Erskine, Thomas, Lord, 101, 106, 125, 137
Etiquette, see Bar, etiquette
Expenses: professional, 47-8, 55-7; personal, 48, 56, 153-8

Fees, 25-6
Field, William Ventris, Lord, 159
Flitcroft, Henry, 148
Follett, Sir William, 109

General Council of the Bar (Bar Committee), 26
George III, King, 4, 89, 93, 97-8
George IV, King, 4, 74, 80, 90
Giffard, Hardinge, (Earl of Halsbury), 82n
Gilbert and Sullivan, 164
Gordon Riots, 100-1, 148

Grove, Sir William, 80, 143, 150
Guidebooks, professional, 29-32, 38, 55, 57-8, 63

Halford, Sir Henry, 82
Harvey, Daniel W., 14n
Hay, Sir George, 94
Heath, Sir John, 81-2
Henley, Robert (Earl of Northington), 100, 116, 121
Holroyd, Sir George, 160
Horne, Sir William, 83n
Hotham, Sir Beaumont, 81
Huddleston, Sir John, 8, 23-4

Ideology: professional, 5, 168, 175-82; social, 143-4, 167-8, 170,
    172; see Professionalization
Incomes, at the bar, 72, 105-7, 154; eighteenth-century, 107-8, 110;
    nineteenth-century, 108-11
Incomes, judicial, 22, 112-3, 122-4, 141-3
Independence, judicial, 96-7
Industrial revolution, 52, 180-2
Inns of Court, 7, 10, 14-15; benchers, 14-15; education at 15-17, 173-4;
    affiliations of judges, 45-6

Jeafferson, John C., 12n, 14
Jenner-Fust, Sir Herbert, 143
Jervis, Sir John, 9, 106, 109-10
Jessel, Sir George, 58, 87, 106, 110, 143
Journalism, as career, 48, 60, 151
Judges: administration of the criminal law, 99, 101; ages on appointment,
    72-3, 181; ages on retirement, 73; attitudes towards trades unions,
    103-4; attributes of, 132; as civil servants, 2n; club membership
    160; estate management, 132-5; family position, 53-4; geographical
    origins, 42, 66-9; as lawmakers, 1; life styles, 153-60; marriage
    partners and patterns, 161-5; as members of the cabinet, 97; as
    MPs, 21; non-Anglicans, 42n; non-landed investments, 135-9,
    182; non-professional activities, 149-53; patronage, 22, 116-25;
    pensions, 121-2; 124-6, 165n; popular image of, 99-101; probate
    settlement patterns, 169-72, 182; purchase of landed estates,
    128-32, 139, 142-4, 182; reputation and status, 25-6; residences,
    123, 145-9; retirement, 125; salaries and fees, 22, 111-16, 119,
    122, 125-6, 141; security of tenure, 97n; social aspirations 143-4;
    167, 170, 172, 180-2; social bias, 102-4; social origins, 50-3,
    102, 179-81; sons of, 165-8, 170, 181; suppression of riots, 100;
    tenure of office, 97; titled 21-7, 84, 87, 132; wealth, 140-4; Welsh,
    75-6; see also individual judicial offices

Judges, Court of Admiralty and Prerogative Court of Canterbury, 2, 17, 21, 78-9; salaries, 22n, 113, 115-16, selection of, 96
Judges, puisne, 2, 17, 78-9; salaries, 22n, 112, 115; selection of, 79-84
Judiciary, dimensions, of, 17-18, Welsh, 25

Karslake, Sir John, 83
Kelly, Sir Fitzroy, 106, 110
Kenyon, Lloyd, Lord, 37, 48, 119, 132, 135-7; income and wealth, 58, 106, 108, 128, 143; judicial appointment of, 83n, 85-6

Lamb, Charles and Mary, 150
Landed classes, 50-2, 54-5, 63, 180-1
Landowning, 127-9, 132, 139, 143-4, 149; estate management, 132-5; purchase of estates, 129-32, 142-4
Law, Edward, (Lord Ellenborough), 97, 119, 135, 143
Law List, 8-9
Law Lords, 21
Law reporters, 60
Law students, 33, 48
Lee, Sir George, 94, 136
Lincoln's Inn, 28, 45-6, 53, 168
Littledale, Sir Joseph, 83n, 137
Lloyd, Sir Richard, 40
London: allurements of, 35; Bayswater, 146-7; Belgravia, 146-7; Bloomsbury, 100, 145-7; City of London, 7, 20; courts in, 7, 20, 22; Hampstead, 100; Holborn, 20, 145; Hyde Park, 146-7; judges from, 67-8; judicial residences, 145-7; Kensington, 146-7; Knightsbridge, 146-7; Lincoln's Inn Fields, 145-7; Mayfair, 146-7; Notting Hill, 146-7; Regent's Park, 146; riots in, 100-1; St. James's, 146; St. Marylebone, 146-7; Soho, 146; Westminster, 7, 20
Lord Chancellors, 2, 17, 78-9; clerical patronage, 22, 118-19; functions of, 20-1, 97; legal patronage, 22, 116-18; as politician, 20, 88, 97-9; salaries and income, 22n, 111, 112, 114, 124, 143; selection of, 87-95
Lords Justices of Appeal, 2, 18, 78-9; selection of, 84-7, 95
Lushington, Stephen, 74, 92, 94

MacDonald, Sir Archibald, 86
Maine, Sir Henry Sumner, 11
Manners-Sutton, Thomas (Lord Manners), 143-4
Marriot, Sir James, 122, 152
Maseres, Francis, 150-1

Masters of the Rolls, 2, 7, 19, 21, 78-9, salaries, 22n, 112, 114; selection of, 84-7; 95
May, John, 69
Mellish, Sir George, 83n
Middle classes, 52-5, 63, 70
Middlesex, 24n, 67, 69
Murray, William (Earl of Mansfield), 15-16n, 58, 85, 97, 100-1, 148; finances, 139, 156-8

New Domesday Book, 105, 127, 141
Newspapers and Periodicals: *British Critic,* 60; *Edinburgh Review,* 151; *Morning Chronicle,* 60; *New Monthly Review,* 60; *Quarterly Review,* 60, 151; *The Times,* 60, 90
Nicholl, Sir John, 153, 159n; income, 106, 108, 154; finances, 137-8, 143, 148, 154, 158; estates, 130-2, 158
Noel, William, 40
North, Frederick, Lord, 81, 89, 93

Offices, professional, 74-5; admiralty and king's advocates, 14, 94; king's counsels, 12, 14, 73; law officers of the crown, 13, 75-6, 82, 84-5, 87-8; law officers of the royal family, 74, 90; recorders, 73-4; serjeants-at-law, 12-13; *see* Attorney-General and Solicitor-General

Oxford and Cambridge, 13, 16, 34, 42-6
Oxford, University of, 13, 16, 42-5

Palmer, Roundell (Earl of Selborne), 21, 48, 58, 60, 65, 173, 175
Parke, James (Lord Wensleydale), 47
Parker, Thomas (Earl of Macclesfield), 64, 116
Parker, Sir Thomas, 40, 64, 122
Parliament, 13, 21-2, 77-8; *see also* Politics
Pelham, Henry, 83
Pepys, Charles Christopher (Lord Cottenham), 37, 65, 138, 143, 160
Perrot, Sir George, 122
Pitt, William, the elder (Earl of Chatham), 89
Pitt, William, the younger, 85, 89, 98
Plunket, William, Lord, 85-6
Politics: careers in, 75-7, 93, 96-9; and judicial appointments, 80, 84, 87-96; *see also* Lord Chancellor
Pollock family, 170
Pollock, Sir Frederick, 83n, 106, 109

Pratt, Charles (Earl Camden), 58, 100, 121, 133, 136
Professional men: bishops, 40-1, 43-4; foreign office clerks, 40-1, 44; medical practitioners, 40, 43
Profession, legal: division of labour, 10-11, 25, 179
Professions, 14; dimensions in c. 1850, 9; lower, 4, 10; reform, 4-5, 173, 182; structure of, 176-80; trait definition, 176; upper, 4-5, 10, 29, 54, 70, 182; see Ideology, professional
Professionalization: administrative, 5-6, 18-20, 173-5; definition of, 4-5; internal, 4-6, 173-4; social and attitudinal, 5-6, 165, 167-8, 170, 172-3, 175-82; and social class, 50, 172; types of, 4-5, 173

Reeve, Sir Thomas, 136
Richards, Sir Richard, 86
Richardson, Sir John, 80, 83n
Rolfe, Robert Monsey (Lord Cranworth), 83, 86, 92
Rolt, Sir John, 48
Romilly, Sir Samuel, 21, 58-9, 106, 108-9
Royal Society, 150
Russell, Lord John, 13, 80, 83, 87
Ryder, Sir Dudley, 85n, 132, 136

Salaries, judicial, 22, 112-16, 141-3
Scarlett, James (Lord Abinger), 86, 91, 106, 109, 110, 122
Schools, grammar, 40-1, 47; Litchfield Grammar School, 38, 40
Schools, public, 33-4, 38-41, 46-7, 62; Clarendon, 39-41; Charterhouse, 39-40, 47; Eton, 39-40; Harrow, 39-40, 47, 80; Merchant Taylors, 39-40; Rugby, 39-40; St. Paul's, 39-40; Shrewsbury, 39-40; Westminster, 39-40; Winchester, 39-40
Scientists and mathematicians, judicial, 150-1
Scott, John (Earl of Eldon), 37, 98-9, 174; judicial appointments, 80, 82, 86, 90; income and wealth, 106, 108, 111, 114, 135, 143; as landowner, 128, 130-2, 135; patronage, 117-19
Scott, William (2nd Earl of Eldon), 117
Scott, William (Lord Stowell), 131-2, 141, 143
Self-made men, myth of, 30, 54-5, 63-4
Serjeants' Inn, 3, 13
Servants, 159
Sewell, Sir Thomas, 106
Shadwell, Sir Launcelot, 92
Shelley, Percy B., 100
Sinecures and patronage, 5, 17, 22, 116, 121, 125-6, 174; reform of, 22, 54, 117, 119, 124
Smith, Adam, 31, 97
Smith, Sir Montague, 143

Smollett, Tobias, 8
Soane, Sir John, 20
Social mobility, 70-1, 102, 164
Society for the Diffusion of Useful Knowledge, 152
Solicitor-General, 75, 82-5, 89, 92-3
Solicitors; *see* Attorneys
Special pleader and conveyancers, 8-9, 11-12, 37-8, 57, 60-2
Statutes: Appellate Jurisdiction Act (1876), 21; Judiciary Acts
    (1873 and 1875), 2, 18, 21, 175; Municipal Corporations Act
    (1835), 73
Stephen, Sir James Fitzjames, 27
Street, G.E., 20
Sugden, Edward B. (Lord St. Leonards), 83n, 106, 109

Talfourd, Sir Thomas N., 56, 60, 77, 106, 150, 160
Temple, The, 7, 45-6, 146; Inner Temple, 28, 45; Middle Temple,
    28, 45, 52
Thackeray, William, 31
Thesiger, Alfred, 82n
Thesiger, Frederick (Lord Chelmsford), 82, 117-18
Thomson, H. Byerley, 10
Thurlow, Edward, Lord, 82, 85, 89, 93, 98, 121
Tindal, Sir Nicholas C., 74
Tocqueville, Alexis de, 11, 70, 102, 180
Tory Party, 99

University of London: King's College, 42; University College, 42,
    153

Vaughan, Sir John, 82
Vice-Chancellor, 2, 78-9; 118; salaries, 22n, 112, selection of, 79-84
Victoria, Queen, 21, 99

Wallace, James, 83n
Warren, Samuel, 32
Wedderburn, Alexander (Lord Loughborough and Earl of Rosslyn),
    89-90, 93, 98, 128, 139
Wigan, 81
Wilde, Thomas (Lord Truro), 74
Willes, Sir John, 40, 137
William IV, King, 12, 91n
Williams, Sir John, 74
Wilmot, Sir John Eardley, 81, 121-2
Wives, judges'; *see* Judges, marriage partners and patterns

Wood, William Page (Baron Hatherley), 173, 175
Working classes, 53, 55, 70; judicial attitudes towards, 102-4
Women, inheritance by, 171-2
Wynne, Sir William, 152

Yorke, Charles, 58, 106-7
Yorke, Philip (Earl of Hardwicke), 64, 81, 136, 147-8; as landowner,
    128-33; political career, 97-8; sinecure offices, 117, 121
Young, Arthur, 134-5

Other volumes in this series

1	The Politics of Stability : A Portrait of the Rulers in Elizabethan London	Frank F. Foster
2	The Frankish Church and The Carolingian Reforms 789-895	Rosamond McKitterick
3	John Burns	Kenneth D. Brown
4	Revolution and Counter-Revolution in Scotland, 1644-1651	David Stevenson
5	The Queen's Two Bodies : Drama and the Elizabethan Succession	Marie Axton
6	Great Britain and International Security, 1920-1926	Anne Orde
7	Legal Records and the Historian	J. H. Baker (ed.)
8	Church and State in Independent Mexico: A Study of the Patronage Debate 1821-1857	Michael P. Costeloe
9	An Early Welsh Microcosm : Studies in the Llandaff Charters	Wendy Davies
10	The British in Palestine : The Mandatory Government and the Arab-Jewish Conflict	Bernard Wasserstein
11	Order and Equipoise : The Peerage and the House of Lords, 1783-1806	Michael McCahill
12	Preachers, Peasants and Politics in Southeast Africa 1835-1880: African Christian Communities in Natal, Pondoland and Zululand	Norman Etherington
13	Linlithgow and India : A Study of British Policy and the Political Impasse in India 1936-1943	S. A. G. Rizvi
14	Britain and her Buffer State: The Collapse of the Persian Empire, 1890-1914	David McLean
15	Guns and Government: The Ordnance Office under the Later Stuarts	Howard Tomlinson
16	Denzil Holles 1598-1680 : A Study of his Political Career	Patricia Crawford
17	The Parliamentary Agents: A History	D. L. Rydz
18	The Shadow of the Bomber : The Fear of Air Attack and British Politics 1932-1939	Uri Bialer
19	La Rochelle and the French Monarchy: Conflict and Order in Seventeenth-Century France	David Parker

20   The Purchase System in the British Army   *A. P. C. Bruce*
         1660-1871

21   The Manning of the British Navy during   *Stephen F. Gradish*
         The Seven Years' War

22   Law-Making and Law-Makers in British History   *Alan Harding (ed.)*

23   John Russell, First Earl of Bedford: *Diane Willen*
         One of the King's Men

24   The Political Career of Sir Robert Naunton   *Roy E. Schreiber*
         1589-1635

25   The House of Gibbs and the Peruvian   *W. M. Mathew*
         Guano Monopoly

26   Julian S. Corbett, 1854-1922 : Historian of British   *D. M. Schurman*
         Maritime Policy from Drake to Jellicoe

27   The Pilgrimage of Grace in the Lake Counties,   *S. M. Harrison*
         1536-7

28   Money, Prices and Politics in Fifteenth-   *Angus MacKay*
         Century Castile

Copies obtainable on order from
Swift Printers (Sales) Ltd., 1-7 Albion Place, Britton Street, London EC1M 5RE